Men in Caring Occupations

Also by Ruth Simpson

VOICE VISIBILITY AND THE GENDERING OF ORGANIZATIONS (*with Patricia Lewis*)

GENDERING EMOTIONS IN ORGANIZATION (*with Patricia Lewis*)

Men in Caring Occupations

Doing Gender Differently

Ruth Simpson
Brunel University, UK

First published 2009 by
PALGRAVE MACMILLAN

Palgrave Macmillan in the UK is an imprint of Macmillan Publishers Limited,
registered in England, company number 785998, of Houndmills, Basingstoke,
Hampshire RG21 6XS.

Palgrave Macmillan in the US is a division of St Martin's Press LLC,
175 Fifth Avenue, New York, NY 10010.

Palgrave Macmillan is the global academic imprint of the above companies
and has companies and representatives throughout the world.

Palgrave® and Macmillan® are registered trademarks in the United States,
the United Kingdom, Europe and other countries.

ISBN-13: 978-0-230-57406-9 hardback

This book is printed on paper suitable for recycling and made from fully
managed and sustained forest sources. Logging, pulping and manufacturing
processes are expected to conform to the environmental regulations of the
country of origin.

A catalogue record for this book is available from the British Library.

Library of Congress Cataloging-in-Publication Data
Simpson, Ruth, Professor.
   Men in caring occupations : doing gender differently / Ruth Simpson.
      p.   cm.
   Includes bibliographical references and index.
   ISBN 978-0-230-57406-9
   1. Professions—Sex differences.   2. Occupations—Sex differences.
   3. Men—Identity.   4. Men—Employment—Psychological aspects.
   I. Title.
   HD8038.A1S55 2009
   331.70081—dc22   2008034889

10   9   8   7   6   5   4   3   2   1
18   17   16   15   14   13   12   11   10   09

Transferred to Digital Printing in 2010

I dedicate this book to my three children, Rachel, Matthew and Alexander and to my two grandchildren Joshua and Molly

Contents

Part I
Identity, Visibility, Emotions

1
Introducing Men in Non-Traditional Occupations

Introduction

This book is about men who serve and care. In other words, it focuses on men who enter what have been identified as 'feminine' occupations. These are occupations that are traditionally held by women and which are notable for requiring feminine skills and attributes (for example, sensitivity, service, nurturance and beauty) that society normally attributes to women (Heilman, 1997; Hochschild, 1983). It explores specific themes that are key to understanding men's experience in these roles – identity, visibility and emotions – and sets out the results of a recent research project based in Australia and the UK on men working in four 'non-traditional' occupational groups: nursing, primary school teaching, librarianship and flight attendance. The study addressed career issues (for example motivations, aspirations), implications of men's 'token' status for experiences in the organization, perceptions of gender differences in occupational practices (specifically in terms of performances of service and emotional labour) and how men manage potential mismatch between gender and occupational identity.

Evidence suggests continuing and strong 'sex typing' of jobs with built-in assumptions concerning their suitability for women or men (Acker, 1990). Occupations are consequently labelled as masculine or feminine and carry gender-linked associations concerning the skills required for effective performance (Fletcher, 2003; Williams, 1995). Such skills and attributes are then hierarchically arranged in that occupations that carry power and influence are seen to require attributes associated with men while those lacking power and authority become associated with women – so preserving the gender order (Ely and Padavic, 2007). The prevalence of these associations can be seen in the high levels of gender segregation by occupational groups. In the UK, for example, 84 per cent of service workers and 81 per cent of administrative and secretarial staff are women, while 92 per cent of skilled trades, 84 per cent of machine operatives and 66 per cent of managers and senior officials are men (EOC, 2006). In fact, a recent report by the EOC (2006) has indicated that over 60 per cent of occupations are performed mainly by men or by women.

Despite this, there has been a trend for men and women to move into gender-atypical areas (Hakim, 2000). For example, men now account for 9 per cent of all nurses in Australia (AIHW, 2007), while the figure in the UK is currently 10.9 per cent (Information Centre for Health and Social Care, 2008). However, while the proportion of women moving into 'male' jobs has increased, there has been a slower movement of men into traditionally 'female' jobs – perhaps reflective of the sacrifices in both pay and status, as well as the possibility of encountering disapproval from family and peers, that can accompany these career decisions. So while there is extensive literature on women who have previously been excluded from 'male' jobs and who have now moved into these male-dominated occupations (e.g. Cross and Bagilhole, 2002; Kanter, 1977; Simpson, 1997, 2000), with a few notable exceptions (e.g. Lupton, 2000, 2006; Sargent, 2001; Williams, 1993) relatively little research has been conducted on the small but growing number of men who perform what could be seen as 'women's work'.

This absence may not only reflect the lower numbers of men who 'cross over' into female-dominated occupations, but also a tendency, until recently, for research on gender and work to focus on women. This gap has been partly redressed by recent work on the dynamics of masculinity (e.g. Collinson and Hearn, 1994; Connell, 1995, 2000; Kerfoot and Knights, 1993). These dynamics are particularly highlighted within the context of work and organizations which, as important arenas for the definition of gender, help produce, as we have seen above, characterizations of 'masculine' and 'feminine' work. Such characterizations carry strong implications for occupants of non-traditional posts. For example, token women can be severely disadvantaged by their minority status through isolation and negative stereotyping (Kanter, 1977; Simpson, 1997, 2000) while, as some studies of male nurses have indicated (Floge and Merrill, 1986; Heikes, 1991), some positive career outcomes can accrue for token men. However, the fragmentary literature on men in non-traditional occupations means that little is known about the challenges they face in the organization and how they negotiate the potential mismatch between the (feminine) nature of the job and a gendered (masculine) identity.

An understanding of the experiences of men in these non-traditional roles is vital if sex-stereotypic work–career boundaries, and all their ramifications, are to be challenged and breached. Implications of 'breach' may be especially pertinent in the context of the continuing move of employment opportunities out of manufacturing into services and the resultant 'feminization' of local labour markets whereby employment is increasingly to be found in a range of what might previously have been thought of as 'women's work' – incorporating customer services and 'care'. Men may therefore be 'pushed' into considering jobs that do not fully conform to sex type.

Furthermore, labour shortages in traditionally female occupations such as teaching, nursing and social work, as well as a desire to have a more 'balanced' workforce, have led to calls for more men to enter these professions. Both these 'pull' factors and the 'push' factors outlined above suggest a need to understand the experiences of men who choose such work. More generally, a study of men in non-traditional roles furthers our understanding of gender and work, where conceptualizations of masculinity and femininity are 'on the line', highly visible and vulnerable to challenge (Morgan, 1992). Being both a man and a nurse for example involves occupying two contradictory subject positions in the 'discourse on work' (Fletcher, 2003). It is at these intersections that new knowledge can be gained and, as Connell (2000) argues, greater potential to understand and challenge the gender order. We can thus throw light on the implications of and dynamics behind such a career choice as well as on specific gender-related issues concerning identity, visibility and the practices and processes of 'doing' service and care.

Traditional or non-traditional occupations

Notions of traditional (gender typical) and non-traditional (gender atypical) jobs are not static concepts but vary over time. What we now see as gender-congruent occupations may well be gender-atypical in a different context or time period and vice versa. While, as Acker (1990) points out, gender segregation is an 'amazingly persistent' pattern, the gender identity of jobs is repeatedly produced and reproduced, often to emerge in new forms. As Walby (1986) has argued in the context of 'dual systems theory', capitalism's drive to lower costs through the employment of cheap and biddable (that is, female) labour and patriarchy's desire to maintain the gendered order of male power have combined to create the sex-typing of jobs. These are organized so that men receive the highest social valuation (Bradley, 1993) and so that men can control and if necessary exclude women. However, social and organizational change is constantly altering the nature and boundaries of work – so this positioning is never complete. Occupational boundaries and the sex-typing of jobs are thus subject to reinterpretation and change.

New technology for example can lead to a rearrangement of job typologies and a new gendered order. From Cockburn's (1983, 1985) work, this can define new technology as 'men's work', maintaining the definition of skilled work as 'masculine' and consigning unskilled labour as suitable for women – so reconstructing gender segregation. As she has pointed out, such segregation is an integral part of technological and organizational change. In the context of the medical profession, Witz (1992) has described how the new occupation of radiography that emerged in the 1920s and 1930s became 'feminized' and how men sought, through a strategy of demarcation, to draw gendered (and hierarchical) boundaries between 'bundles' of skills, assigning (seemingly superior) technical skills to men and patient care to women.

In what we see now as 'gender-atypical' occupations, most of the so-called 'feminized' jobs now dominated by women were at some stage thought to be suitable for men. In the context of Australia, Biskup (1994) charts the feminization of librarianship and its shifting identity from the early days of male dominance to the current position in which 83 per cent of librarian positions are occupied by women. Similarly, Mills (1995) demonstrates how airlines initially hired male stewards to serve passengers, replicating the white-coated stewards of first-class rail and ship travel. Positioned against the highly masculine and technico/militaristic image of pilots, the masculinity of the steward was 'imaged out' and, as Mills suggests, paved the way for the introduction of women in the post-war period. Women were initially presented by airlines in asexual terms, that is, as 'surrogate' men (uniforms for example were very similar), and it was not until stewarding became established as a female occupation that sexuality was used as a selling point – and the few men in the occupation 'marked' as gay. In nursing, Evans (1992) notes how both men and women were employed in the early charity hospitals, with men assigned to the care of male patients and the mentally ill. Men's association with nursing ended in the mid-nineteenth century when Florence Nightingale, the founder of modern nursing, established it as a female occupation – based on the belief that nursing care was an extension of women's 'natural' caring and domestic role within the family.

The term 'non-traditional' or 'gender atypical' must therefore be set in the context of changes in occupational demography that lead to different interpretations of 'men's' and 'women's' work. As Cockburn (1991) points out, jobs and skills are not gender-neutral but are conceptualized in terms of their suitability for men or women. These conceptualizations are not, however, fixed and will evolve with movements in the labour market and the wider economy. What does emerge, however, is a tendency for work thought contemporarily as the domain of women to be undervalued and work deemed suitable for men to have a higher status. This can be seen in the way the status of some occupations is eroded as they become feminized – with implications for men when they attempt to enter these roles.

In this respect, Bradley (1993) distinguishes between three patterns of male entry to female-dominated occupations: takeover, invasion and infiltration. With takeover, a job that was originally assigned to women is taken over exclusively by men. This relatively rare phenomenon – rare because of the few status and monetary advantages of such a move – is likely to occur with major economic change such technological innovation. Bradley cites the case of cotton spinning, previously a female-dominated and cottage-based specialism, which with the advent of mechanization was taken over by men. The new technology increased production and hence the economic rewards from the job and the location of spinning in the new factory-based structure of production meant that the job now entailed the supervision and control of other workers, deemed more suitable for men. Invasion occurs when men move into an occupation in large numbers but do not drive women out completely. This is likely to be accompanied by processes of demarcation whereby men monopolize certain (higher status) specialisms. Bradley refers here to primary school teaching, human resource management and social work – where men enter in the expectation of rapid promotion to leadership positions and where, in the case of personnel, men originally took over a newly expanded (tough, demanding) industrial relations component leaving women to deal with more gender-congruent welfare work (see also Legge, 1987). Finally, infiltration occurs when men move slowly and in relatively small numbers into an occupation – such as childcare, nursing or supermarket cashier. This may emerge as a result of high unemployment and lack of opportunities elsewhere – or may reflect personal inclinations or dissatisfaction with a more gender-congruent career.

Theories of occupational choice and the non-traditional career

While research has demonstrated that women pursue male careers because they offer prestige, higher pay and opportunities for advancement (Chusmir, 1990; Galbraith, 1992), little is known about the entry decisions and career orientation of men in non-traditional occupations. The advantages for men in what are generally seen as 'women's jobs' are less clearcut, involving as we have seen probable sacrifices in terms of pay and status as well as raising questions over their masculinity and suitability for the job (Bradley, 1993; Lupton, 2000; Williams, 1993). Men therefore have less to gain and much to lose by choosing a non-traditional career.

Various theories, drawing on psychological, social and cultural factors, have emerged to explain occupational choice. With a focus on psychological factors, Holland (1959, 1962, 1966, 1982) for example has highlighted the importance of 'fit' between individual's personality and career choice, while Gottfredson (1981), with an emphasis on the social as opposed to the psychological self, sees perceptions of and preferences for gender roles, through circumscription and compromise, as central to occupational choice (Gottfredson, 1981; Gottfredson and Lapan, 1997). Circumscription occurs as young people remove occupations as being incompatible with their developing self-concepts while compromise occurs as they eliminate their preferred choices through perceptions of inaccessibility (for example, wrong sex type, low prestige). The theory postulates that gender, as a core element of one's social image, is the first aspect of self-concept against which young people judge the desirability of different occupations and that gender is the aspect of self that young people, particularly boys, are least willing to violate when making occupational choices. Therefore, career choices reflect efforts to implement preferred self-concepts, and satisfaction with career choice depends on how well that choice fits or matches that concept.

Other theories which focus on the importance of gender emphasize the effect of socially prescribed gender roles (e.g. Eagly, 1987; Eagly *et al.*, 2000). From this perspective, men choose to enter male-dominated occupations (calling for masculine personal qualities) because of gender socialization processes (e.g. Jacobs, 1989; Wigfield *et al.*, 2002). Such research accordingly suggests gender differences in occupational choice and aspirations. Other studies focus on possible gender similarities and suggest that women's occupational aspirations are becoming more like men's (Farmer and Chung, 1995; Powell and Butterfield, 2003; Shu and Marini, 1998). Powell and Butterfield, for example, found that men and women who saw themselves as possessing an abundance of male characteristics were more likely to aspire to top management positions than those who saw themselves as possessing female characteristics – indicating personality and self-concept were significant factors in career choice and aspirations rather than gender. However, while some women may be conforming to male patterns, this does not explain the small but growing number of men who choose female roles and female professions.

Dynamics of career entry and career choice

Looking at the dynamics of entry into female-dominated occupations, Williams and Villemez (1993) differentiated between three broad groups of men: seekers, who actively sought female-dominated jobs; finders, who were looking for other types of work but who ended up in a non-traditional occupation; and leavers, who were in 'female' jobs and left them. This typology has been further refined (Simpson, 2004, 2005) to include a further category of 'settlers'. Factors identifying each group include the location of the current occupation in respondents' scale of preferences, whether the occupation comprises a first or subsequent career, the nature of any previous occupation and relative levels of satisfaction compared to that job.

Thus for seekers and settlers, current occupations are high on their preference scale and are 'first best' choice at the time the decision was made. By contrast, the decision to enter a non-traditional occupation is 'second best' for finders and involves some compromise around an alternative and preferred option (for example, a decision to enter librarianship may be taken because of lack of necessary credentials in relation to the preferred choice of academia). The career decision of finders also has an unplanned element ('I just fell into it'). Settlers stand out in that the majority have undergone a career change and have moved out of careers that are radically different, in terms of sex type, from their current choice (for example, management, engineering, finance, the army). After periods of dissatisfaction in their previous (more masculine sextyped) roles, they frequently claim high levels of job satisfaction in their current occupation.

As a result, unlike seekers and finders, settlers prefer to remain close to professional practice at 'grassroots' level rather than adopting a careerist strategy and ascending the hierarchy into management (possibly because they have already rejected a masculinist career model in their non-traditional occupational choice). They thus prioritize intrinsic over extrinsic rewards. In nursing and teaching, for example, settlers prefer to work closely with patients and to have responsibility for their own class at school in a context where seniority might remove them from this day-to-day professional contact. As I have argued elsewhere (Simpson, 2005), the common notion of 'fast track' or 'straight through' careers for men (e.g. Williams, 1993), where upward mobility is facilitated by assumptions of leadership capabilities associated with the masculine gender, may not therefore be representative for all men in these non-traditional roles.

Despite this, greater opportunities for promotion may present themselves as key motivating factors for some groups of men – as well as a possible desire for professional status not open to men in more 'masculine' occupations (Lupton, 2006). In accordance with the 'settler' category above, men may be motivated by a desire for fulfilment not available in male sex-typed jobs (Chusmir, 1990). In short, while men in non-traditional careers are more likely then women to have leadership aspirations (Williams, 1993), they may also choose to develop the affective domain of their lives (Galbraith, 1992; Schann, 1983).

Challenges faced in a non-traditional occupation

As Williams and Villemez point out, some men choose to leave their non-traditional occupation and many are denied access, despite having a preference for such a job. Men face limiting factors due to societal and personal barriers that discriminate against free choice (Jacobs, 1989; Williams, 1993). Society understands why a woman would want a male job because it raises her status and her quality of life. Non-traditional jobs for men are likely to be low paid and of low prestige. Men's identity as a man may be challenged as well as their sexuality (Lupton, 2000; Mangan, 1994) and their ability to compete in a man's world (Cameron, 2001; Chusmir, 1990; Williams, 1993). Accordingly, some incongruity is likely between gender identity and occupational stereotyping.

For example, emotional labour such as teaching, nursing and social work may call for special abilities that only women are deemed to possess (Hochschild, 1983). This can create problems for men (Heikes, 1991) who call into question their competence and suitability if they assert a traditional masculinity and yet who invite challenges to their sexuality and masculinity if they adopt a more feminine approach. In primary school teaching, men have been found to be in a double bind: their presumed masculine interests in sport and male bonding give them an initial hiring advantage but these same characteristics can alienate them from female staff (Williams, 1993).

These challenges raise issues about how male workers reconcile the feminine nature of their work with the demands of a hegemonically masculine gender regime. Work in the area suggests that men engage in various practices that involve a distancing from the feminine. One strategy may be a 'careerist' one, that is, to move into management or supervisory positions (Williams, 1995); to identify with more powerful male groups, such as hospital doctors or head teachers (Floge and Merrill, 1986); to emphasize the male and downplay the female elements of the job for example by moving into what may be seen as a more 'masculine' specialism (Williams, 1993). In nursing for example men often gravitate towards mental health, with historic (and 'masculine') links to custodialism or accident and emergency, seen as more 'adrenalin charged' than general nursing care (Squires, 1995; Williams, 1995). Other work suggests that men create a sense of comfort with their occupational role through a process of 'naming and reframing'. Piper and Collamer (2001) in the context of librarianship found that men often renamed the job (for example, information scientist, information manager) to redress the weak image of the occupation and chose 'masculine' specialisms, often involving new technology, within its domain. Such strategies suggest a tension for men in non-traditional roles between the 'feminine' nature of the job and dominant discourses of masculinity – and the need for identity work to restore a comfortable sense of self.

Theoretical focus: Doing gender, doing masculinity

The work discussed above on career motivation, career orientation and challenges faced by men in non-traditional occupations has furthered our understanding of the experiences of men in these work roles. This book builds on these important contributions. However, it moves away from a 'role based' perspective or one which conceives of responses to 'role strain' in these contexts as instances of separation or distancing from the feminine. A focus on roles can lead to a neglect of underlying processes or practices that may be saturated with power, while responses to challenges to masculinity around separation and distance can overlook the complex ways in which gender is 'managed' and maintained.

A more dynamic approach conceives of gender, not as the property of the individual or as a simple, unambiguous category, but as 'situated doing' (West and Zimmerman, 1987, 2002) or performance (Butler, 1990). From the work of West and Zimmerman (1987, 2002) and Fenstermaker and West (2002), drawing on symbolic interactionism and social constructionism, difference and the gender binary are actively produced as part of the work of gender in everyday interactions while for Butler (1990), from a post-structuralist perspective, gender is conceived as a 'performance' produced through discourse. Both focus on how gender-differentiated practices take place in the light of normative and localized conceptions of what it means to be a woman or a man (Moloney and Fenstermaker, 2002).

Doing gender thus involves creating, re-creating and sometimes resisting difference in specific interactional and institutional contexts, so underpinning existing hierarchical arrangements. These provide a 'repertoire of practices' (Martin, 2003) concerning the doing of gender at work. In the institutional context of teaching, for example, men 'do' masculinity in that they are often called upon to be the disciplinarian or to take on difficult or challenging groups (Simpson, 2004) while within hospitals male nurses are expected to do heavy lifting work and to manage angry or abusive patients (Evans, 1997). However, in their interactions men may conform to, resist or partly dismantle these normative pressures. Institutions, as gendered (Acker, 1990) and purveyors of gendered narratives (Ashcraft, 2006) as well as individuals are thus implicated in the appropriate doing or 'undoing' (Deutsch, 2007; Pullen and Knights, 2007) of gender. Organizations may therefore 'prompt conformity' (Ely and Padavic, 2007) which may appear as sex differences but which may also trigger resistance (Deutsch, 2007; West and Fenstermaker, 1995). From Ely and Padavic (2007), deconstructing and understanding difference requires an emphasis on the reciprocal influences of organizational and institutional practices as well as internal processes of identity construction.

From their early work on 'doing gender', West and Zimmerman moved to a focus on 'doing difference' (West and Zimmerman, 2002). This allows a more nuanced understanding of how men and women create, deny and draw on difference as well as the significance of other identities apart from gender to aid an understanding of how men and women create a sense of self. As Ashcraft (2006) notes, a focus on doing difference enables a more complicated inquiry into the varied articulations of and meanings attached to difference as well as into the implications of intersectionality for identity performances. Here difference exists only to the extent that it is manufactured and given meaning through situated performances and in relation to multiple discourses of identity for example around race, class, sexuality.

Thus, for Butler (1990, 1993), prioritizing the latter, gender must be understood in relation to sexuality in that gender performances are shaped by and viewed in relation to heterosexual norms. Gender is 'marked' by heterosexuality (Butler, 1990) and can therefore give rise to vulnerabilities at their intersection. In the context of the non-traditional career, associations with homosexuality for example can collide with dominant discourses of masculinity with sometimes painful implications for men in these roles (Lupton, 2000). As West and Zimmerman (2002) point out, failure to do gender appropriately may call individuals (their character, motives, predispositions) rather than institutions to account – with implications for the individual performances of men in 'feminized' roles. Individuals are thus 'accountable' for appropriate performances of gender in that they are subject to the regulatory force of what it means to be a woman or a man in specific contexts.

As mentioned earlier there is potential for men and women to resist these normative pressures. It could be said for example that men's decision to enter a non-traditional career is in some ways a resistance to dominant conceptions of masculinity. However, as Deutsch (2007) argues, the concept of 'doing' may leave little room for the incorporation of the challenge to and dismantling of difference. Recent work (e.g. Butler, 2004; Pullen and Knights, 2007) has therefore focused on the 'undoing' of gender, defined by Deutsch as those social interactions and associated discourses that reduce, dismantle or challenge gender difference. This has particular resonance with the experience of men in non-traditional roles, in that performances of masculinity in these contexts may well involve both the doing and the undoing of gender and of difference. Moreover, given the potential for dissonance, such performances are likely to render the salience of doing as well as the potential for undoing gender more visible and alert us to the complications of doing and the undoing of difference in particular contexts.

This suggests a need to move beyond the binary of male/female, masculine/feminine inherent within a gender role approach as well as an associated view of difference as a stable 'gap' between the two (Ashcraft, 2006) to consider how men may draw on, resist and play with difference as well as the implications of dominant discourses of heterosexual masculinity for the 'doing of difference' at work. This poststructuralist perspective (Connell, 2000) takes on board such issues of instability, complexity and fluidity to explore the dynamic nature of gender and how gender identities are constructed and reconstructed as a 'relational' and situated project (Pullen, 2006). Gender may therefore be constructed differently in different situations, with several masculinities (and femininities) present in any one context. As Connell (2000) states, these masculinities will be hierarchically arranged around a dominant or hegemonic form – with some forms of masculinity marginalized and devalued as a result. Different forms of masculinity will therefore emerge in different organizations and even within the same organizational site – each delineating variations in power and access to a privileged status.

This allows for a more complicated enquiry into how men in non-traditional occupations 'do gender' in their work contexts, how they experience their Other status at a subjective level and how they draw on, create and resist difference as they manage their identity at work. In other words, as Ely and Padavik (2007) point out, organizations' gendering processes shape gender identities and this can sometimes lead to sex differences and sometimes to similarities. Perceptions of such similarities and differences form a major focus of this book.

The study

The following chapters are based on interviews with 74 men working in four occupational groups: nurses, primary school teaching, librarianship and cabin crew. Six female nurses were also interviewed about their experiences of working with men. The research was conducted in two stages over a 4-year period. The first stage took place in the UK between 2002 and 2004; the second stage consisted of a smaller-scale Australia-based study, funded by the Nuffield Foundation, conducted in 2006. In both contexts, the research was deemed pertinent given widespread changes in the occupational structure and the diminution of traditionally 'male' jobs in many sectors, the growth of services and the need to address labour shortages in traditionally female occupations such as teaching and nursing.

The sample

The UK study comprised 49 in-depth interviews, conducted in London and the South-East, with male workers from four occupational groups: librarianship, primary school teaching, cabin crew and nursing. Seven interviews took place with academic librarians from two different universities, five of whom were at assistant librarian level. Ten primary school teachers were interviewed from six different schools in and around London. Two were on the senior management team, one was nursery manager and seven were mainscale class room teachers. Of the 15 nurses, from six different hospitals, who took part in the study, five were involved in mental health, four in accident and emergency, one in palliative care and the remainder in general nursing. Data were collected between 2002 and 2004 from 17 male cabin crew. Crew were employed in five different airlines, two of which were short-haul low-cost airlines with the remaining three long-haul global carriers. Sixteen male nurses, six female nurses and nine primary school teachers took part in the smaller Australia-based study. All were located in and around Sydney, New South Wales. Of the male nurses, four were senior managers, two were midwives and two were psychiatric nurses. The remainder were located in various specialisms (intensive care, HIV, accident and emergency, working in operating theatres) or were still in training and/or working in general nursing on the ward. All but two of the nurses were registered, a professional status, having completed a university-level course. The two remaining nurses were 'enrolled'. Enrolled nurses in Australia usually spend 12 months training at the equivalent of a further education college, followed by practical experience in hospital wards for the remainder of the time. Of the sample of teachers, all worked in primary schools in Sydney. Two were at a more senior (head of year) level. Four had come from teaching positions abroad (UK, South Africa, Malta).

UK-based samples of cabin crew and nurses were established by advertising the project on the intranet site of a UK-based airline and through a professional nursing journal. Teachers were found through personal contacts, many of whom then drew on their own friends and acquaintances in the profession. Librarians were approached directly, from university library staff lists, through an e-mail explaining the nature of the project. In Australia, use was made of some limited contacts in the nursing and teaching community. In the main, samples of each profession were established through advertisements in appropriate professional journals and associated websites.

This sampling technique can have certain drawbacks. Interviewees who 'self-select' by responding to requests for help may be more aware of and reflexive about the significance of gender at work or may have more 'issues' in relation to their non-traditional occupational choice than other men in these occupations. Equally, reliance on personal contacts may lead to a sample that is not wholly representative. However, such techniques have been used in other exploratory research on non-traditional occupations (see Chung and Harman, 1994; Murray, 1996) and may therefore be seen as acceptable, given the above reservations, in this case.

In terms of sexual orientation, between one-quarter and one-third of the sample identified themselves as homosexual. Issues around sexual orientation were not pursued specifically as a line of inquiry in interviews, on the grounds that this was likely to be a particularly sensitive area of discussion. The significance of sexuality was only discussed if it was raised, unprompted, by interviewees. As Fassinger (1991), cited in Chung and Harman (1994), has argued, it is difficult to locate and adequately sample gay men because they are a hidden minority group. Their sexual identity cannot usually be discovered without their cooperation. Gay men may be reluctant to participate in studies which require disclosure because they fear potential risks such as misunderstanding and discrimination. However, as Chung and Harman (1994) point out, gay men may be more likely to have non-traditional career interests and aspirations because they are more likely to endorse non-traditional sex-role orientations for men. While some aspects of sexuality were explored during some interviews, and while for all men homosexuality was an issue if only because they were subject to assumptions from others that they had that sexual orientation, it was likely that the significance of this aspect of identity was under-represented in the data – and the exact nature of the sample in terms of sexual orientation remains unknown.

Research approach

The research adopted a social constructivist approach in that it explored how men give meaning to their experiences at work and how they make sense of their reality. The goal of constructivism is to understand the world of lived experience from the point of view of those who live it (Schwandt, 1994). It seeks to understand 'how the seemingly 'objective' features, such as industries, organizations and technologies, are constituted by subjective meanings of individuals and inter-subjective processes (Eriksson and Kovalainen, 2008: 19). From Burr (1995), cited in Eriksson and Kovalainen, there are four basic assumptions of the social constructionist philosophical position. Firstly, it challenges the hegemonic status of taken-for-granted knowledge on the grounds that 'the world does not present itself objectively to the observer, but is known through human experience' (ibid.: 20). Secondly, in that human experience is mediated through language, language does not simply describe 'reality', it also produces and creates meanings through social interaction. Thirdly, knowledge is sustained by 'conventions of communication' and, finally and relatedly, knowledge and social interaction are intertwined.

This orientation has an alignment with both critical theory and post-structuralism. The former rejects positivist philosophical assumptions of an objective, stable reality independent of the researcher in favour of emancipatory research and interpretations based on shared meanings. Similarly, post-structuralism focuses on the social construction of what is taken as real (Johnson *et al.*, 2006). In both cases, the aim is to challenge previously taken-for-granted understandings and to reveal alternative meanings.

These meanings and understandings are often produced through interaction and language, interpreted through historical and cultural norms that operate in peoples' lives and in specific contexts (Creswell, 2007). They are thus complex, contingent and fragmented – and shaped through discourse (Alvesson, 1998). It is through discourse (that is, signs, labels, expressions, rhetoric that form our thinking, attitudes and behaviour) that we are persuaded to think and act in a certain way and through which we interpret our own and others' behaviour. From this post-structuralist perspective, rather than supporting the possibility of a universal objective knowledge, meaning and knowledge are 'subjectively shared social constructions' (Pullen, 2006) – open to multiple interpretations, some of which are privileged over others. There is no 'single discoverable true meaning' (Johnson *et al.*, 2006) but different interpretations that are implicated in the social construction of subjectivity. This approach therefore lends itself to an exploration of the dynamic nature of masculinity, how it is constructed and reconstructed through sameness and difference, how it is experienced at a subjective level and how multiple masculinities exist in relation to the dominant (hegemonic) form.

This critical stance, in supporting the possibility of multiple realities, also sees research as a 'processual project that emphasizes researchers' and participants' reflexive and dialogic interrogation of their own understandings' (Johnson *et al.*, 2006: 143). Such research is oriented towards insight, tension and the emergent nature of identity and prefers to focus on local phenomena as the site of 'decisional constraints' (Alvesson and Deetz, 2000). Guided by concept formation, the researcher seeks to explore how individuals give meaning to their experiences and to uncover the 'otherness of the other (the way people and events exceed categories and classifications of them)' (Alvesson and Deetz, 2000: 30). On this basis, interviews became an active resource for exploring identity in that the stories and interpretations offered were seen as part of an identity management process. The question was not whether interviews reflected 'true' attitudes, feelings or experiences but how interviewees constituted themselves with reference to their work contexts.

Interviews were semi-structured, following a set of themes that concerned career issues (career background, motivation, aspirations, attitudes of friends and family to career choice); issues relating to minority status (potential advantages/disadvantages; experiences of marginalization and inclusion); perceptions of 'caring' (significance and perceptions of personal attributes, of gender difference in performing emotional labour, of challenges faced in this work); and issues concerning implications of career choice for identity and self-image (image of the job, its fit with self identity and self perception, possible challenges to masculinity and associated response). Interviews mainly took place in the place of work and lasted between 1 and 1.5 hours. All interviews were recorded and subsequently transcribed.

In recognition of the researchers' implication in the production of accounts (Pullen, 2006), interviews took the form of a dialogue. Reflexivity was sought through a shared process of exploration. Here, interviewer and interviewee discussed the meanings of recounted experiences and respondents were encouraged to consider, in the manner of reflexivity put forward by Martin (2006), their attitudes, emotions and behaviours. As Whitehead (2002) has pointed out, located in the 'mainstream', men often fail to reflect on themselves as gendered subjects or to understand experiences in the margin. Men in this study were unusual in the sense that they had to some extent 'broken the mould' in their occupational choice and had thought carefully about their decision. As one nurse pointed out, he came into nursing 'against all the odds' in terms of giving up a previous career and coping with the disapproval of family and friends. Reflexivity had accordingly been involved in their journey and was in some ways built into everyday practice as men coped with challenges to their masculinity and as they performed, in many cases, care and emotional labour. Therefore, while conversations in interviews often took a turn which was new, in the sense that respondents had not thought about certain issues before, many reflected ably on their attitudes and experiences.

Concerns that the gender difference between the two parties (female interviewer/male interviewee) might compromise willingness to explore sensitive issues were kept in mind during the interview situation. However, a reluctance to disclose did not emerge as a particular problem during these encounters. As Evans (2002) has suggested, research

collaboration between women and men can potentially raise epistemological issues concerning from whose standpoint we can develop a truer
understanding of men and masculinity. She subsequently concludes
that it is the standpoint of women rather than men that offers this possibility on the grounds that men 'tend to remain imprisoned within
established epistemological theoretical and methodological frameworks
which have historically been at the centre of knowledge production'
(Frank, 1993: 337 cited in Evans, 2002), while women's marginalized
position offers a broader and more 'accurate and comprehensive' lens
(Harding, 1987). In the context of the present study, men spent a large
part of their day working and communicating with women and there
was thus an ease in terms of shared reflections and disclosures in the
interview situation. As one man pointed out when asked about this
issue, he would in fact feel more constrained if talking to a man.

Data analysis

The analysis took place in two stages. First, the data was divided into
broad 'slices' that related to each of the themes above (careers; perceptions of gender difference in skills and aptitudes; emotions and
emotional labour; management of tensions between gender and occupational identity). Open coding, where data is broken down into discrete
parts and examined for similarities and differences, was used to find
common patterns and themes. These patterns were explored firstly
across all occupational groups and then within each group. Part A of
the book reflects some of the themes, relating to those specified above,
that emerged across occupations around identity (incorporating difference), visibility and emotions. These themes included, for example, the
colonization of the feminine (identity), struggles around the dominant
centre (visibility), and the gift exchange (emotions).

Within each occupational group, a specific 'lens' was chosen as a
framework with which to analyze the data. This lens emerged partly
from the data, as a particular issue or as a means of making sense
of men's experiences in that context, and partly from existing work
relating to that area of practice. For example, perhaps because of a
commonly felt fascination with aircraft as well as the confined nature
of crews' working space, dictating the content and parameters of the
service encounter, male crews' descriptions of their work were deeply
embedded within the 'spatialities' of their work context. Space therefore
emerged as a 'lens' through which to explore and make sense of how

they enacted and performed gender as well as of some complications involved in that performance.

The analysis comprised a critical reading of the text, paying attention to, from Essers and Benschop (2007), what was said, how it was said and the context in which the statements, descriptions or interpretations were made. Interviewee responses provided 'thick descriptions' (Geertz, 1973), that is, multi-layered accounts of their experiences and of identity construction. Some of these accounts have been presented in the following chapters – selected because they appeared to be of significance to the interviewee, because they served to throw light on experiences, particularly in relation to gender, and because they resonated with accounts given by others. This is not to say, from Pullen (2006), that these accounts are necessarily representative of a wider population or dataset – or that other fragments of data might not also yield useful results. A post-structuralist-influenced methodology does not seek to produce unified or exclusive accounts of reality, but is reflective of the fragmented nature of experience and of the possibility of multiple meanings. There are therefore many possible interpretations of the same data, all of which are potentially meaningful (Eriksson and Kovalainen, 2008). In this respect, this book makes a modest claim – namely to further our understanding of men's subjective experiences in the specificities of their gender atypical work contexts and of how they themselves make sense of those experiences as they manage a sense of self.

Structure of the book

In the chapters that follow, we accordingly explore how men 'do' and 'undo' gender in their work context. Part I of the book starts with an overview of key issues that relate performances of gender in atypical work situations. Chapter 2 discusses identity as part of 'doing difference' and of how men manage some of the insecurities of a masculine identity when masculinity is 'on the line' and subject to challenge. Chapter 3 explores issues of visibility – both in the context of men's 'token' status in non-traditional roles, the implications of the 'gaze' for men in gender atypical roles and in the context of their relationship with the 'dominant centre'. Chapter 4 considers the hitherto neglected area of gender and emotions – neglected in the sense that emotions have been implicitly tied to notions of femininity. The chapter accordingly explores links between emotions, emotional labour and masculinity.

In Part II, we consider the four occupations on which the study was based. In each case, a particular 'lens' is adopted to explore the diverse experiences of men in their specific work contexts. These 'lenses' or themes emerged as being of particular significance in terms of understanding the occupationally specific nature of these experiences and in terms of appreciating the 'work' men undertake to manage potential mismatch between gender and occupational identity. This is not to say that another lens might not have been revealing – or that the 'view' created is the only one of significance. As discussed above, post-structuralist-influenced research is based on the principle of the possibility of multiple understandings. The interpretations presented are not the only ones possible – but serve to highlight key aspects of men's accounts of their work context. Thus, Chapter 5 explores how space is implicated in how male cabin crew manage their identity; Chapter 6 considers the implications of bodies for how male nurses perform emotional labour and other work practices; Chapter 7 discusses the implications of professional identities and of the 'professionalization project' for male primary school teachers; and Chapter 8 discusses social identity and how male librarians draw on different categorizations to negotiate around the negative image implied by their job. Chapter 9 draws on the data from female nurses as well as male nurses to explore issues of gender reflexivity and perceptions of gender difference. Through these chapters, we throw light on how men both do and undo gender in the context of their (gender atypical) work.

2
Identities

With contributions from Alison Pullen

Introduction

In the last chapter, I positioned the theoretical orientation of the book as one of 'doing' gender. In other words, rather than seeing gender as a stable attribute or category that 'attaches' to the individual, gender is performed in action and interaction. Thus, gender can be seen to be a dynamic: an accomplishment (West and Zimmerman, 2002) or achievement (Bruni and Gherardi, 2002) produced through discourse (Kerfoot and Knights, 1998), symbolism (Gherardi, 1995) or performances (Butler, 1993, 1994).

This conceptualization of gender has implications for how we see identity in that gender identity and how it is experienced at a subjective level (how it feels to be a man, how it feels to be a woman) is likely to be made up of a variety of different discourses and interactions. Gender identities are thus constituted through relations of power (Kerfoot and Knights, 1998) and will vary in different contexts and different institutions. The way individuals 'do' and sometimes 'undo' gender will be context-specific as gender norms, from an institution's past history and present cultural configurations, impress on expectations of appropriate behaviour – and as individuals draw on institutional symbolic and cultural resources in their gender performances. There are therefore a number of different masculinities and femininities which are produced in different contexts, with some being more dominant or privileged than others.

This post-structuralist approach moves away from seeing identity as a stable trait or as a process that results in a form of harmony or unification through, for example, appropriate learning and performance of roles (for example, parent, team-worker, manager, volunteer).

Rather than focusing on consistency and singularity, as an unchanging identity unfolds in different contexts, identity can instead be seen to be a product of discourse, relationship and interaction. Discourse refers to those signs, labels, expressions and rhetoric that help to construct meaning. Discourses serve to shape our thinking, attitudes and behaviour as well as our sense of self. Consequently, meanings about gender can be framed by rhetorical strategies about the 'appropriate' placing and behaviour of men and women which then define institutional attitudes and practices (Fondas, 1997; Leonard, 2002; Maddock, 1999). As discourses structure the world, they also structure the person's subjectivity providing him/her with a particular social identity and 'ways of being' as well as the potential to resist or redefine a sense of self. Identity is thus a 'process rather than a product – a process which involves societal factors, psychological factors, interaction, reflection practice and performance' (Pullen and Linstead, 2005: 3).

In this chapter we explore identity issues firstly through the concept of the One and the Other which has the potential to capture the relational nature of identity, discussed below. We then consider the insecure nature of masculine identities and how men manage insecurities in their non-traditional roles. Finally, we look at the implications of sexuality and ascriptions of homosexuality, a common assumption associated with men in these occupations, and how men resist uncomfortable, subordinated and marginalized identities. These issues help to highlight the fragmented and ongoing nature of identity work and the complexities involved as men move between masculinity and femininity in these roles.

Gender identity: The One and the Other

Rather than surfacing and reading gender as comprising static categories, a relational approach, as a consequence, sees identity as actively produced in day-to-day relations and interactions; in other words, gender is something that we 'do' together (Ashcraft, 2006). As Beech and McInnes (2005) point out, the 'multi-authoring' of identity relies as much on others, as the individual both constructs him/herself in relation to others and is in turn mirrored in their own constructions. Masculinity only has meaning in terms of its relationship with femininity, so the masculine is given meaning through its culturally constructed difference from the feminine. Through this One/Other relationship, men and women produce their sense of self.

In this respect, the 'One and the Other' have been a source of much attention in gender and organization studies, with a great deal of work focusing on the 'Other', that is, on the marginal and abject position of minority social groups (e.g. de Beauvoir, 1949; Gatens, 1991; Grosz, 1994). Here women have been conceptualized as Other with research on masculinity largely concentrating on their position as 'One' – a source of privilege and power (e.g. Connell, 1995, 2000; Hearn, 1994; Kaufman, 1994; Kerfoot and Knights, 1993, 1998).

De Beauvoir (1949) in her classic text *The Second Sex* presented one of the first systematic accounts of women's Otherness as a formation of self produced through situations of oppression and subjugation. De Beauvoir contends that throughout history women have been reduced to objects for men and denied their own subjectivity and autonomy. Woman is constructed as man's Other – an unequal pairing imposed on women by men. De Beauvoir gives prominence to how the 'One' is superior to and depends upon the 'Other' in gender relations (see also Irigaray, 1985; Jardine, 1985; McDowell and Pringle, 1992). In the latter respect, man attains himself 'only through that reality which he is not' (de Beauvoir, 1949). The Other accordingly conforms to man's 'onto-logical and moral pretensions' and is appropriated by the One in that his often precarious and fragile sense of power is founded on an Other of powerlessness and derided weakness (ibid.). The Other is thus the 'mirror of its essence' (that is, the One) and is distinctive only through default (McDowell and Pringle, 1992) or 'lack' (Irigaray, 1985). Kerfoot and Knights (1998) for example refer to a privileged form of masculinity prevalent in some management and organizational settings (rational, competitive, goal-driven) which both generates and sustains feminine dependency – a passivity that is partially created by masculine identity practices and which serves to support the hierarchical order between men and women.

As Tyler (2005) suggests, de Beauvoir's articulation of gender as 'becoming' is resonant with recent work on identity as a process. Wom-anhood, the primary focus of her work, can be seen as a project situated in Otherness (that is, in inequality, constraint, oppression). However, as Czarniawska and Hopfl (2002) point out, the post-modern concern with plurality of difference may have rendered the construction of the Other problematic. In this respect, the dualism inherent in the One/Other relationship (Butler, 1990; McDowell and Pringle, 1992) may serve to reinforce an interpretation of gender as a series of opposites, leaving lit-tle room for gradation or overlapping categories – as well as preventing a more nuanced understanding of Otherness that can embrace men (Grosz, 1994).

Nevertheless, as Tyler (2005) argues, the conceptualization in general, and De Beauvoir's work in particular, has potential to highlight marginalization and the perpetuation of hierarchies in difference as well as to understand identity processes at work. In this respect, the conceptualization does not in itself deny the existence of multiplicities of gender. Kerfoot and Knights (1998), for example, from an orientation to gender based on the existence of multiple masculinities and femininities, illustrate the nature of oppositional identity practices that separate privileged forms of masculinities from the feminine. In exploring the creation and meaning of difference, various authors in Czarniawska and Hopfl's (2002) edited book *Casting the Other* address issues relating to how individuals experience alterity – and the ways in which the Other is cast. Similarly, Hearn (1996) calls for a 'deconstruction of the dominant', the One, to explore the unspoken, invisible centre of organizations and their occupants and subject them to the scrutiny normally reserved for the Other ('Making the One(s) the Other(s)').

This suggests that we can apply the lens of One and Other to explore how men become/experience the Other in feminized spaces, how men move between visibility and invisibility, and how the discourse of 'Otherness' is employed as part of the identity project. This allows us to move beyond the binary suggested by De Beauvoir and others in the field to explore the significance of changing boundaries – as men create, draw on and complicate difference – in the ongoing project of 'identity work' (Sveningsson and Alvesson, 2003; Thomas and Linstead, 2002). Rather than denying complexity and multiplicities of difference, we can thus use the One/Other relationship to consider how men in gender-atypical occupations simultaneously experience and move between both subjective modes. In so doing, we can throw light on how they respond to being 'cast' as the Other and on how they can draw on Otherhood and alterity to support rewarding and unconventional identities as well as increase the value of their skills. After considering the insecure nature of masculine identities, we return to these themes below.

Insecurity and masculine identities

In so far as gender is a meaning that is produced through discourse and interaction with Others, we have seen that issues of complexity, ambiguity and fluidity become central themes. This highlights the fragmented, insecure and uncertain nature of identity (Collinson, 2003; Kerfoot and Knights, 1998; Pullen, 2006). Here identity is a constantly emerging process or 'doing', characterized by confusion and conflict within the individual (Pullen and Linstead, 2005). From this perspective, work on masculinity (e.g. Connell, 2000; Kerfoot and Knights, 1993, 1998; Whitehead, 2002) has similarly focused on issues of complexity, ambiguity and fluidity and on the roles of agency and symbolism in its construction as well as on institutions and social practices. Such work has explored the dynamic nature of masculinity, how it is constructed and reconstructed, how it is experienced at a subjective level and how multiple masculinities exist in relation to the dominant (hegemonic) form. From this, masculinity is seen to be internally divided, ambiguous and often contradictory (Alvesson, 1998; Collinson and Hearn, 1994; Connell, 2000; Kerfoot and Knights, 1998) as men manage their identities against these dominant conceptions of 'how men should be'.

This highlights the insecure nature of identity as men construct themselves as masculine subjects. Collinson (2003) locates this insecurity in the release of identities from the 'old' order of birth, religion, class and the rise of paid employment, with all its uncertainties, as the source of a valued sense of self. For Kimmel (1994), insecurity emanates partly from a failure to live up to a masculine hegemonic ideal while Kerfoot and Knights (1998) see it as part of a quest for, and failure to achieve, control. In terms of the former, as Connell (2000) argues, while discourses of masculinity are not always and everywhere the same and while different masculinities exist in definite (hierarchical, exclusionary) relations with each other, there is in most situations some hegemonic form – the most honoured or desired – which can be expressed and represented in everyday interactions. Accordingly, despite differences and variations, successful performance of masculinity is, more often than not, equated with being heterosexual, successful, capable, reliable and in control (Alvesson, 1998; Collinson and Hearn, 1994; Connell, 2000; Hearn, 1994; Knights and McCabe, 2001). From Kimmel, failure to achieve this 'ideal' in all its manifestations is thus a constant source of anxiety and insecurity for most men. These problems and insecurities often surface under the 'gaze' of male family members and peers (Kimmel, 1994) as 'guardians' of the masculine ideal. As Ely and Padavic (2007) note, anxiety about being sufficiently masculine is a form of self-surveillance that gains much of its power because it goes unnoticed – driving men to seek to secure a stable sense of self (Kerfoot and Knights, 1993, 1998).

This quest, as Kerfoot and Knights (1998) point out, can become an end in itself, the driver behind the masculine desire for control (over self, over others, over environment) and for a knowable and predictable world. In this respect, competitive masculinity can afford men some comfort among considerable insecurity, but its foundation is shaky in that it is based on an identity that 'generates and sustains feminine dependence and along with it support for a masculine self that is continuously feeling threatened and vulnerable as a consequence of the failure, potential or otherwise, to maintain control' (Kerfoot and Knights, 1998: 9). Moreover, the end is 'never fully specified, out of reach and constantly in motion' (ibid.: 13) – threatened by failure to fully achieve control as well as by femininities that do not conform to (stereo) types. As Collinson (2003) tellingly points out, the inevitable difficulties that arise in this quest may further reinforce rather than resolve the insecurities such strategies were intended to overcome.

The often contradictory and insecure nature of masculine identities has been highlighted by several authors who have explored the diverse and shifting nature of masculinities in different contexts. Barrett's (1996, 2001) study of US navy officers, discussed in Collinson (2003) found that dominant masculinity based on physical toughness, aggression, rugged heterosexuality and lack of emotional expression contributed to insecure identities. As Barrett demonstrates, attempts to achieve a secure masculine identity created 'conditions that undermine the possibility of such an achievement' (Barrett, 2001: 96). In this respect, he points to the demanding nature of the military where degradation and humiliation often accompany continual surveillance and testing and where men invest in masculine discourses in order to compensate for these negative experiences. Here differentiation from women (as emotional, deficient) was key to the management of masculine identities:

Preoccupation with differentiating self and discounting others creates an enduring sense of subjective insecurity. This persistent sense of fragility and precariousness generates a greater need to display worth. Such defensive posturing – differentiating self by outperforming others, validating self by negating others – is not only unlikely to lead to the achievement of a secure identity, it creates the very conditions that drive men to strive for a chance to demonstrate exceptionality. These officers are chronically aware that their peers are eager to surpass them. The achievement of masculinity in this culture is never secure. It must be continually confirmed and exhibited.

(Barrett, 2001: 97)

This supports the necessity for identity management as men negotiate and renegotiate their conditions of insecurity in an ever-incomplete process of identity work. Given that the cultural resources available for identity management will vary from organization to organization and given the way in which interactional repertoires and practices impress on subjectivities will be equally context-specific, 'doing masculinity' will be multiplicitous, fluid as well as multidimensional. Organizations also 'do' gender and have codes for performing gender identities. They are thus home to a variety of masculinities (Collinson and Hearn, 1994), with implications for how the dynamics of different masculinities – some prioritized, others suppressed – inform men's gender identities at work.

In terms of the One and the Other, this also suggests that location as the One is never secure but can form the site of struggle as individuals manage its inherent contradictions as well as challenges to that status. As Hearn (1996) argues, the location of the One is composite and shifting, based on hierarchies, difference and similarities, hierarchies over Others and relations of similarity with similar selves. Similarly, from Robinson (2000), we can think of the normative, the One, as being constantly under revision – shifting in response to the changing social, political and cultural terrain. The status of the One is thus 'surprisingly fragile' (Hearn, 1996) and is simultaneously and paradoxically a site of privilege and power and a source of ontological insecurity – reflecting the interdependent, ambivalent and complex nature of the relationship with the Other.

Managing masculinity in non-traditional roles

Consequently and from the previous discussion, managing masculinity in non-traditional occupations is likely to throw up particular challenges for men. As Leidner (1991) has argued, all workers seek ways to reconcile the work they do with an identity they can accept. The 'feminine' nature of as well as the often low status afforded to such work may well lead to tensions between gender and occupational identity as well as, in some para-professional occupational positionings, few 'status shields' (Hochschild, 1983) in the negotiation of a comfortable sense of self. In terms of the service role, often integral to such occupations, service providers are increasingly being asked to 'inhabit' the job (Forseth, 2005) in that the personal characteristics of the individual (for example, gender, age, appearance) as well as his or her personality and skills are integral to the quality of its delivery (Leidner, 1991). This has likely implications for the subjectivity of the worker and, in the context of the work environment, for his or her sense of self – causing difficulties for men as they negotiate a masculine identity.

More broadly, discourses of service and care can collide with dominant conceptions of masculinity arraigned around rationality, competition and profit (Ross-Smith and Kornberger, 2004) while organizational interactions and practices may reflect non-masculine ways of working. Men may find such femininity 'unlivable' in that its constituent elements (nurturance, passivity, service) have been defined and rejected by masculine identities. Moreover, the insecurities referred to earlier as integral to masculinity may become exacerbated in non-traditional roles. As Williams (1993) argues, men who 'cross over' upset the gendered assumptions embedded in such work so they are suspected of not being 'real' men – generating insecurity in relation to their positioning, as discussed above, against the hegemonic ideal.

This is supported by Lupton (2000) who suggests that men in non-traditional roles fear feminization and stigmatization – fears which are particularly acute, as argued earlier, under the gaze of other men. Associations with homosexuality for example can collide with dominant discourses of masculinity with sometimes painful implications for men in these roles (Lupton, 2000). In the context of the present study, men had particular difficulties explaining their non-traditional career choice to male peers – often relabelling the job to minimize non-masculine associations (for example, 'I'm in tourism' for cabin crew; 'I teach sport' for a primary school teacher; I'm an 'information officer' for a librarian). Men must therefore manage their identity under specific conditions of insecurity generated by a questioning of their masculinity.

But how do men manage their identity under these conditions? As we saw in Chapter 1, research suggests that responses to these challenges are largely oriented around the creation and maintenance of distance from the feminine. Men have been found to reconstruct the job so as to minimize its non-masculine associations (Lupton, 2000; Simpson, 2004). We will see in Chapter 5, how male cabin crew often focus on the safety and security aspects of the job, thus overriding associations with deferential service and customer care. As male crew variously commented, men are valued for their bodily strength and help instil feelings of security in passengers; they are not there for the 'niceties' of serving food and drink – by implication the domain of women. Equally, male librarians have been found to construct their job in terms of the requirement for high levels of information technology know-how and expertise discussed in Chapter 8. These practices serve to differentiate themselves from the 'feminine' associations of the job.

Men also engage in compensatory gendered practices so as to 'restore' a dominating position. From the last chapter, we have seen that strategies have included 'careerism' whereby men aspire to (masculine) management or supervisory posts and away from (feminine) day-to-day professional practice (Heikes, 1991; Williams, 1995); identification with more powerful male groups, such as hospital doctors or head teachers (Floge and Merrill, 1986; Simpson, 2004); emphasis on male and de-emphasis on female elements of the job for example by moving into what may be seen as more 'masculine' specialisms (Williams, 1993). Men can emphasize traditional masculine traits such as assertiveness or by being blatantly sexist (Cross and Bagilhole, 2002) while at the same time they can reconstruct a different masculinity, embracing their feminine side to become what they see as a more 'complete' person.

Overall, men have to undertake considerable 'identity work' to create a degree of comfort in their non-traditional role, work which may involve the reinforcement of what may be seen as masculine values and practices through a distancing from the feminine. The potential, as suggested by Cross and Bagilhole (2002) above, to 'embrace' the feminine indicates, however, the possibility of more complicated manoeuvrings that involve resistance to normative conceptions of gender. Issues of identity and resistance are considered in more detail later in the chapter.

Sexualities and identity

As Fassinger points out, studies of gay men are rare because they are a hidden minority group – so relatively little is known about the significance of sexual orientation for identity at work. One notable exception is the work of James Ward (2008) in his recent volume: *Sexualities, Work and Organization*. Here he notes the historic shift in conceptualizations of homosexuality from a behaviour to an identity. As he explains, between the sixteenth and the nineteenth centuries, discourses around sexuality were focused on particular acts, liable to various forms of punishments, rather than on the particular type of person. As Ward points out, it was the work of Foucault in his *History of Sexuality* published in 1976, which developed our understanding of homosexuality and identity. By setting sexuality in an historical context, and by pointing to the new homosexual identity that emerged in the mid-to-late nineteenth century, Foucault helped to challenge our understanding of sexuality as a biological given and homosexuality as a form of deviance. From

Foucault's work, we can see how homosexuality is given social meaning and constructed through discourse leading, as Ward (2008) points out, to a body of work referred to as Queer Theory.

These ideas are based on the view that sexuality is socially constructed. From this perspective, sexuality is discursive and a product of power and knowledge. The meanings we give to and our understandings of sexuality are thus, as we have seen above, historically contingent as well as contextually specific. The aim of Queer Theory is to challenge the power relations inherent within taken-for-granted assumptions about sexuality and its stereotypical representations. Thus, as Ward states:

> Queer Theory encourages analysis of how the creation of a reviled gay identity in Western societies has often been a method by which heterosexuality assured themselves of their superiority through the construction of minority sexuality as an inferior identity and as a reviled category of knowledge.
>
> (Ward, 2008: 15)

With strong post-structuralist leanings, minority sexual identity is seen as multiple, unstable and fluid – thereby challenging the notion of a unified, stable homosexual identity. The homosexual/heterosexual binary is problematized and rendered unstable (individuals can after all embrace both or move between one and the other) with instead a focus on how the hierarchically structured binary is constructed and maintained. Thus, for Butler (1993), an eminent queer theorist, gender has to be seen within a regulatory frame of heterosexuality. In this respect, the illusion of two 'core' genders as well as the regulation of sexuality itself is maintained through dominant discourses of heterosexuality. Men and women who do not conform to the 'norm' of heterosexuality are negatively sanctioned and so controlled. The binaries of gender and of sexuality are thus socially constructed and 'policed' through normative conceptions of what it means to be male, female and heterosexual.

Through stories of gay men in different organizational contexts, Ward gives voice to some of these practices of sanction and control – from different forms of bullying to less visible hostility and negativity – which 'through language, policies and procedures, physical arrangements, signs and symbols all impact on the dynamics around inclusion and exclusion which operate within the organization' (Ward, 2008: 134). In the context of the present study, several men spoke of the 'stigma' and shame of the associations drawn between their non-traditional work role and homosexuality. In this respect, men were often aware of being subject to the conventionally gendered gaze of parents, patients, colleagues or passengers, often with uncomfortable consequences. As one cabin crew commented:

> ... *being thought homosexual, I say the general public out there that don't accept gay men look at you in disgust and look at you as if you're filth and I don't like that, I don't appreciate that.*

There is thus a hierarchical system of sexual values, with homosexuality denigrated and devalued. Sexuality must therefore be seen in historical, social and cultural terms. In this respect, from Butler, both sexuality and gender are performative and the product of discourse; in other words, they are produced through repeated performances (citational practices) which signify or inscribe what that discourse (of gender, of sexuality) has named. Sexual identity is therefore not stable and intact 'once and for all' but has to be performed again and again according to these dominant meanings. For cabin crew, with its historic associations with femininity and deferential service (often signalling, with the help of promotional advertising, sexual availability) intimations of homosexuality were particularly strong and often keenly felt. 'Straight' men therefore had to continually establish their heterosexuality in this context. This might include, from one (gay) man's description, repeated displays of interest in women.

> *Talking about women, they* (heterosexual men) *talk about women all the time and in the galley, this is where we actually talk about life and some people can have pictures of their life like their husband or wife or the dog or the house or whatever and these straight men like to keep showing a point, oh yes she looks good.*

Referring to sexuality as discourse implies that it carries meanings – often inscribed on the bodies of women and men. These meanings may or may not accord with those embodied in the job. Thus, as Ward points out in the context of the police force, gay men are seen as unreliable as police work is 'inextricably linked with the body and its performance, it is assumed that gay people cannot express outwardly the physical signs of being a police officer' (Ward, 2008: 133). Officers need to perform a form of hegemonic masculinity to be authentic in the role and in order to be taken seriously by fellow officers and the public alike. Gay officers were accordingly often victimized or seen as a source of humour and fun. Similarly, in the context of airlines, where homosexuality is considered the norm and where meanings of pleasure and gratification (for example, giving satisfaction as part of quality service) were attached to the job, gay men were seen as 'good for a laugh' in their sometimes 'outrageous' and 'flamboyant' camp behaviour.

As Ward notes, and as discussed later in this chapter, power relations can be seen in the response to difference and this can apply to sexual orientation as much as to gender. Dynamics of exclusion and inclusion that operate within organizations can have a profound effect on how we express our identities in the workplace. In this respect, within the regulatory framework of heterosexual masculinity, men in female-dominated occupations, irrespective of sexual orientation, are marked by assumptions of homosexuality and subject to the judgements implied in the conventionally gendered and sexed gaze of other women and men. Through repeated performances of heterosexuality, or by 'camping it up' in oppositional displays, men in non-traditional contexts must in their daily practices negotiate their sexuality at work.

Identity and resistance

The problems and challenges to identity experienced by men in non-traditional roles suggest a close alignment between identity practices and resistance. At a micro-political level, resistance occurs when individuals challenge or refuse to accept subjectivities and identities defined by dominant discourses. This moves conceptualizations of resistance away from more structurally based analyses of workplace resistance, through for example the activities of trade unions or work councils, to oppositional practices that take place at the discursive level. As Thomas *et al.* (2004) point out, discursive forms of resistance focus on identities and meanings to accommodate 'the ambiguities and complexities' in the 'dialectics of freedom and constraint involved in the process of subjectification' (Thomas *et al.*, 2004: 6). Here they refer to Rajchman's (1991) 'moments of difficulty' as an individual's notion of self, derived from discourse, collides with the subjectivity offered in a dominant discourse. Individuals may seek to challenge that subjectivity in a myriad of small ways, and in so doing help to recast a more favourable or comfortable sense of self. Resistance from this perspective concerns individual struggles over meanings and subjectivities rather than specific behaviours or acts. As Davies and Thomas (2004) point out, resistance arises at 'points of contestation and contradictions within discursive fields, presenting spaces for alternative meanings and subjectivities, and new forms of practice' (Davies and Thomas, 2004: 105). This can occur as individuals exploit 'looseness of meanings' and respond in 'unanticipated and innovative' ways, in a process of 'resistance, reproduction and re-inscription' (ibid.).

Individuals thus strive to subvert and evade the identities imposed on them by dominant discourses and associated attempts at classification. Men in non-traditional occupations, as we have seen, may struggle to align discourses of masculinity with their (feminine) occupational identity and may resist the categorizations and subjectivities that are imposed. The resources open to individuals are varied. Overt resistance can be seen in Chapters 5 and 6, as cabin crew express hostility to pilots, an embodiment of the hegemonic masculine ideal, and in the context of nursing, as male nurses resist the subordinated identity impressed by their proximity to higher-status medical men. In both contexts, feelings of hostility and anger are expressed to more privileged men in the workplace. Many told stories of how they overturned the norms of deference – putting pilots and male doctors/consultants 'in their place' – by withholding service or openly challenging decisions made, refusing to be marginalized in day-to-day interactions and exchange.

As intimated above, resistance can take more subtle forms. It can be activated through humour as, for example, employees make fun of customers or management and in so doing recapture a sense of dignity in what may be seen as a powerless or demeaning role. Humour was particularly evident among cabin crew, discussed in Chapter 5. Here men encounter asymmetric relations of deference in their interactions with passengers, where those interactions are driven by discourses of consumer sovereignty and the need to please. They also have limited resources from which to draw, such as those around professional care or vocationalism, to create a compensatory and more valued identity. Making fun of passengers in the safety of galley, subtle changes in intonation (for example, exaggerated yes sir, no sir) to convey ironic service, similar to Kondo's (1990) 'ironic twists of meaning' that create possibilities of subversion, were some of the tactics used.

Individuals may draw on other, more valued identities that are located outside the work context. In Chapter 8, we see how librarians often overcome the negative and rather 'stuffy' image of their job to draw on other categorizations, such as those around their involvement in sport or by drawing on identities that relate to a preferred and future aspiration – such as music, studying or writing. They may activate more favourable or oppositional aspects of an identity. Some nurses for example distanced themselves from a 'feminine' vocationalism and from discourses of care by presenting their occupational choice in (oppositional) hedonistic terms. Here nursing was presented by some men as an occupational choice that allowed the freedom to travel and the opportunity to work anywhere in the world. Others gave priority in their interview accounts to 'professional' and 'academic' selves, as they presented themselves as being in the forefront of knowledge through a commitment to read widely about latest research and developments in their field.

As Davies and Thomas (2004) argue, individuals can also construct themselves as Other and facilitate the uptake of alternative identities. In the context of women managers working in a male-dominated public service organization, they describe how, positioned as Other, women were able to challenge the status quo (in this case, the expectation of long hours and attendance at late meetings), so calling up a 'maverick' trailblazing identity. In this way, the subject position (that is, devalued Other) on offer was resisted and challenged. In the present study, and as discussed further in Chapter 5, some male cabin crew embraced an Other status and used it to their advantage. Here the purpose was to cause discomfort in the flight deck – epitomizing a dominantly masculine and heterosexual One and seen as the source of a conventionally gender-based 'gaze' consigning them to a devalued (homosexual) alterity. As some crew reported, even heterosexual men would occasionally act out a flamboyant and parodic homosexuality – for example, teasing pilots with sexually charged comments (as one crew reported saying to a pilot in this vein: *'you're a big boy, aren't you'*). Male crew can thus reify and celebrate alterity. Through recognition and deployment of self as Other, they play on difference and exploit proximity to unsettle the mainstream.

Some men deliberately invoke gender and acknowledge the power of masculinity and some of its conventional (and undesirable) understandings such as those relating to threat, violence and intimidation. Here, men present themselves as special in their reflexive capacity to manage their bodies, such as adopting a gentle tone or remaining seated to reduce body size before children or patients in their care. Men are thus able to create a satisfying identity that builds on yet also subverts traditional notions of gender. Men recognize the power of masculinity but reject it in such a way as to also reinforce its status. As Davies and Thomas (2004) argue, 'to resist something is also to reify it' privileging it, legitimizing and reproducing 'the very subject position that is being denied' (Davies and Thomas, 2004: 115). As they argue, dominant discourses and the self work in a matrix of power relations that is both dynamic and highly contradictory.

This points to the complex ways in which individuals respond to dissonance between subjectivity and the context in which he or she moves, where that context may mean a subject position on offer that is disconfirming to a sense of self. The relationship with alterity may well be fragmented and incomplete – and form space for effective 'attacks' on the privileges and status of the One. The One/Other relationship goes further than dichotomy or a binary divide – a theme pursued in the next section.

Doing difference through the One and the Other

As we have seen, perspectives of 'doing' gender and 'doing' identity may point to more complex identity practices that go beyond separation and distance. This suggests the need to consider how men may draw on, resist and play with difference (Ashcraft, 2006; Pullen, 2006) – as well as the implications of dominant discourses of heterosexual masculinity for the 'doing of difference' at work (Pullen and Simpson, forthcoming). While gender can be seen to be a created system of difference, this moves on from seeing difference as a 'static' dichotomy of masculine and feminine (Ashcraft, 2006) to an orientation towards seeing how difference is created, resisted and disrupted (Deutsch, 2007; Pullen and Knights, 2007) and to how men and women draw on difference to create a sense of self in specific contexts and interactions.

Thus, from the present study (also see Pullen and Simpson, forthcoming) it can be argued that men experience 'Otherness' in partial and fragmented ways – sometimes reinforcing, sometimes resisting and dismantling difference, and sometimes playing with the boundaries between masculine and feminine. Some men attempted to reinvigorate a traditional masculinity. Nurses for example can perform a protective masculinity, doing heavy work or shielding women from threatening situations with patients. As one nurse commented:

> *I believe in the old system where women are weaker than men and that men open the door for women and if there is somebody to be lifted up that the men do the lifting not the women. And I will argue with anyone who goes the other way round.*

Difference could also be reinforced through a colonization of the feminine. Here, men often reframed discourses of care to privilege the masculine by presenting rationality and emotional distance as desirable for effective performance. One young Australian nurse described his approach working in palliative care:

> *I'm not going to get too emotional with these guys* (patients who are likely to die), *I'm going to do whatever I can to help them without getting too close, and I know a lot of my female colleagues found it very hard because they got really emotional to patients, and on top of the work load as well. They just went home and cried every day and you know, if something happens to a patient they cry. I guess I try and distance myself as much as I can without putting the patient . . . making them uncomfortable.*

Men thus differentiated their attributes (disciplined, detached) from those possessed by women (emotional, over-involved). Through a masculinization of emotion (discussed in more detail in Chapter 4) men co-opted the essence of the Other to support a status as One – calling on images of stoicism, stamina as well as, in the above case, a studied casualness and distance ('these guys') towards the patients in their care.

Some men sought to 'slip out of' Otherness through strategies of assimilation. Here, male nurses in particular drew on ties of fraternity to seek entry into the 'dominant centre' of male medical practice – discussed further in the next chapter – and male cabin crew went out drinking with pilots at the end of their shifts. At the same time, men would sometimes escape Otherness within which they were framed, by becoming, from Fournier (2002), 'not that Other' but something else. Thus, Australian nurses in particular, when asked why they chose nursing as an occupation, often spoke in an instrumental manner of their desire to have the means and freedom to travel in the context of the worldwide demand for nursing and the portability of nursing skills:

> *I can move on whenever I want . . . I don't have to stay here, I can go anywhere with my qualifications and experience. The whole world wants nurses – I'm not tied in any way to one place. I'm free and easy that way. That's partly why I chose it.*

Nursing was accordingly presented as a choice that could allow a more adventurous, almost bohemian lifestyle. In this way, men created distance from (feminine) discourses around vocationalism, service and a desire to 'care' and moved towards a hedonism and freedom more associated with the One – as well as another Other, based on lack of careerism and alternative lifestyles.

Even though elements of the 'hegemonic ideal' found purchase in men's negotiation of identities, creating uncomfortable feelings of difference, many men sought to maintain distance from some common or traditional notion of masculinity. Men thus played with the boundaries of the One and the Other by resisting identification with traditional, heterosexual masculinity and by minimizing difference from women. Men claimed distinctiveness in their caring skills and attributes, to be in touch with their 'feminine' side unlike other men of their acquaintance. Feminine skills were valued across both occupations and actively performed through a narrative of care. As argued elsewhere (Pullen and Simpson, forthcoming), by drawing on a discourse of distinctiveness men can partly subvert their location as One, that is, by claiming special status within the sphere of Other. In this way, possession of 'feminine' skills is afforded a valued and non-essentialized specificity, privileging their owners over other men.

Moreover, men drew on sexuality and humour to celebrate as well as bridge difference from a heterosexual masculinity, playing with sameness and femininity as they embraced the Other and gaining pleasure from that discursive domain. As one (heterosexual) nurse commented in relation to his female colleagues: *'I'm quite happy in the company of women and talking about woman things'*. A comfort with the feminine and enjoyment of the company of women was widespread across all occupations, and was seen by some as a welcome relief from the competitiveness often encountered in the company of men. Thus men enjoyed being 'one of the girls', particularly in informal spaces, engaging pleasurably with 'feminine' practices and interactions – often using exaggerated femininity to embrace the Other. On occasion, particularly with cabin crew, this involved 'camping it up' in displays of sexual alterity and banter when in the company of heterosexual men.

Through various gendered and situated practices, men can thus reinforce, resist and play with difference – both 'doing' and 'undoing' gender (Butler, 2004; Deutsch, 2007; Pullen and Knights, 2007) – drawing on margins to create as well as to dismantle difference. Men 'do' masculinity through colonization of the feminine within masculine discourses of emotion, rationality and detachment and by drawing on ties of fraternity with men – thereby seeking security and legitimacy within their non-traditional role. At the same time they 'undo' gender through femininity and through feminine performances as they seek to demonstrate genuineness and authenticity in their claim to inhabit a 'feminine' space. While this involves to some extent a differentiation and distance from the feminine, it also demonstrates how men can move between the masculine and the feminine and how they can draw on discourses of the Other to subvert and sometimes support their position as One. Therefore, as Fournier (2002) argues, remaining Other requires disconnection and versatility – the ability to resist being framed, to withdraw from categories of difference and to stand apart – providing lines of movement into the One as well as into an Other.

In these circumstances, as Bruni and Gherardi (2002) have pointed out, the boundaries between the symbolic universes of male and female may merge, become fluid and negotiable. Men's subject positioning, as a dynamic process of performance and accomplishment, may therefore be activated through an alignment of male/female – creating a kind of 'hybrid' universe – as well as through distance and separation. Men thus do appropriate as well as inappropriate gender enactment in processes of assimilation and differentiation that, as Bruni and Gherardi argue, are never complete and which are managed by all actors involved. As they point out in the context of 'Omega's story' of a young woman working in the male-dominated area of consultancy, 'gender switching' occurs as 'she takes up a masculine positioning, acts from within it, leaves it and defends her gender identity, is second sexed by colleagues, affiliates herself with other women or differentiates herself from them' (Bruni and Gherardi, 2002: 191).

Men in gender-atypical occupations may become similarly adept at entering and leaving masculine and feminine discursive positions. Thus men seem to defend a masculine identity fraught with insecurity and undermined by feminine associations and must manage their encounters with Otherhood, brought painfully home particularly in their relations with higher-status men. They both affiliate with such men and separate from hegemonic masculine associations as they colonize the feminine and (often playfully) enter the feminized symbolic and discursive domain. Identity work at the boundaries thus comprises a set of manoeuvres that encompasses but is more complicated than and which may go beyond a separation or distance from the feminine.

Conclusion

This chapter has explored issues of gender identity, with particular relation to the construction and maintenance of masculinity. Through the concept of the One and the Other, we have explored how men manage tensions between gender and occupational identity in non-traditional roles and resist subordinated identities. We have demonstrated that, unlike de Beauvoir's original account of the dichotomy, in which the

Other was always and everywhere the domain of women, that alterity can also be an experience and identity for men.

Furthermore, rather than seeing Otherhood as an 'abject' state (de Beauvoir, 1949) located as 'lack' in victimhood and oppression, this suggests that the Other can be a source of pleasure and comfort and for men perhaps a welcome relief from the demands and insecurities of maintaining an identity as One. As Fournier (2002) has pointed out, Otherness has been imagined as 'an unfortunate position ... from which the Other no doubt wants to be saved' (Fournier, 2002: 68). However, by assuming we can, with greater understanding of the Other condition, 'invite the Other in' to possibly join the One is, from Fournier, to flatten it and to conceive it (accommodate it, manage it) as various degrees of the same. Instead, the Other is contextual, versatile and slippery. It continually moves, 'withdrawing from the categories of difference in which it is framed' (ibid.).

While Fournier, drawing on an ethnographic study of female farmers in Italy, describes in a similar vein to Bruni and Gherardi (2002) how women experience multiple Otherness, sometimes deploying sometimes resisting lines of division, for men the 'doing of difference' is further complicated by their (albeit fragmented, incomplete, insecure) location as One. Like the women in Fournier's study, men both activate and dismantle difference, drawing on and responding to the 'casting' of an Other status and reframing lines of Otherness (as a man working in a feminized occupation, as a homosexual, as an itinerant 'non-careerist'). At the same time, Oneness (for example, masculinity) can be contaminated, undermined, threatened by proximity with the Other (femininity) – and the Other can be colonized and partly framed into the One. From men's particular position, they may have more opportunity to move in and out of the One – as well as the Other – sometimes re-establishing a traditional masculinity, sometimes co-opting or colonizing the feminine, sometimes having the 'luxury' from their association with the One to dabble with, play with and enjoy the Other domain. This moves us away from some post-structuralist accounts of identity which privilege, from McNay (2000), an exclusionary dynamic vis-a-vis the Other and rejection of difference that is unsettling to self, to a conceptualization that can seek to understand, be sympathetic to and embrace or accommodate alterity. This particular issue is explored more fully in Chapter 9.

Issues of identity run throughout the rest of the book. In the next two chapters, the implications of visibility and token status for the masculine subject and the links between emotions, emotional labour and identity are discussed. Part II explores different dimensions of identity management in the four occupational contexts, drawing on issues of space, bodies, professionalism and social categorizations. In Chapter 9 some issues considered above are revisited to explore reflexivity and identity transformation in non-traditional work contexts. In short, identity is central to understanding how individuals make sense of themselves in organizations and how they relate to One an(Other). In particular, how men relate to (resist, reject, dismiss, embrace) what they see as the non-masculine is key to understanding their experiences in a gender-atypical terrain.

3
(In)visibility

Introduction

Issues of visibility have emerged as key for understanding the experiences of both men and women in non-traditional occupations. One aspect concerns the heightened visibility that accompanies 'tokens' of either sex as 'exceptions to the rule'. Men and women 'stand out', visible in their gender-atypical occupational choice and as gendered subjects. They can be subject to surveillance, scrutiny and negative appraisal. This can be a difficult experience for men who, in a wider context, can be thought of as enjoying a status of invisibility – their gender as well as their privilege and advantage hidden within the 'norm'. In 'feminized' occupations by contrast masculinity is 'on the line' (Morgan, 1992) and available for scrutiny. Men are seen as different in these situations where women's dispositions and women's experiences serve as the 'unmarked' case. In other words, while in general terms gender can be seen to be a problem that attaches to women, in non-traditional work contexts it becomes an issue that is visibly associated with men.

A further aspect that relates specifically to men in these contexts concerns the invisible nature of much of the work involved. Here service and care can be rendered invisible through associations with femininity whereby skills and attributes required to do the job are 'disappeared' (Fletcher, 1999) into the embodied dispositions of women. As Fletcher argues, areas of work that are congruent with masculinity are seen as such (that is, work) while those aspects associated with femininity disappear into the private realm. This means that men who undertake such work must manage the incongruity between their masculine status and the devalued, invisible nature of both the work itself and of the skills and attributes required.

Issues of visibility and invisibility are therefore integral to understanding the experiences of men in gender-atypical roles. These issues are addressed in this chapter, firstly by exploring how men overcome the devalued and often invisible nature of feminized service work as well as the implications for such work for how men manage their identity. The chapter then considers the significance of (in)visibility in terms of the heightened visibility that can accompany men's occupational choice – how they respond as 'tokens' in their organizations, the implications of the 'gaze' for behaviours and practices at work and men's struggles around the norm. In terms of the latter, we shall see how some men can be seen to be seeking the privileges of invisibility, granted to higher-status men as invisible gendered subjects and as sources of privileges and power.

The (in)visible worker

The invisible nature of work involving emotions and service is based on the notion that they are the 'natural' domain of women (Guerrier and Adib, 2004; Taylor and Tyler, 2000). Gendered assumptions about the natural abilities of women mean that some work is seen as suitable for women by virtue of their difference from men – care-givers as opposed to care-receivers – with the result that such activities are concealed and devalued (Fletcher, 1999; Hall, 1993). Management and organizations consequently assume that women will use interpersonal skills in their work – skills which through their gender they are supposed to possess. In support of this, Taylor and Tyler (2000) found in the context of the airline industry that women were judged on 'hard' and 'soft' standards (that is, getting a sale *and* interaction with customers) while men were only judged by the 'hard' standard of getting a sale. It was expected that women would draw on interpersonal skills necessary for successful service interactions because they were women. As Fletcher (1999) points out, the attribution of relational activity as something women *are* and not what they *do* 'disappears' any responsibility for reciprocity and for recognition. Such activities therefore remain devalued and invisible within conceptions of work.

What are the implications of invisibility when men undertake this work? Two processes have emerged which suggest that men present themselves as emotional labourers and 'do' service in such a way as to afford those activities a higher value and a greater level of visibility. Firstly, as we saw in the last chapter, men have been found to 'do difference' by conferring a rationality on the skills required for the job whilst differentiating themselves from what they see as the 'emotional dysfunctionality' characteristic of the majority of men. Secondly, there is a tendency for men to present in Bolton's (2005a) terms their relational work as part of a 'gift exchange'.

In terms of the former, men in 'feminine' occupations have been found to differentiate their skills from those practised by women (Simpson, 2007). Men often described themselves as having 'a different form of compassion', caring in a more 'detached' way, as being 'more rational' and having 'more authority' than women. They saw themselves as able to deal with difficult or demanding situations without becoming 'over-emotional' – a 'female' tendency which was seen to interfere with the ability to meet the challenges of the job.

> *They're* (female colleagues) *always here there and everywhere – they can't put things aside to for example, talk to a distressed relative or patient. They say they haven't got time – but then you see them later chit-chatting away at the desk so I don't know what that's all about. Or they talk to the patient or whatever and end up crying as well – which isn't helpful. You have to listen and do what you can – but you need a sense of detachment to be able to do that, to help sort things out for them like get someone to visit them or whatever. They often need practical help and you can't give it if you're sobbing with them as well.*

(nurse)

Masculine characteristics were thus employed to 'add value' to caring skills, rendering them superior to those of their female counterparts. At the same time, many men sought to maintain distance from some common or traditional notion of masculinity, locating themselves within feminine discourses of care. Men commented on and placed value on their 'feminine' side, distancing themselves from traditional notions of masculinity as being out of touch with their own and others' feelings. Men distinguished themselves in different ways from what they described as the 'average male'. They recounted their feelings of pride in their 'nurturing' skills and ability to relate to, for example, children in their care which, as one teacher commented, 'the Dads don't have time or the inclination to do'. Feminine skills were thus prioritized and actively performed through a narrative of care. Positioning themselves favourably against the masculine norm and by calling upon and activating discourses of 'new manhood', men challenged the devalued status of relationality and, from the last chapter, by colonizing the feminine enhanced the value of associated skills when practised by men.

In this way, while the caring performed by women could be devalued through associations with essentialized notions of femininity, such work performed by men was rendered visible and celebrated as an asset, divorced from Other and from nature. This special status arose because of claimed differences from women (more rational, more detached) as well as claimed differences from and privilege over other (that is, traditionally masculine) men. Emotions and underlying skills and attributes were thus appropriated and expressed as part of 'masculinist' rationality while gaining value through their specificity and specialized status in relation to skills and attributes normally associated with men.

A second process of 'revealing' concerns a tendency by men to present their work involving service or care as a gift exchange (discussed further in the next chapter). From Bolton (2005a), the gift exchange occurs as part of 'philanthropic' emotion management when workers 'go the extra mile' – going beyond the call of duty in their caring role. This may include for example spending time with distraught relative or mobilizing resources to assist a child. As Williams (2003) has argued in the context of cabin crew, greater service demands are made on women compared with men. It is expected that women will, as 'care-givers' (Fletcher, 1999), go beyond the call of duty in the service interaction so that these 'extra services' are largely invisible and rarely recognized as such. From this, greater recognition may be likely when such philanthropy is practised by men. As discussed elsewhere (Simpson, 2007), male nurses in particular have been found to differentiate themselves from women by presenting their emotional labour skills in terms of the gift exchange. Unlike women who were seen as bureaucratic and rule-bound, men took pride in and recounted examples of their ability to mobilize resources, to circumvent procedures to satisfy individual wishes or to spend extra time with needy patients despite other demands on their time.

I think that's partly why I'm a nurse... I also have a deep sense of nourishing that makes me able to empathize, like hold their hands and put patients' minds at rest – rather than sitting like a truck driver by the side of the bed.....I went and I held her hand (a dying patient) and we talked about her job as a seamstress and I was quite happy to sit there doing all the things I had to do while talking about embroidery and crotchet work because I think it's easy to talk to old ladies and put their minds at rest.

(cited in Simpson, 2007: 65)

Rather than sitting like a truck driver by the side of the bed (a masculine configuration) this nurse presented himself as being able to offer extra time and support that went beyond the call of duty. Some men thus saw themselves in terms of their ability to go the extra mile and to be a donor in the gift exchange. Together with the masculinization of skills and attributes associated with service and care and differentiations from traditional masculinity through discourses of new manhood, the location of activities associated with performance of such work within the gift exchange serves to render the work visible and to increase the value of associated skills and attributes. In other words, the invisible and hence devalued nature of such work can be reversed when these activities are undertaken by men.

The visible 'token' male

As we saw earlier in this chapter, issues of visibility are particularly pertinent in the context of men's 'token' status in non-traditional occupations. Men in these contexts 'stand out' and their gender is rendered visible (they are seen as gendered subjects, as *men* working in a gender-atypical role). Work on the implications of visibility in organizations draws extensively from Kanter's (1977) seminal study of 'token' women. Arguing that outcomes apply to any group that is numerically in the minority, Kanter pointed to systems of bias and discrimination whereby the numerically dominant group controls the group culture and through various processes marginalizes and excludes the minority. In particular, tokens (so called because they are seen as representatives of their category) encounter three processes which are detrimental to their experiences within the organization and to their careers. Each is related to the problems of being conspicuous as a minority within a numerically dominant group. High *visibility* creates increased performance pressures and a cautious approach to work tasks through a fear of failure; *polarization* occurs as differences between the dominant group and tokens are exaggerated leading to separation and isolation; finally *assimilation* means that individuals are made to fit into stereotypical roles associated with their group. In Kanter's study, younger women were either pressed into a 'seductress' sexually charged role or seen as a cute and asexual 'pet'. Older women were expected to perform the 'mother' role as emotional specialists. If none of these fit, women were seen as an 'iron maiden', hard and rather masculine. In general terms, each role trap defines and constrains behaviour according to stereotypical expectations – and from Kanter's study, women often exhibited highly cautious behaviour in order to avoid being consigned to one or other of the constraining (and largely powerless) role traps.

Following from this, and given the supposed universality of some of these results (that is, effects of token status were seen to apply to *any* minority group), a body of work has explored the extent to which these detrimental effects of high visibility apply to men. In this respect, token men have been found to experience visibility in advantageous ways. Men can be prioritized in terms of developmental and training opportunities and can be given special consideration by being subject to more relaxed organizational rules. Arriving late for work or making mistakes can be treated more leniently when perpetrated by men. In the following quote, cited in Simpson (2004) a male nurse recounted an incident when, as a student, he committed what he described as the 'cardinal sin' of being late for duty – a situation that would normally demand a reprimand from the nurse in charge:

> *On one particular occasion I overslept for an early shift and I was woken in the nurses' home by somebody hammering on my door at nine thirty to say the ward's on the phone. So I went to the phone and it was the sister saying 'You've overslept'. And I said 'Yes, I'm ever so sorry'. And she was going 'No, no, not a problem, have you had your breakfast?' 'No, I haven't had breakfast'. 'Well you get your breakfast inside you and then you make your way up to work and don't worry we'll see you when you get here'. So I got ready, had my breakfast, sauntered up to the hospital and got onto the ward about eleven o'clock.*
>
> (Simpson, 2004: 357)

As this nurse later admitted, surprised himself at the way his lateness had been accommodated, it was unlikely that his female colleagues would be treated so leniently.

In addition, ascriptions of authority aligned with a masculine status can lead to exposure to difficult or demanding situations (for example, giving advice, taking the lead at meetings, dealing with difficult children or demanding patients). One nurse recalled how as a student his female supervisor routinely asked his advice as if she did not know herself what to do – deferring to his judgement even though he was not yet trained. A teacher recounted how he was often expected to be the 'spokesman' at staff meetings and raise controversial issues on behalf of female colleagues. Other male nurses were expected to step in and take charge of difficult situations with patients, such as where there was a danger of physical aggression. These expectations, however, can have positive outcomes. Rather than leading to highly cautious behaviour as in Kanter's study of women, these situations may be developmental for men. In other words, heightened visibility and assumptions of authority and expertise may accelerate confidence and learning through exposure to challenging situations that demand initiative and resourcefulness.

In terms of polarization, whereby the dominant group excludes and isolates members of the minority, studies suggest (e.g. Cross and Bagilhole, 2002; Heikes, 1991; Simpson, 2004, 2005) that in non-traditional occupations, it is often men (that is, the minority) who are active in creating distance between themselves and the majority group of women. In nursing, from Chapter One, men often choose more 'masculine' specialisms such as mental health or accident and emergency and male primary school teachers often take up sport as a key component of their job. Some men pursue a careerist strategy and move quickly into management roles and away from 'feminine' practice. In fact, studies suggest that, rather than experiencing marginalization, men are generally welcomed into the profession by women (Williams, 1993). From the present study, many men commented on how much they enjoyed working in a female dominated group.

> *I actually like being one of the few men or even the only man in a school full of women, because they treat me like one of the girls to be perfectly honest and that's absolutely fine, I love it, I don't have a problem at all.*

In contrast to the isolation experienced by women in non-traditional roles (Kanter, 1977), men by and large encountered a welcoming and comfortable environment. Therefore, while some polarization may well occur in these contexts, far from women creating an uncomfortable working environment based on the marginalization and exclusion of men, it is often men who, resonant with the differentiation strategies discussed in the last chapter, choose to distance themselves from the majority female group.

The third condition discussed by Kanter – assimilation – refers to how through heightened visibility, individuals are assumed to take on the stereotypical characteristics of their group and so be confined to corresponding 'role traps' with sanctions imposed (for example, ridicule, negative labeling, isolation) for non-conformity. In this respect, evidence suggests that men are subject to pressure to take up particular behaviours associated with 'father' and 'son' roles (Sargent, 2001; Simpson, 2005). In terms of the former, as we have seen, men are often expected to be the disciplinarian, to take charge of demanding situations and to be authoritative in formal work settings while younger men can find themselves in a 'son' role – looked after by older female staff. Here men can be encouraged to take advantage of developmental opportunities. In nursing, for example, men were encouraged to attend courses, accompany doctors on their rounds or to be present at operations. Men were thus subject to gendered expectations – to having gender 'done to them' by women. This suggests a more apt conceptualization of 'role pressure' (Simpson, 2005). There are expectations that men conform to stereotypical roles – but they may be less likely to become 'trapped'. Men often do refuse to comply with these expectations (they resist demands that they perform heavy work or that they should take the lead) with few long-lasting sanctions for stepping outside the 'role'. Outcomes of these expectations may also be less detrimental than in Kanter's analysis of role traps which constrain independent action and prompt cautious behaviour as an avoidance and coping strategy. Rather than being confining or belittling, having gender 'done' to men (for example, pressure to adopt 'son' or 'father' roles) may, as discussed earlier, be developmental through exposure to learning opportunities.

Therefore, contrary to the predictions of Kanter, who saw heightened visibility and associated processes of polarization and assimilation as disadvantageous and as applicable to all minority groups, men may well benefit from preferential treatment and from exposure to situations that are challenging and developmental. For many men in the study, visibility was welcomed – captured in the following quote from a nurse:

God yes for me being in a minority is fantastic! Especially if you're liked as that minority, people know who you are, people come to you for things. I guess I'm relatively popular.

This more positive experience suggests, in accordance with Bradley (1993) and Heikes (1991), a need to include social and cultural factors into the analysis – specifically the cultural valuation given to male attributes in society and the devaluation of the feminine (Heikes, 1991; Zimmer, 1988). Thus, women in the minority have undesirable social experiences because they are women and men benefit from visibility because they are men. In the context of the non-traditional occupation and heightened visibility, doing gender for men (and having gender done to them by women) can lead to benefits that are denied to similarly placed women.

From the study, not all men however experienced visibility in such a positive light. As intimated above, many resented the pressures of having to take the lead. Some commented on how they were often watched in the expectation that they would make a mistake – that they would not be able to cope, particularly in the area of giving care.

> *You can't display bad nursing skills because they're watching you all the time. You've got to keep your skills you know spot on. You've got to do all those things, be a caring person, be empathetic towards the patients, don't shirk your responsibilities, take responsibility for what you're doing, be the technical expert... it's not always easy.*

> *She thought I was a smart alec – she told me so – and that I wouldn't last five minutes. It was like she was watching and waiting for me to fail.*

Visibility therefore can be potentially problematic for some men as they experience similar performance pressures to token women. In many of these cases, however, men felt spurred on by pressures to perform or by the expectations that they would fail. One man recalled how he broke the rules and took a ventilator home from intensive care to dismantle – so that if it went wrong he was 'technically ready for it'. Another confessed that he studied his medical texts into the night to prove to a particularly exacting ward manager that he could excel at the job. Visibility could be problematic – but generally not in ways that were confining or constraining. In the main, results from this study and from other work suggest that visibility and token status are experienced by men in ways that may be less detrimental than those experienced by women.

The power of the gaze

Inherent in work on 'token' women is the notion of surveillance. For Kanter, tokens are subject to scrutiny. As we have seen, this scrutiny serves to constrain women into defining 'role traps' and to limit available repertoires of power and influence. Women may respond to constant scrutiny by avoiding conflict, by being over cautious or by exhibiting a fear of failure in order to avert possible retribution. Keeping a low profile is thus a common strategy for women. This appraisal or 'gaze' can therefore be seen to have a disciplining and normalizing effect in that it helps to structure thought and action into pre-existing norms, categories and behaviours. For women, these would tend to be stereotypically 'female' self-effacing, powerless behaviours.

The concept of the gaze, and its power, is captured in Foucault's (1977) Panoptican. Originally conceived by the utilitarian philosopher Jeremy Bentham in the context of the need to control the behaviour of convicts, the Panoptican comprised a 12-sided polygon with a central tower through which surveillance could take place. Inmates may or may not be actually under view – but there was always the possibility that they were so. It was through the constant possibility of surveillance that conformity and discipline would eventually take place.

For Foucault, the gaze is a source of power and discipline. It need no longer be incorporated into an external edifice but can be institutionalized and projected through internal systems and procedures. A managerial gaze for example can be exercised through targets, accountability and control or through performance appraisals. As Townley (1992) argues, the gaze is thus a form of government achieved through the practice of total visibility. Moreover, if individuals can be encouraged to 'want' what these systems deliver, then the 'inspecting gaze' can become internalized and discipline, regulation through self-surveillance can be achieved. Being constantly seen or able to be seen produces the disciplined individual – influencing individual experiences as well as organizational structures.

The concept of the gaze therefore captures the disciplinary power of surveillance. Through systems of classification, codification and measurement, it constitutes for Foucault (1977) both power and knowledge. In terms of the latter, a partial reality or form of invention (Townley, 1992) is created through the gaze. The knowledge is partial because it leaves those aspects which it does not highlight or classify 'in the dark'. Townley points out:

> What is involved is the assessment of the individual in relation to the desired standard of conduct: a means of knowing how the individual performs, watching his or her movements, assessing his or her behaviour and measuring it against a rule – allowing incidents of non-conformity or departures from set standards to be recognized and dealt with. By referring individual actions to the 'population', a 'rule' or 'norm' is established. What is acceptable or normal, a conformity which must be achieved comes into operation. Through observation, differentiation and assessment, the characteristics of the individual are recorded over time and in comparison with others.
>
> (Townley, 1992: 192)

Through examination and surveillance, knowledge of the individual emerges but this is incomplete in that the individual is visible only in relation to a 'hypothesized essence' (ibid.) – a norm from which it is characterized and derived. In other words, the individual is known through a series of normative judgements. From Kanter's work, we have seen for example how heightened visibility leads to token women's assimilation into a series of stereotypical and constraining 'role traps'. These are accompanied by strong sanctions, in the form of marginalization and ridicule, if women step outside of these roles. There is a reality created around women irrespective of individual and personal dispositions. In this way, the gaze allows knowledge to develop and control (through correction, classification, exclusion) to be exercised over those in view.

The practices and relations embodied in the gaze have strong gender associations. In this respect, a gendered vision is often bestowed on women by the 'gazer' (Perriton, 1999), capturing the power asymmetry that exists between the viewer and the viewed. As Snow (1989) points out, the 'male gaze' is founded on voyeurism, objectification and patriarchy – as well as phallocentrism. Tyler and Abbott (1998) for example refer to how female flight attendants are subject to instrumentally imposed aesthetic codes and manage themselves as 'ornamental objects'. Through the gaze of airlines in particular and patriarchally determined aesthetic codes of femininity more generally, women are expected to manage and maintain their bodies to reach an aesthetic ideal. As Tyler and Abbott argue the production and maintenance of 'gendered bodies' is part of the control of women's behaviour through appearance (see also Adkins, 1995; Hall, 1993). Saturated with male values embodied in the gaze, this 'panoptic management' prompts conformity as employees internalize beliefs and as individuals appraise each other.

As Wolf (1990) and Faludi (1992), cited in Tyler and Abbott, have argued, the control of women's appearance norms has intensified with the political and economic gains made by women in Western Societies. An intensification of the gaze may therefore be a form of male 'backlash' which affords men the power of the appraising viewer and consigns to women the subordinate and passive, objectified 'viewed'. In support of this idea, Alvesson (1998) has examined how men working in the 'feminized' context of an advertising agency, where a focus on team-working and the need for creativity and sensitivity in relationships put strains on gender identity and afforded few opportunities for displays of traditional masculinity, activated a sexually appraising 'gaze' on women in the firm. This was manifested in sexual jokes at the expense of women and by referring to female staff in a degrading and objectifying way. The emphasis on the sexual attractiveness of female employees, a 'hyper-feminization' of women, therefore placed women in a subordinate position and allowed men to recapture a masculinity undermined by the symbolically feminine of their organizational context. In general terms, the gaze thus has a constitutive role (of subjectivity, of knowledge) which results in and emanates from the operation of power, so helping to define organizational reality.

Reversing the gaze

I remember walking down the corridor one day in the hospital and there were visitors waiting to go onto a ward for visiting time and I heard them say look there's a male nurse, I've never seen one of them before and actually feeling them staring at me as I walked down the corridor and I found that so odd because I thought why are they saying it, I'm not a male nurse, I'm a nurse, a student nurse.

As we have seen, and as the above quote indicates, men in nontraditional occupations are highly visible. As exceptions, they stand out in the crowd and are subject to scrutiny. What are the implications of the gaze for men, when it is men who are appraised? How do men respond to this 'reversal of gaze'? The implications can be both pleasurable and a source of pain.

In terms of the former, as we shall see in Chapter 5, male cabin crew often enjoyed the presentation of their bodies to fit a corporate image as well as the high levels of visibility on the job. As with female crew (Tyler and Abbott, 1998; Williams, 2003), men were expected to embody the organization in that physical appearance was symbolic of the organization 'brand'. All men spoke of the need for a smart and clean image. One senior crew reported that he had occasion to reprimand male crew for a sloppy appearance (for example, a '5 o'clock shadow' or a crumpled shirt) highlighting the importance placed on the presentation of an aesthetic, corporate ideal. Like women in Tyler and Abbott's (1998) study, men routinely exercised a form of self-surveillance, undertaking body work to comply with managerial prescriptions of presentation. However, as we shall discuss further in Chapter 5, men often gained pleasure and pride from their bodies and from aesthetic displays. Rather than experiencing the 'panoptical gaze' as oppressive, male crew instead appeared to celebrate their bodies as the bearers of an aesthetic ideal, aligning their appearance with professionalism – relishing and enjoying the visibility their work afforded in the terminal and the aisle:

> *That's partly why I chose the job. I love being clean* (laughs) *I love looking smart, the uniform and that. It's expected that you be like that, to look professional and I don't mind at all, I enjoy looking good and parading if you like up and down the aisle – though it's sometimes difficult to keep it up after a 10 hour flight!*

In other contexts, however, the gaze is more oppressive, containing critical appraisal of men in their non-traditional roles. Unlike the appraisal of women, embodied in the gaze of men in these contexts is a suspicion of their motives and of their sexuality. In this respect the gaze is traditionally gendered and fundamentally heterosexual. The gaze is felt particularly keenly in the company of male peers, supporting Kimmel's (1994) argument that it is men rather than women who 'police' the gender boundaries in terms of the appraisal of male behaviour.

> *I can see it in their eyes – I can see them* (male acquaintances) *wondering why has he chosen that job? Library work is for women – that's an odd job for a man to go into.*

> *Men in particular – they laugh and say oh you're a man for goodness sake, why have you chosen to do nursing? Why can't you be a doctor?*

From Sargent's (2001) study of male primary school teachers, men's motives for entering the profession were often scrutinized and in the process men came under suspicion, their bodies marked as potentially dangerous in their work with children. As Sargent argues, the social construction of homophobia acts as a ritualized mechanism of social control especially when it is conflated erroneously with paedophilia. For men to nurture children is to judge them as also being dangerously close to molesting them. In this respect, from men's accounts, the gaze is a construct that is a hybrid of two 'symbolic statuses': homosexual male and child molester – the person that parents fear most to have in charge of their children. One teacher from Sargent's study described his feelings:

> *I've been teaching second grade now since I started teaching. I guess I wanted to teach little kids all along. Actually I'm kind of offended by this constant reminder from other teachers and from the principal that, as a man, I have to be particularly careful how I behave with children.*

I know what has happened. I know, um, how do I say this. I understand I guess that there have been some horrible incidents and most of them have involved men, but you know there have been some pretty terrible incidents that have involved women too. They're just not all over the headlines. Molestation is one issue but you know slapping kids around, yelling, calling them names, demeaning them – that's pretty awful too. And that happens more in the women's classrooms than in the men's classrooms, I've noticed. There isn't this big push on to make women understand they're being you know watched more closely. I think that's just because people assume that just because a child is in a class with a women a child is safe. Hey that's just not true look at the evidence.

(Sargent, 2001: 69)

The gaze therefore does not just fall on women (in this context, they evade it) but has strong implications for men. In fact, intimations of homosexuality were encountered by men across the four occupational groups in the present study (though the rather 'stuffy' image of the librarian precluded strong ascriptions in this respect). For cabin crew, as we have seen, these intimations were particularly prevalent and men spoke with feeling of the abuse they often had to endure in the course of their work. Men's accounts of the gaze – from male and female passengers, from pilots – were infused with negative imagery:

They (the pilots) *look at you in disgust sometimes like they assume you're gay and you're going to jump on them.*

I was leaving the plane and these guys started shouting at me, like where's your boyfriend then you dirty bugger.

The gaze can thus be experienced as pleasure or as a source of discomfort and pain. The corporate gaze can be a source of gratification – through which men manufacture and celebrate a clean and professionally turned out body. In other contexts, the gaze highlights and conceals – supporting partial truths and obscuring what remains outside of its view. From the quote above, we have seen how male teachers are marked as potentially dangerous while female teachers lie outside its line of vision. Men may seek to escape its sights and strain against its ideological framing – but its disciplinary power remains. As Sargent argues, many of the behaviours that men adopt (moving into management and away from classroom teaching; minimizing physical contact with children) are intended to distance themselves from this symbolic status – symptomatic of the disciplinary and normalizing power of the gaze. Across the occupational groups, men encounter an appraisal that is based on traditional notions of gender and of sexuality – often incorporating homophobia and with painful implications for those under view.

Overall, while the gendered nature of the gaze has been based in the main on a masculine source of vision with women as its object of appraisal, we can see that men can also be part of the 'viewed'. Men in 'feminine' occupations challenge traditional notions of masculinity and in so doing become subject to a conventional, disciplinary appraisal in these contexts from peers, acquaintances, parents, patients and passengers. The gaze has discursive and material consequences as men resist subordinated identities and as they conform to (or evade) its normalizing tendencies in specific work practices. In the reversal of the gaze, men become aware of and resent their marking as gendered subjects – and resist an Other status. As the nurse took pains to emphasize in the quote at the start of this section, I'm not a male nurse, I'm a nurse, a student nurse . . . .

The desire for invisibility

Men can therefore be visible in their difference and positioned uncomfortably as Other. This is in contrast to more traditional contexts where, as Butler (1999) has argued, men and masculinity are concealed within the norm. Here men (their gender, their power, their privilege) are largely invisible – bearers of a 'body-transcendent universal personhood' (Butler, 1999: 14). Men stand for all people. As 'the absolute One', they are therefore gender-neutral and, unlike the teachers in Sargent's study and the nurse quoted above, their bodies go unmarked within a 'disembodied normativity'. Those outside (for example, women) are by contrast marked as Other, problematized and made to embody their difference from the One. In support, Whitehead (2004) refers to the 'invisible gendered subject' to describe men's inability to see themselves as gendered or to see gender as an issue that 'attaches' in any way to them – preferring instead to see it as a 'problem' that only concerns women. As we have seen, this invisibility is challenged when men enter non-traditional work contexts. In this respect, while women are visibly defined by their gender, visibly categorized and essentialized by their femininity, in 'feminized' non-traditional work occupations men can also be so defined – gendered, categorized and essentialized by their masculinity. Men as a gendered subject are thus visible in these contexts.

As Foucault suggests, occupancy of the normative position and associated invisibility are essential to the maintenance of power. The norm escapes scrutiny so that masculinity as gendered is 'unseen' and its attendant privileges inside and outside organizations go unrecognized as gendered effects (Collinson and Hearn, 1994; Lewis, 2005). The patriarchal power and privileges that male doctors enjoy are not on this basis scrutinized or problematized because they are not 'seen' as such. Patriarchy goes unrecognized in this context – its attendant privileges taken for granted because they are not perceived as a gendered source of power. The dominant accordingly have an interest in remaining unmarked and invisible (Haraway, 1991; Pierce, 2003; Robinson, 2000). However, as Hearn (1996) and Robinson (2000) argue, and as we pointed out in the last chapter, the location within the dominant centre (the One) is never secure and can be a site of struggle and resistance. Different groups (identified as Other) can accordingly challenge the dominant position to promote the visibility of social difference and to render the dominant's hold on cultural and material advantage less secure (Simpson and Lewis, 2005).

Visibly gendered and Othered in their non-traditional role, men have been found to engage in such struggles around the 'dominant centre' of their organizations (Evans, 2002; Simpson, 2007). Male nurses in particular have been shown to draw on ties of fratriarchy and expert knowledge to seek entry into the centre of male medical practice and to have exhibited conflict and resentment when they felt outside of that sphere (Simpson, 2007). They accordingly present themselves as having special ties with male doctors, based on shared 'masculine' interests such as sport and on an expertise associated with their often specialist status. Women located in 'feminized' general nursing are presented as having less to offer in either respects and are often seen as too deferential and unassertive for any such entry claim.

> *I do have a close relationship with the (male) doctors – I find that I can be pally with them and sit down and chat with them and we can talk about men things.*
>
> (cited in Simpson, 2007: 64)

Associations with femininity and men's marginal occupational status mean, however, that entry into the dominant centre is never fully secure and there can consequently be tension around male nurses' uncertain position in relation to this 'norm'. Tension is evidenced in stories of encounters with (always male) doctors where practices of deference and of hierarchy were challenged by male nurses and overturned.

I do know that the junior doctors have been afraid of me because I've told them off, if I don't think they're doing something safely I'm quite happy to say let me do it, or I'll show you.

(cited in Simpson, 2007: 64)

I've sent doctors out of my unit before – I've sent them off because I felt they were behaving inappropriately in front of my patients and I've said don't come back to my unit until you either apologise or you can conduct yourself appropriately.

(cited in Simpson, 2007: 64)

I was at a meeting yesterday and there was three consultants just chit chatting away while I was trying to discuss something and I asked them if they could keep quiet and they just carried on chatting so I said if you don't **** shut up I'm going to walk out of here . . .

(cited in Simpson, 2007: 64)

Similar dynamics emerged from interviews with male cabin crew, discussed in Chapter 5, where relationships with male pilots were often confrontational and where crew actively resisted a subordinated status.

The need to enter and the subsequent antagonism towards the (masculine) dominant centre can be interpreted as resistance to a visible Other status and to its hierarchical implications. As we have seen, in other contexts men may well have experienced the privileges of invisibility, their gender and cultural advantage hidden within the norm. They may have had few occasions to reflect on or problematize the privileges of men. These privileges may become more visible 'from the outside', from their position as Other. The struggles around this centre – of resistance and overtly aggressive displays – may be interpreted as firstly, a recognition of the material and cultural rewards associated with that location and secondly as a desire to enter that domain. The quest for invisibility – for an invisible gendered subjectivity unmarked by alterity and for access to the cultural rewards of the norm – may partly explain the levels of antagonism when those privileges are effectively denied.

Conclusion

In this chapter we have explored some of the implications of (in)visibility for men's positioning in a non-traditional role and for associated practices of gender. Issues of visibility and invisibility are pertinent to men in these contexts in several ways. Men often claim to enjoy the visibility their token status brings and the 'doing' of gender on the part of women often means special consideration for men and exposure to opportunities for development and challenge. At the same time, visibility and marking can be an uncomfortable experience when that is associated with Other (different, devalued) identities. In this respect we have seen how the reversal of gaze can be a pleasurable as well as a painful experience for men. Moreover, location as visible Other can imply a devalued and 'disappeared' work content and associated attributes and skills. Doing gender then involves the 'revealing' of work practices and skills to enhance their value – differentiating from essential notions of femininity as well as, through discourses of 'new manhood', from traditional (and emotionally dysfunctional) notions of 'average men'. Identity work can also be seen in the struggles that take place around the dominant centre as men resist Otherhood and seek the invisibility and privileges of the norm. Men thus move sometimes strategically and sometimes as a result of pressures and expectations between visibility and invisibility as they do gender and difference in their non-traditional work roles.

4
Gender, Service and Emotions

Introduction

This chapter considers issues of gender, service and emotions. While there have been several studies on the gendered nature of services (discussed below), there has long been a 'gender gap' in studies of emotion (Knights and Surman, 2008) – a gap that reflects the implicit assumption that emotions are the domain of women. This implicit assumption has meant that gender has tended to have been overlooked altogether in the study of emotions. In this respect, Ross-Smith *et al.* (2007) have argued that emotions have been considered a 'supplement', or Other, to cold organizational rationality – and that the failure to acknowledge the gendered nature of emotions ignores the 'inherent relationship between rationality and masculinity and between emotionality and femininity'.

In addressing this, the chapter explores the gendered nature of service and emotions as well as the way men 'do' gender as they undertake such 'emotion-related' work. Both service and emotions are involved to greater and lesser extents in non-traditional occupations for men. This may include professional 'caring' roles as in nursing, teaching, social work or 'para-professional' roles – what MacDonald and Sirianni (1996) refer to as the 'emotional proletariat'. This category includes front-line service workers (for example, cabin crew, hotel workers, call centre operators, retail assistants) engaged in interactive work where management largely dictate how that work is carried out. Both groups are of interest because of the growth of such work in post-industrial economies and the consequent service occupational uptake by small but growing numbers of men. Both categories have cultural connections with femininity through associations with nurturance and care or through the domestic nature of some of the tasks involved (Adib and Guerrier, 2003; Tyler and Abbott, 1998).

Gender and the service role

Social interaction with a customer or client is a key feature of service work (Forseth, 2005). This interaction forms the intangible service product – with production and consumption occurring simultaneously, diminishing 'role distance' (Goffman, 1980) and blurring boundaries between the product and the service provider (ibid.). As Morgan and Knights (1991) argue, the move from bureaucratic to market logics has meant that customer needs and consumer sovereignty are foregrounded and the quality of the product and the climate of its delivery have become a potential source of competitive advantage.

These features of modern service, notably the emphasis placed on the sovereignty of the consumer (Sturdy, 1998) and the blurred boundaries between the person and the product, have strong associations with an earlier 'servanthood' where deference and subservience were part of the job (Forseth, 2005). As Macdonald and Sirianni (1996) argue, asymmetry in the exchange of respect is built into the structural features of service – supporting Goffman's view of the deeply hierarchical as well as ceremonial nature of deferential work. Characteristics of modern servanthood (being caring, polite and deferential) may be called upon to 'manage' (Bolton and Boyd, 2003) customer behaviour as well as customer expectations that have been heightened by general discourses of consumer sovereignty (Sturdy, 1998) and promotional advertising by the service-providing organization. Providing service may therefore involve 'doing deference' particularly within the para-professional or proletariat role.

The gendered nature of these roles and encounters has been highlighted by a body of research in the area, linking service to the 'natural' domain of women (Guerrier and Adib, 2004; Taylor and Tyler, 2000; Tyler and Abbott, 1998) so that such work is constructed (and hence concealed and devalued) as a 'natural' part of doing gender (Adkins, 2001; Hall, 1993). Such work has explored the gendered consequences of giving 'good service' in the airline industry; how women 'do' service as overseas tour reps by conforming to 'patriarchally determined aesthetic codes of behaviour' (Guerrier and Adib, 2004); how femininity is mobilized in the work of cabin crew to deliver deferential service (Williams, 2003); how gendered notions of servanthood infiltrate the delivery of service in banking (Forseth, 2005). Other work has explored strategies of resistance to expectations of deference (Amble and Gjerberg, 2003;

Bolton and Boyd, 2003) including the significance of bodily attributes such as size and voice (Forseth, 2005). Contextual factors influencing the gendered nature of the service include the cultural expectations of consumers in a situation where there is close proximity between production and consumption. Thus expectations of deferential service from discourses of consumer sovereignty can shape the interaction (Guerrier and Adib, 2004; Hall, 1993; Mulholland, 2002), can activate gendered scripts in service encounters (Forseth, 2005) and can fracture status shields from possible associations with the employing and 'expert' organizations (ibid.). From the above, women often have more service demands made of them than men (Macdonald and Sirianni, 1996) while men can draw on other voices and repertoires (for example, of authority, of expert) to side-step both the practices and identity implications of such work.

The gendered nature of service work, together with the blurring of the boundaries between service provider and product, therefore has implications for men as they enact gender and masculinity within the particularities of the role. MacDonald and Sirianni (1996) for example argue that men are less likely to embrace some service demands, particularly those involving deference, because they do not fit their notion of gender-appropriate behaviour, while Hochschild (1983) and Taylor and Tyler (2000) suggest that some male service providers tend to distance themselves from the 'niceness' demanded by the job. As Hochschild (1983) argues, men are more likely to adopt 'surface acting' whereby feelings displayed (friendliness of the smile) are 'put on' for the occasion so that the worker maintains a distance from the requirements of the role.

In other professional occupations, such as nursing, teaching and social work, discourses of consumer sovereignty have also placed demands on the service provider, partly displacing 'old' conceptions of deference and respect (Dent and Whitehead, 2002). Customer-oriented values and expectations as well as market-based principles are thus taking precedence over knowledge and practices of a professional 'elite', subjecting occupants to some of the pressures experienced in para-professional or service proletariat roles. Despite these pressures, the allure of a professional status, from relatively high levels of autonomy and from vestiges of the 'old' order concerning respect afforded to specialist knowledge, can often account for men's decisions to enter these occupations (Lupton, 2006).

Feminine associations however are still strong and, as we have seen, men have been found to engage in compensatory gendered practices so as to minimize its non-masculine associations and to restore a dominating position (Alvesson, 1998; Lupton, 2000). This can be achieved by emphasizing the male and downplaying the female elements of the job (Williams, 1993) and through a preference for roles that require technical expertise and/or physical strength (Heikes, 1991; Simpson, 2004). As discussed in Chapter 2, such strategies suggest a tension for men in non-traditional roles between the 'feminine' nature of the service encounter and dominant discourses of masculinity and for the need for 'identity work' to help manage such tensions.

Emotions and emotional labour

The above suggests a close link between service and emotions. The practice of service will generally require some conscious manipulation of self-presentation on the part of the service worker in order to display 'feeling states' and to create feeling states in others (Macdonald and Sirianni, 1996). This is referred to as emotional labour and concerns the ways individuals change or manage emotions to make them appropriate with a role or an expected organizational goal (Hochschild, 1983; Sturdy, 2002). Fineman (2000) draws a distinction between emotional labour and emotion work. The latter concerns the effort we put into ensuring our private feelings are controlled or manipulated so they are in line with socially prescribed norms – which may include managing the feelings of others. Emotional labour is the commercial exploitation of this principle. In other words, emotional labour (being nice, caring, polite) may be required for 'quality' delivery in service encounters referred to above – where the guiding principle is productivity, quality and profit – as well as in public sector caring roles such as teaching, nursing, social work to which the concept has also commonly been applied.

The importance of emotional labour skills has been intimated in our discussion of service work. Specifically the growth of services and the culture of the customer have led to a greater emphasis on such skills as a source of competitive advantage (Sturdy, 1998). Caring for others, the need for personal and interpersonal skills, and the presentation of a 'happy face' have therefore become part of the production process and there is now a body of work exploring the emotional labour process and the costs or otherwise to the individual (e.g. Morris and Feldman, 1996; Wouters, 1989). Hochschild (1983), in her study of cabin crew and debt collectors highlighted the costs in the form of alienation as individuals attempt to comply with the 'feeling rules' prescribed by the organization while others have suggested positive outcomes from emotional labour in the form of self-affirmation and job satisfaction (Morris and Feldman, 1996; Wouters, 1989).

Either way, emotions are viewed as market-based commodities (Morris and Feldman, 1996) to be controlled and organizationally ascribed (Mumby and Putnam, 1992) for instrumental ends such as in the pursuit of greater competitive edge and profit. However, as Bolton (2005a) points out, this conceptualization of emotional labour may not apply in all contexts. In particular, it may be inappropriate for the analysis of public sector caring roles where a service is provided that is not directly for profit and where individuals can often exert an active and controlling force in how that service is carried out – through for example-specific and often personalized relationships with customers, clients and managers. From this perspective, we need to revisit the definition in order to distinguish between emotional labour produced for profit, where processes are often controlled by managers, and that work which conforms to professional non-profit-oriented norms of conduct. As Bolton argues, it is difficult to see how nurses caring for the dying or teachers dealing with an upset child do emotional labour according to a single definition based on commercial gain.

Bolton accordingly developed a typology of emotional labour based on different feeling rules. Firstly, pecuniary emotion work is based on Hochschild's original definition in that it refers to feeling rules dictated and prescribed by the organization and its management and is geared towards profit. Here the product is customer satisfaction. Secondly, prescriptive emotional labour refers to those feeling rules which are dictated by professional norms of conduct (for example, codes of conduct that relate to how some aspects of the job are carried out). Finally, Bolton introduces presentational emotional labour to capture those feeling rules which rely on social norms and which are geared towards the maintenance and facilitation of the interaction order. This concerns the ways in which individuals are socialized into conforming to conventions of feelings in particular interactions. The latter may include for example philanthropic emotion management (discussed in Chapter 2) whereby emotional labourers give a 'bit extra' by going beyond the call of duty in their caring role such as supporting a stressed colleague or spending time with a patient's distraught relative. Studies drawing on this typology have demonstrated how, in a hospital context, prescriptive feeling rules, based on 'masculine' norms of self-discipline, professional conduct and control, are prioritized over 'feminine' norms embedded within the gift exchange (Lewis, 2007) – as well as, from a different perspective, how men 'add value' and specificity to emotional labour skills by presenting their work philanthropically (Simpson, 2007).

Gender and emotional labour

In common with much of the discussion on gender and service above, a strong association exists between gender and emotional labour. Emotional labour can be seen as gendered at several levels (Simpson, 2007).

Firstly, emotional labour has been associated with the sexual division of labour whereby men have traditionally been located within the world of (rational) production while women have been assigned to caring and nurturance in the private sphere of the home (Mumby and Putnam, 1992; Sturdy, 2002; Taylor and Tyler, 2000;). The apparent location of emotions in the private domain has led to their gendered connection with the domestic and with femininity – in contrast to the rationality of the public domain which has core assumptions with masculinity (Ross-Smith and Kornberger, 2004) and which carries patriarchy as a dominant value system (Mumby and Putnam, 1992). As Sturdy (2002) points out, the sexual division of labour has meant that emotions have been sidelined as irrational, 'hysterical' and essentially feminine and, from Mumby and Putnam (1992), the emotional devalued in a gender-based process as a 'weak appendage' to reason.

The division between the private domain of home and the public domain of workplace accordingly compounds the already low status of 'natural' unskilled women's work. This brings us to the second and related gendered aspect of emotions and emotional labour namely the belief that emotions and care are the 'natural' domain of women (Guerrier and Adib, 2004; Taylor and Tyler, 2000; Tyler and Abbott, 1998). Such work is constructed and hence concealed and devalued as a 'natural' part of doing gender (Adkins, 2001; Hall, 1993). It is assumed that women can 'do' service and care because they are women (Fletcher, 1999). From Ross-Smith *et al.*'s (2007) study of executives, women were perceived as better able to manage the emotional side of organizations. They were seen as 'naturally' more intuitive, empathetic and genuinely caring just because they were women. In this respect, as Guerrier and Adib (2004) point out, women are simply doing at work what is expected of them from society and undertaking activities which are required of them in the private sphere. However, as Ross-Smith *et al.* argue, women's custodianship of emotion work does them few favours, despite the supposed feminine advantage that women are supposed to bring to leadership and despite recent valorization of so-called 'feminine' skills. Such work is undervalued, unrecognized and reinforces traditional gender stereotypes that might 'narrow down the actual repertoire of women – prescribing to women what they should do and what they might be expected to do' (Ross-Smith *et al.*, 2007: 49). In fact, while mothering, care-giving or peace-making roles may be valued in the domestic sphere, none of them are necessarily aligned with contemporary models of good leadership behaviours.

A third orientation towards gender and emotions conforms to the theoretical orientation prioritized in this book namely the construction of gender (and hence emotional labour) as a cultural performance (e.g. Butler, 1994; Sass, 2000). Cultural performances are episodes through which members construct organizational reality (Williams, 2003) such as through performances of sociality. As Butler (1994) argues, gender provides much of the meaning for these performances through repeated acts which conform to norms of what constitutes male and female. Therefore as Hall (1993) and Williams (2003) point out, giving good service through emotional labour is 'doing' gender, involving for example the performance of culturally defined and gendered scripts. Similarly, Ross-Smith *et al.* (2007) demonstrate how narratives concerning the expectation that women take up mothering, care-giving and peace-making roles 'were deeply coloured and structured signifiers of gendered performance' constructed within the 'regulatory fiction' of gender binaries. Accordingly women both struggled against and conformed to these gendered scripts and the 'grain' of essentialization. This also has implications for men, discussed below, as they do or undo masculinity in their performances of emotional labour, performances which are themselves embedded with gendered norms and expectations.

Men, masculinity and emotions

Much of the above draws explicit or implicit links between emotional labour and femininity. On this basis, both men and organizations are assumed to be unemotional, associated instead with rationality, with emotions consigned to the private sphere and embodied in femininity. Rationality, discussed in more detail below, is conventionally seen as the 'opposite' of emotionality – even though as Albrow (1992) has argued, rationality itself involves emotions and emotion work to present a controlled and logical state. Moreover, as Hearn (1993) points out, men are far from unemotional and organizations are far from unemotional arenas. Instead he suggests, in terms of the former, that men may be too emotional: 'too out of control (or indeed too in control), especially when it comes to anger, sexuality and violence' (Hearn, 1993: 143). In terms of the latter, emotions are involved in the day-to-day interactions with colleagues, clients or employees – emotions which may become intensified in times of drama. Many male nurses, for example, described their strong emotions in their dealings with death and illness as well as what they saw as the appropriate expression of emotion in these settings. In the following story, a nurse recalls his first day on clinical placement:

> *I'll never forget when my very first clinical day as a trainee enrolled nurse clinical placement, it was only like for a morning and I worked with this nurse doing a bed bath on a very ill man and it was the first time I'd ever done any kind of nursing with a real person, so I was quite, you know concerned and I was doing everything gently and everything and this poor man, he was ... oh, you know really ill, almost comatose sort of thing, and he had a broken leg which hadn't been able to be fixed because he was so ... we had to roll him over to try and, you know, give him a proper wash and to make sure he was going to be comfortable, it really hurt him then and he came out of his comatose situation and he was being rolled by the nurse from this side towards me, but he rolled towards me, the pain of this caused him to open his eyes and he looked straight at me and he said 'you bastard!' And I thought ... and I really took that home and that really upset me, you know and I ... because even before I was off the ward that man died that day, he had a cardiac arrest and died like within a half an hour of us doing that bed bath ... I think when you first come into nursing and you're doing these sorts of things, they really have a tremendous impact on ... you know and I was in tears outside with the educator that had us on the ward. She said 'oh what's wrong?' And I said 'oh I'm sorry but a patient just died', you know and I was in tears and felt really embarrassed ... you know it's pretty unusual for me to burst into tears! (laughing) I can assure you.*

This suggests that emotions are more than just inner states and that we need to take into account the social context and the meanings attached to emotional displays. From the above story, memories of the pain of the patient's death have remained – as well as the embarrassment over what he saw as an inappropriate expression of feeling. Emotions and displays of emotion were frequently recalled during nurses' accounts of their experiences at work. From Hochschild (1983) and Hearn (1993), emotions therefore need to be seen as social and ideological constructs which can only be fully understood in their social context. Men for example are generally con-structed as rational and decisive while the same behaviour can be seen as cold or controlling when enacted by a woman. From Hearn (1993), men often feel free to express anger, perhaps because this complies with expressions and practices of dominance, while this emo-tion is strongly sanctioned in women. Some emotions are not seen as suitable for men. Fear for example has associations with 'feminine' vulnerability (even though anxiety and fear of not living up to the 'hegemonic' masculine ideal may be the experiences of most men) and it is often seen as inappropriate if men shed tears. In fact, as the above story illustrates, open displays of sorrow and sadness are often seen by men as out of place in the workplace and a source of embarrassment – even if the circumstances are painful. Several male nurses in the study were disapproving of female colleagues who they claimed had a tendency to cry with patients or relatives – preferring instead that they maintained a 'professional detachment'. This sup-ports Parkin's (1993) claim that ethos of control over emotions is seen as part of being professional – and the further up the hier-archy the less acceptable it is to demonstrate feelings of pain and sadness.

In terms of emotional labour, work suggests that men face challenges in performances of 'care'. Here, men can be marked as Other in caring work (e.g. Heikes, 1991; Hochschild, 1983; Simpson, 2007; Williams, 1993) on the grounds that work such as teaching and nursing call for special abilities that only women are deemed to possess. In the context of teaching and nursing, there are several implications for men in terms of how they perform gender and emotional labour. Firstly, as we saw in the last chapter and in terms of Bolton's typology outlined above, men are more likely than women to present their work as part of philan-thropic emotion management, that is, as part of a 'gift exchange'. High standards of care may be seen as a 'natural' part of femininity and hence undervalued and invisible (Taylor and Tyler, 2000; Williams, 2003). One outcome is therefore that emotional labour is more likely to be pre-sented and received as philanthropic and given a higher value when performed by men. In this respect, men often combined philanthropic and maverick performances as they presented themselves as 'going the extra mile' as they circumvented bureaucracy and mobilized resources for those in their care.

> *What do I mean by care? Well, for me it's being able to do the best for*
> *the patient, and if that means breaking rules then so be it ... so you've got*

*to understand it from a patient's point of view ... if a patient is obviously
dying, he wants a cigarette, there's no point refusing him a cigarette, I would
take him outside whereas my female colleagues would say 'no you're not
allowed to smoke'. You try and give him a cigarette when they're going to
die anyway. They're at the end of the road and what he needs most in this
case is a cigarette, he wanted a cigarette. Now, with the women he'll get a
hard and fast, 'this is what's good for you' and that's it, that's the way ...
I don't feel that way. You tell me what's good for you, what you want – and
I'll do it ...*

Presenting women as 'rule-bound' and cautious allows the uptake of a
more satisfying oppositional identity around independence and non-
conformity. Secondly, meanings attached to men's bodies constrain, in
terms of Bolton's prescriptive emotion management (work performed
according to professional norms of conduct), the way aspects of emotional labour are carried out – a theme we develop further in Chapter
6. As Connell (2000) points out, it is easier for meaning around masculinity and femininity to take hold when the body complies with its
social definition. In primary school teaching and nursing, for example, drawing on essential notions of femininity, the masculine body
is very much at odds with its social definition (for example, as rational, disembodied). While men may be valued for their bodies in work
that demands physical strength or discipline (Evans, 2004), in caring
roles men's bodies are also viewed with suspicion and seen as potentially dangerous and disruptive. They are accordingly subject to codes of
conduct concerning how aspects of caring (comforting a crying child,
examining a female patient) are carried out. Thus, from Bolton's typology, prescriptive feeling rules (emotional labour dictated by professional
norms) and presentational feeling rules (emotional labour based on
social norms) can be seen as gendered to the extent that different standards of professional and social engagement for men and women are
likely to apply.

Thirdly, a gendered division of emotional labour can be identified
whereby men gravitate towards more 'masculine' specialisms within the
occupation, take on authority roles and those demanding discipline or
more challenging emotion work. For example, we have seen that in
teaching men are often called upon to take on the role of disciplinarian
and authority figure – to adopt a father role – while in nursing men are
given more challenging and difficult tasks such as dealing with suicidal
patients or breaking bad news to relatives. Men do not always actively
choose these roles but are pressed into them. One nurse commented on
his own situation:

> *I think sometimes as a man you're expected to, there's an expectation on you as a leader, which is something I don't feel particularly comfortable with, but I have time after time been offered leadership roles, leadership positions and it's not something I'm particularly good at or confident at, so I often find it bemusing that I'm offered the roles. For example there's this job which is a leadership role, I was approached by the director of nursing and invited to apply for the job. Now I'd demonstrated no ability to do the job in my previous position, so I often think there's an expectation that men will be more ambitious.*

The gendered division of emotional labour therefore reproduces wider divisions based on traditional notions of masculinity and femininity and which channel men into authoritarian roles or those demanding discipline and personal challenge. At one extreme, men characteristically manage the emotional labour of others, controlling the emotional labour of women and less powerful men (Hearn, 1993). More generally, from Pierce (1995) and Brannen (2005), activities around emotional labour may provide men with repertoires of 'doing' emotional labour and gender that, by drawing on displays of risk-taking, authority and control, have positive identity implications. Women, by contrast, may perform emotional labour through traditional, devalued notions of passivity, service and care. This supports James's (1993) view that it is possible to identify '*differential* divisions of emotional labour based on equal-status work and *deferential* divisions of emotional labour which are characterized by submissions to authority' (James, 1993: 95). On this basis, the gendered division of emotional labour may imply gender difference based on deferential divisions, that is, which carry different valuations and which are hierarchically arranged.

The 'masculinization' of emotions

As we have seen, rationality, as the antithesis of emotion, has been largely predicated on the exclusion of the feminine with close connections with qualities considered masculine such as efficiency, effectiveness and calculating self-interest (Knights and McCabe, 2001; Morgan, 1992). Technical rationality for example conforms to masculinity both in the gendered engineering metaphor that forms its roots and in the value placed on the mastery of techniques as the means of achieving managerial control. By the same token, instrumental rationality, based on the identification of the most efficient means to achieve given ends, is quintessentially male in the emphasis given to monetary calculations for determining the most effective, most efficient means for realizing one's material self-interest. As Bologh (1990), cited in Ross-Smith and Kornberger (2004), argues, this process:

> implies reliance on precise measurements, comparison and quantitative calculation of costs and benefits... Instrumental calculating rationality brings with it qualities considered masculine: smart and decisive self-determination or free, confident aggressive action.
>
> (Bologh, 1990: 126)

As Knights and Surman (2008) point out, the pre-eminence given to rationality in pursuing organizational goals does not mean that we leave emotions 'on the doorstep' as we enter. In this respect, following from Hochschild's pioneering work on emotional labour, attention has been given to emotions as an integral part of organizational life. However, as Lewis and Simpson (2007) argue, in 'adding emotions on' to the conventional rational paradigm they have in the process become 'masculinized'. This can be seen in several ways.

Firstly, we can identity a masculinist preoccupation with measurement and performance in the recent interest in emotional intelligence and the perception of its primacy in the effective operation of organizations. Emotional intelligence is defined by Goleman (2004) as the ability to manage one's emotions as well as the emotions of others and includes capacities for self-awareness, empathy and self-motivation. From Goleman's work, these capacities have been shown to increase organizational performance. In other words, as Lewis and Simpson (2007) point out, emotions have been harnessed as an organizational asset and used, measured for instrumental ends – trends that can be identified as a masculinization (or rationalization) of emotion. Here, emotions are not afforded any intrinsic value but are valorized simply because they enhance productivity and production (Knights and Surman, 2008).

Secondly, we can identify masculinist discourses of quality and accountability currently driving many practices in the service and caring professions. Bolton (2007) for example refers to the masculinized model of professionalism embedded in some teaching contexts, whereby concepts of a 'good teacher' are increasingly associated with masculine competences of management, control and technical expertise (discussed further in Chapter 7). Metcalfe and Linstead (2003) in a study of team-working, often characterized as 'feminine' through associations with cooperation, empowerment and relationships, have pointed to the prevalence and take-over of 'masculine' behaviours around output, efficiency and performance while Fletcher (1999) has similarly argued that relational capabilities, as in arguments relating to emotional intelligence above, have been 'captured' by organizations and put to instrumental use in the masculinist project of efficiency and control. Emotions are thus being rewritten as masculine in contrast to their conventional reading as feminine. As Lewis and Simpson argue, by being presented as masculine, emotions are taken out of the private realm and an association with female bodies, and institutionalized:

> Thus in this way emotion which is culturally associated with women is taken out of the realms of 'the body', 'nature' and the 'private sphere', given authority and scientific weight through the development for example of quantitative measures (emotional IQ, performance indicators) and placed in the masculine public world of work and organizations. The placing of emotion in the realm of the intellect through the association with 'intelligence', quality, performance or outputs signals that emotion has been disembodied, demonstrating the strong association that is being made between masculinity and emotion.
>
> (Lewis and Simpson, 2007: 7)

Finally, the 're-gendering' of emotions has been highlighted in several studies of service work and emotional labour. These include management attempts to harness and deploy emotions as part of the drive to deliver 'quality' service (Korczynski, 2001); the squeezing out of the feminine nurturance and care in primary education by the masculine cultural project emphasizing quality, efficiency and performance (Bolton, 2007); the use of statistical information relating to the monitoring of emotional labour provided by call centre operatives (Brannen, 2005) and other forms of 'customer-oriented bureaucracy' (Korczynski, 2001) designed to rationalize the service and emotional labour process. In this way, masculine logics of efficiency, price, quality and speed are imposed on and take precedence over feminine dimensions of customer service and care.

As Lewis and Simpson argue, the rewriting of the emotion in masculine terms serves not only to demonstrate a current emphasis on the control and management of emotions but also to provide men with a positive image in their performance of emotional labour. As we saw in Chapter 3, men often present their emotional labour skills in masculinist terms (as rational, detached, objective) and so render them visible and disengaged from the embodied dispositions of women. In other words, as Knights and Surman (2008) point out, the positive enhancement of the sense of self often associated with deployment of social skills at work, is gender-differentiated and skewed towards men. In fact, men's emotional displays are often interpreted as appropriate and signalling a valued assertiveness and leadership while women's emotions are seen as inappropriate – women themselves perceived to be irrational, excitable or unstable (ibid.). Moreover, it has been suggested that in the appropriation of emotional and personal attributes in client or customer services or in the emotional support of colleagues, it is women who are drained of emotional reserves in the process. This is supported by Ross-Smith *et al.*'s (2007) study in which women were often expected to undertake 'maintenance' emotion work in the organization (caretaking, 'toxic handling', conflict resolution) and who complained of exhaustion and burn-out as a result.

Conclusion

In this chapter we have explored the gendered nature of the service encounter and of emotions at work. Both have core associations with femininity. While the service sector has been recognized and investigated as explicitly 'feminized', the gendered nature of emotions and emotional labour – perhaps because of their association with the private sphere and with the 'natural' embodied dispositions of women – has been, until recently, often implied rather than the subject of critical analysis. In this respect, we have seen how emotions and emotional labour have become the subject of rationality and can be seen to have become 'masculinized'.

In this respect, as Swan (2008) has argued, the mobilization of feminine emotions can be a source of power for men. Swan refers here to the work of Robinson (2000) who suggests that men restore power and privilege (threatened for example by the feminization of work practices) through a number of 'appropriating moves'. These may include the co-option of the feminine, as discussed in the last chapter in the context of men's performance of care. As we have seen, by imposing a masculine rationality and detachment on descriptions of these skills, and by drawing on discourses of the New Man, men were able to enhance the value and specificity of emotional labour skills *when they were performed by men*.

Despite the primacy afforded to instrumental and technical rationality in pursuing organizational goals, we have seen from this chapter that emotions are integral to understanding organizations and their day-to-day practices and operations. This is not confined to service work, but as Kelan (2008) has pointed out, is also integral to work typically defined as masculine such as engineering or ICT. However, in the context of the present study (of male cabin crew, nurses, primary school teachers and librarians), the nature of the work means that emotions and emotional labour are central to activities and practices as well as to gender identity and performance.

In the latter respect, as Marsh and Musson (2008) point out, emotion and identity are intertwined in that emotion is one of the key ways in which identity is expressed or performed and in the sense that emotional effort is required for the construction of identities. This effort may be particularly great in ambiguous settings, such as those encountered by men in gender-atypical roles – aspects of which were discussed in Chapters 2 and 3. Overall, emotions, emotional labour and identity are themes that run throughout this book – and are central to accounts by men as they make sense of their experiences in their non-traditional work contexts. It is to these contexts and these accounts that we now turn.

Part II
Occupational Contexts

5
Gender, Performativity, Space: Male Cabin Crew and the Negotiation of Identity

With contributions from Margaret Patrickson

Introduction

This chapter sets out to explore how men who occupy 'para-professional' service roles, specifically cabin crew, mobilize and utilize the spaces of their working lives as they manage their identity in a non-traditional role. Authors from social geography (e.g. Gregson and Rose, 2000; Lefebvre, 1991; Massey, 1994, 2005) as well as from organization studies (e.g. Halford and Leonard, 2006a, 2006b; Keenoy and Oswick, 2003; Kornberger and Clegg, 2004) have argued for a greater attention to context and to the discursive aspects of space as an identity resource. Addressing the latter, Halford and Leonard (2006b) examine in a hospital context how generic discourses such as those associated with gender and occupation are mobilized by individuals within and through the specificities and associated temporalities of space. This and the above-mentioned literature have played a key role in highlighting the complexity and instability of space as well as, to a lesser extent, its performative nature (Gregson and Rose, 2000; Massey, 1994). Informed by post-structural accounts, performativity alludes here to how spaces as articulations of power relations are brought into being by the embodied performances and citational practices of individuals within them. Through an analysis of the practices of male cabin crew as they manage their identity in and through space, this chapter explores the creativity and complexities inherent within space–identity relationships.

As we have seen, all workers seek ways to reconcile the work they do with an identity they can accept (Leidner, 1991). In this respect, the work of cabin crew has specific spatial characteristics (for example, close proximity to service recipients, inability to leave the site of the service encounter) which may have implications for how individuals manage a comfortable sense of self. 'Para-professional' service work, where man-agement largely dictate how that work is carried out, traditionally has (as in the case of crew) both low status and, through the domestic nature of the tasks involved, cultural connections with femininity (Adib and Guerrier, 2003; Tyler and Abbott, 1998). The routine work of crew, as Tyler and Abbott (1998) point out, is largely of a domestic nature (serv-ing food and drink, clearing trays, seeing to passenger comfort) and while management are absent from the site of the service (that is, the aircraft) there are strong prescriptive elements, supported by training, concerning how that service is to be carried out.

Service, gender and identity

As we saw in the last chapter, social interaction with a customer or client is a key feature of service work (Forseth, 2005), with ser-vice quality depending on the skills (for example, emotional labour skills) and attributes of the service provider (Hochschild, 1983; Leidner, 1991). Personal characteristics of that individual (for example, gen-der, age, appearance, personality) are thus integral to the service with implications for subjectivity. Moreover, the emphasis placed on the sovereignty of the consumer (Sturdy, 1998) as a source of competi-tive advantage – and the airline industry has been subject to particular pressure in this respect – has contributed to deference as increasingly characteristic of the job (Forseth, 2005). As Macdonald and Sirianni (1996) argue, asymmetry in the exchange of respect is built into the structural features of proletariat service. An identity of deference (being nice, caring, polite) may therefore be integral to the service encounter within the para-professional role. The work of cabin crew, for example, involves a relentless friendliness even in the face of angry or abusive passengers (Tyler and Abbott, 1998; Tyler and Taylor, 1998).

The gendered nature of such work has been well documented (Forseth, 2005; Hochschild, 1983; Tyler and Abbott, 1998; Williams, 2003) with strong association between 'doing deference' and feminin-ity. In terms of cabin crew, the occupation has moved from what was previously a masculine domain, supported by airlines' earlier associa-tions with militarism (Mills, 1995) to a largely feminine one based on the mobilization of a glamorous and subservient female heterosexual-ity. Young and beautiful women have been groomed to provide service to what was largely seen as male passengers – a service that was sex-ualized by promotional slogans such as 'Fly Me' (Singapore Airlines). Cabin work is still largely female-dominated but now employs older, more mature women and, perhaps influenced by recent emphases on safety and security, a growing number of men.

Identity in place, space and time

We have seen how identity can be conceptualized as an ongoing project (Sveningsson and Alvesson, 2003), mobilized, negotiated and renegotiated in day-to-day activities and interactions. Individuals can be seen to 'do' identity through, among others, speech, dress, narrative and body performance (Halford and Leonard, 2006a). Identity is accordingly positional, temporal and relational. In other words, people position themselves in relation to others (Gherardi and Poggio, 2001) and within 'situated discourses' (Pullen, 2006) that have a precise location in place, space and time. As authors have argued (e.g. Keenoy and Oswick, 2003; Thrift and Dewsbury, 2000), these dimensions are more than mere *context* or environmental 'backdrops' to experience and performance. Instead, as Goffman (1959) demonstrated in his analysis of 'front' and 'back' regions, where displays of conformity and resistance, respectively, take place, these time–space relations can form the basis of power, opposition and control. For example, the strong managerial and prescriptive elements of the work of crew in the 'front region' can be undermined by activities in the 'back region' of the galley which resist attempts at such control (Williams, 2003).

As Halford and Leonard (2006b) argue, place, space and time in organizations combine with more generic resources, such as those afforded by gender and occupation, to offer multiple and competing resources for the construction of working identities. These resources are invested with particular meanings that 'interplay with the discursive and material conditions' in which individuals are situated (p. 11). Spaces can thus be seen to be 'performative' (Gregson and Rose, 2000) in that they are articulations of power produced interrelationally through the performances and subject positions of men and women. Individuals operate and interact with and in space – through gesture and bodily movements and influenced by norms of engagement in these specific contexts. In other words, spaces are 'animated by the embodied performances of the women and men who move through them' (Halford and Leonard, 2006b: 77). As individuals move within the spaces of their working lives, the 'contextual resources of subjectivity open to them constantly change' (Halford and Leonard, 2006a: 660). Space thus constitutes a dynamic resource (Lefebvre, 1991) that is both active and activated in body performances (Butler, 1990, 1993; Rose, 1999) and the management of subjectivity. Rather than being a 'given, neutral and passive geometry' (Dodge and Kitchin, 2005), space can thus be seen to be 'ontogenetic', that is, continually brought into existence by the reiterative practices of individuals within them (Lefebvre, 1991; Mackenzie, 2002; Massey, 1994).

As Halford and Leonard, following from Massey (1994, 2005), point out, these contexts are not gender-neutral but offer resources that are both gendered and gendering. From Baldry (1999), environmental 'variables' such as access to space and opportunities for mobility as well as meanings attached to space can come together to strengthen gender power relations and can be drawn upon to support a performance and subjectivity of 'male' and 'female'. In this respect, spaces can be seen as gendered and can be used or drawn upon to support a performance and subjectivity of 'male' and 'female' (Gregson and Rose, 2000). The cockpit (or flight deck) and the aircraft cabin, for example, can be seen as masculine and feminine spaces, respectively. As Mills (1995) has illustrated, the highly technologized space of the cockpit is underscored with meanings around rationality, danger and expertise that have core connections with discourses of (heterosexual) masculinity. Militaristic uniforms worn by the (mostly male) occupants are symbolic resources (Gherardi, 1995) that further enhance the masculinity of this space. By contrast, the cabin, or main body of the aircraft, can be defined as a feminine space. It is in this arena that consumption, service and the trivia of entertainment occur – culturally associated with femininity.

Moreover, as we have seen above, this space has sexual connotations in that it has been and, to some extent, continues to be the site for the mobilization by airlines of a subordinated heterosexual femininity (Hochschild, 1983; Williams, 2003). This is achieved through the presentation and performance of female bodies (Tyler and Abbott, 1998; Tyler and Taylor, 1998) within the visible arena of the aisles, positioned erotically against the traditional masculinity of the flight deck (Mills, 1995). When men enter this space as crew they too become associated with femininity (Hochschild, 1983) and with a denigrated (homo)sexuality. Thus, as Halford and Leonard (2006b) argue, spaces constitute 'rich resources' for the 'performance' (Butler, 1994) of gender. It is within the feminized and 'sexualed' space of the cabin, positioned against the masculine space of the cockpit, that male crew accordingly negotiate their identity.

More generally, specific temporalities of the service context can combine with space, as in time–space distance, to have implications for the service encounter, for emotional labour and for the management of identities of the service worker. *Firstly,* space and time collectivities involving time–space separation of short distance, as in an aircraft, are likely to be expressed through the physical characteristics and per-ceptual abilities of the individuals concerned. Cultural expectations of consumers, for example, can shape the social interaction within the ser-vice encounter when there is close physical and temporal proximity of production and consumption (Guerrier and Adib, 2004) and this can make specific demands on the public presentation of the (employee) self. Within the context of cabin crew, expectations of passengers, mobilized through promotional advertising that continue to draw on creations of heterosexual femininity outlined above, together with the body proximity inherent in that service work, has helped to create a sex-ualized atmosphere within an encounter that can last for several hours (Tyler and Abbott, 1998).

Secondly, short time–space separation can make it more difficult for individuals to develop 'communities of coping' (Sturdy and Fineman, 2001; Korczynski, 2003) during the labour process – leading to an imper-ative, in a Goffmanesque sense, to create 'off-stage' regions (such as the 'galley') for mutual support. Such spaces, out of sight of customers, can be important arenas for the expression of emotions without the danger of violating organizational display norms (Morris and Feldman, 1996). *Thirdly*, time frequency of the interaction may be important in that, as Gutek *et al.* (2000) point out, personal characteristics ingredient to identity (including gender, size, voice and personality) may be more important in one-off interactions where there is little or no expectation of future contact – such as often occurs between flight attendant and passenger.

Finally, the time length of the interaction can have implications for emotional labour effort in that, as Morris and Feldman (1996) argue, service of a longer duration requires longer emotional displays, are less likely to be scripted and may accordingly require greater attention and emotional stamina. This is likely to be the case in the airline service encounter where, even on short-haul flights, crew are often called upon to perform their role for many hours at a time.

All these factors are implicated in how crew manage subjectivity in and through space. From the present study, three themes emerged that are pertinent in unravelling the complexities of space–identity relations in this context: control, resistance and corporeality.

Authority and control: Power relations in the aisle

As we have seen, spaces are gendered, and hence both support and incorporate power relations in that they can be drawn upon to assist in a performance and subjectivity of 'male' and 'female'. Generic discourses of gender and occupation are accordingly negotiated through daily activities and interactions that are not only spatial in their context, that is, occur *within* space, but are activated, constructed, resisted *through* space. In this respect, the identity management of male cabin crew carried tensions from its contextualization within the largely feminized and also sexualed space of the cabin (where domestic activities and aesthetic body displays take place). Several of the men interviewed sought in some way to distance themselves from these dominant meanings for example by placing emphasis on safety, security and the sometimes dangerous aspects of the job or by claiming bodily advantage in this more masculine role:

> *You are there for safety and security, we are not there for the niceties... and we've all had incidents at 37,000 feet with passengers or whatever and it's not nice, it's not nice... when things go wrong it is extremely stressful... and a lot of people can't deal with that and it takes a very specific type of person to be able to successfully do the job as cabin crew but it's anything but serving tea and coffee.*

> *Passengers feel reassured having men on the craft, they feel that security, they feel that strength, they feel that authority – especially where passengers are irate it's good to have the male strength.*

The gendered nature of their working space could thus be rearranged (from feminine 'niceties' to masculine authority and strength) to help support a masculine identity. At the same time, while the cabin can be seen to be largely feminine through its association with domesticity and female heterosexuality, meanings could shift with the practices occurring within it. These practices related partly to the nature and extent of physical movement and to the maintenance of safety within the aircraft.

In terms of the former, while passengers are able to move within the aisle, their access is restricted and incursions more tentative and there are times when they are confined to their seats. The colonization of this space by crew – confident, visible and active as they perform their service and safety roles – supported an authority over the seated and largely passive passengers.

> *I know everything about the plane, what it does, if it does something its not supposed to do... they don't*

The thing about being on a plane is that the passengers are usually sat down and you're usually standing up so you've already got that advantage over them...

Walking purposefully up and down the aisle (checking seat belts, closing overhead lockers, fetching drinks, serving food) is integral to the work of cabin crew. As Halford and Leonard (2006b) argue, movement such as walking is a particularly important spatial practice which, through comportment, eye contact, posture, tells 'rich stories' of relationships and power. In this context, a 'masculine' freedom of movement of crew is juxtaposed against the 'feminine' confinement of passengers. The high levels of visibility within this space mean, moreover, that certain bodily displays by the crew (a way of walking, facial expressions) can convey powerful meanings to manipulate the emotions of passengers.

You can make them feel comfortable, you can make them feel uncomfortable, you can make them feel scared, you can make them feel happier and that all depends on the way you are in the cabin.

This more masculine 'authoritative space', initiated partly by relations of movement and confinement, can help overlay more feminine meanings outlined above. However, authority conveyed by movement is not fully secure and in this context can be undermined by associations with chore-driven domesticity. Therefore, while movement and walking is often associated with a (masculine) purpose and authority, movement in response to the demands of others can be seen to be part of deferential and hence devalued 'feminine' service. In this respect, crew made frequent references to the need to 'run around' after passengers:

So they'll be asking for things and we're running around and your head just booms.

The men usually... because they had their secretaries running around after them and it was like 'I've dropped my handkerchief, can you pick it up'.

These meanings undermined the authority of 'masculine' behavioural practices associated with the need to secure safety in the cabin. Discourses of consumer sovereignty, mobilized in promotional advertising, could also create tensions between the safety and service elements of the job and cause shifts in asymmetries of power.

...sometimes they sit there by the (emergency) *exit and just throw their bags and clothes and they need to be clear, so you have to go and tell them and... you are the father who tells the child what to do, but then you go there with the trolley and they go right I'll have coffee and can you give them Pringles to my children over there and at that time you serve them.*

In this juxtapositioning of responsibilities and of relations of power, the trolley as feminine artefact supported a feminization of space in the craft, undermining more authoritative meanings and impressing on the identity of male crew (many crew referred to the uncomfortable 'trolley dolly' image of their role).

Overall, the busy routines and 'stand-up performances' of cabin crew, colonizing space within the aisles, combined with the seated and largely immobile audience of passengers to produce particular subjectivities. Masculine discourses of safety and security, heightened by recent terrorist threats, supported the crew in a credible authoritative and knowledgeable performance. This presence however was undermined by activities and meanings concerning the domestic and subordinate task of serving food and was complicated by discourses and practices of consumer power. These meanings can therefore be tension-ridden and contestable and have material (for example, dismissive behaviour from passengers) and discursive (for example, feelings of servility) implications. Space thus emerged as complex and unstable – its meanings shifting with the activities and practices contained – both influencing and influenced by (gendered) identity processes.

Spaces as sites of resistance

As Thomas *et al.* (2004) argue, resistance is not simply a behavioural response in the form of oppositional practices to inequality at work but can also incorporate, at a discursive level, struggles against the potential colonization of particular meanings and subjectivities. At this 'micro-political' level (Weedon, 1993), resistance takes place when tensions occur between 'an individual's notion of self (itself derived from discourse) and the subjectivity offered in a dominant discourse', thereby involving 'contests over meanings and the articulation of counter discourses' (Thomas *et al.*, 2004: 6). Resistance is thus socially constructed in context in that its manifestation and performance will vary between individuals in their specific temporalities and spaces (Prasad and Prasad, 2000).

As discussed earlier, deference and subservience, characteristic of both the emotional proletariat role (Forseth, 2005) and of the work of cabin crew (Bolton and Boyd, 2003; Hochschild, 1983; Tyler and Abbott, 1998; Williams, 2003) can have negative implications for subjectivities (Leidner, 1991). Moreover, specific temporalities of the service context can combine with space, as in time–space distance, to have implications for the service encounter. Close physical and temporal proximity of production and consumption (Guerrier and Adib, 2004) as well as the one-off nature of the contact (Gutek *et al.*, 2000) can put strains on the personal characteristics of service providers (including gender, size, voice and personality) and the public presentation of self. The confined space of the interaction, the inability to leave the site of the service and the duration of the service encounter may well exacerbate the effects of any 'assault on self' (Williams, 2003) associated with the demands of servanthood. As two crew commented:

> *Like say a restaurant is probably the closest* (to airline service), *the customer comes, you treat them they leave. In our sort of industry, the passenger comes, you've treated them and they stay you know, they stay for a long time*

> (passengers) *see you like a servant really. Some of them who wouldn't look at you and it's infrequent these days, please or thank you. I used to let that bother me and after a few years or whatever you know it really used to get on my nerves because you do think you know, hang on a minute I'm still as valued a person as you are and ... because you're in such a confined space and you have them there and it's very hard to explain but you do almost feel like there's nothing else important apart from that person treating you so badly.*

Spaces were mobilized as crew resisted subordinated subjectivities, shaped through discourses of servanthood, to create alternative meanings. Identity repair work often took place in the confines of the galley – a space which was rarely visited by passengers. As we have seen, from Korczynski (2003) and Sturdy and Fineman (2001), short time–space separation can make it difficult for individuals to develop 'communities of coping' during the labour process. The time pressures on the completion of service, particularly on short-haul flights, together with high levels of visibility in the aisles would rule out supportive, as opposed to purely instrumental, exchanges between crew – creating an imperative for off-stage regions as a retreat. The exclusivity of this space was made concrete by an emphatically closed curtain:

> *You can't get away and that's where the curtain comes in and we slam it shut. The galley is our space when we don't have to see passengers*

In this small 'reservoir of occupational life' (Bolton, 2005b), occupational communities developed to offer friendship and support through shared meanings. Here, crew let off steam, referred disparagingly to passengers and indulged in sexual innuendo, gossip and flirtatious banter. The confined nature of this space together with a common antipathy towards passengers created an in-group identity and acted as a 'safety valve' for the pressures of the cabin. As Benwell and Stokoe (2006) suggest, 'boundary talk' is possible only at the point where one piece of space objectively ends and another begins. The private space of the galley, separated by the boundary and exclusivity of the curtain, accordingly makes such talk (for example, gossip) possible.

Resistance was not however confined to the galley as exclusive space. Within the aisle, feminized through the practices of domestic service and sexualized through promotional practices and bodily displays, male crew also resisted a subordinated self. This could be achieved through ironic recognition of its dominant meaning (for example, of deference and sexual availability). In the following quote an interviewee playfully contrasted an acceptance of a subordinated identity with a more authoritative role:

> *So you're a trolley dolly because they see you up and down the aisles with the coffee or tea and I used to laugh and make a joke, I'd say you can't afford me so you might as well have the tea or coffee or whatever but when you collapse in the aisle with a heart attack, this trolley dolly has got to know what to do...*

A community of shared meanings through humour served to support group identity and cohesion and further undermined the dominant discourse of service and deference. Exclusionary tactics, referred to by Collinson (1994) as 'resistance through distance', created alternative meanings around camaraderie and an erotically risky (and risqué) subversion of prescribed behavioural norms. Wording and emphasis of the end of flight farewell to passengers at the cabin door could, for example, be manipulated to convey derogatory and usually sexually charged meanings that were exclusive to crew. Released from the pressures of the trolley, the 'post-dinner' aisle could be vacated – or mobilized in a playful subversion of service:

> *We used to stand in the front of the aircraft at first class and we used to race to the back, not running but walking through the aircraft and make*

sure that nobody (i.e. passengers) *stops you or eye contact or anything because if they stop you, you've lost the race.*

Creative use of space thus disrupted norms of deference and transformed it into an arena of play. Resistance to a subordinated identity was further displayed through status-levelling tactics associated with the masculine space of the flight deck. As suggested earlier, the proximity of this space, culturally associated with a superior and heterosexual masculinity, may serve to underscore the femininity of the meanings and material practices within the cabin. The antagonism displayed towards the flight deck and its occupants (perceived as arrogant, bullying and homophobic) may be testimony to levels of discomfort experienced as status differences impress subordinated identities on male crew. One crew briefly reflected on his negative feelings towards pilots: *'I'm only a steward and you're flight deck ... it's a male thing I suppose'.*

Putting pilots in their place (*'winding them up'*) was a preoccupation of many crew – achieved through potentially embarrassing banter, withholding food and refusing a servile role. Such resistance could be afforded greater license when pilots moved into the space of the cabin:

We had one where he came out of the flight deck and he said there's nowhere to hang my jacket. I said well try the wardrobe, it's in the bloody flight deck and he said yes but there's no hangers, could you go and get me one. I was like, f*** off. I said, who do you think you're talking to?

Similar tensions have emerged in other work (e.g. Simpson, 2005) where struggles around the 'dominant centre' (Hearn, 1996) have taken place. While women are frequently subordinated in organizations, the take-up of an inferiorized identity has been found to be more difficult for men (Lupton, 2000; Simpson, 2004, 2005). This may be particularly the case when men are forced to confront a privileged masculinity in the workplace.

Thus, spaces are mobilized in often creative ways as men resist subordinated identities. In this respect, spaces can be used as a site of retreat and identity repair work as well as a backdrop to and an active resource in playful subversions of their role. Equally, meanings attached to spaces can underpin an inferiorization of subjectivity, triggering overt resistance displays.

Corporeality: Bodies through space

As Lefebvre (1991) points out, conceptions of body and space are insep-
arable in that, from Grosz (1994), individuals move through and occupy
space with their bodies and in relation to other bodies. Spaces are thus
brought into being and activated by the embodied performances of men
and women within them (Halford and Leonard, 2006b). We have seen
for example how bodily movements such as walking can convey an
authoritative claim to space while, in the context of 'running around'
after passengers, can at the same time impress a subservient identity.
Such understandings of body performances may be particularly pertinent for service workers (Warhurst and Nickson, 2007). Such work is
both *embodied* in that 'facial and bodily displays are crucial elements of
the performance of emotional labour' and *aesthetic* in that 'modes of
embodiment' are increasingly being corporately produced in such a way
as to signify the aesthetics of the organization (Witz *et al.*, 2003: 36).

In these respects, crew were aware that facial and body displays had
a powerful impact on passengers. As one crew pointed out, a hurried
walk or anxious look may undermine passengers' feelings of safety on
the plane. These body performances were also critical when dealing with
passenger complaints: crew were trained for example to kneel to maintain eye contact with seated passengers. At the same time, as Warhurst
and Nickson (2007) found in the context of service organizations generally, the need for airlines to present a particular professional 'face' was
associated with aesthetic codes of body management and with corporeal dispositions that express friendly and helpful service. Crew made
frequent references to how they represented (embodied) the organization and to the importance of a smart, clean appearance and welcoming
manner, also discussed in Chapter 3. These aesthetic codes were additionally symbolic of the glamour of aviation, adventure and travel.
Pleasure from visibility and from body performances ('*I love it, I'm like
that, bring it on!*') – referred to in the last chapter as the 'gaze' – were
experienced both inside the aircraft and in the airport terminal:

> So every time you go down the aisle people are watching you and it's because
> it's a glamorous job, it's because they would like to do that job ,it's because
> they think oh what he has got so special that he's there.

These meanings were captured within the airline uniform which, as
Halford and Leonard (2006a, 2006b) argue more generally, can confer
particular subjectivities. In this context, uniforms were seen to bestow

authority in interactions with passengers as well as a subjectivity of glamour and adventure. As Dellinger (2002) points out, uniforms also serve to define the boundaries of the in-group:

I always wanted to strut through the terminal with my uniform on after flying or like going to the plane and it's like the passengers go oh it's the crew.

One crew admitted that he routinely kept his uniform on, as a powerful signifier of adventure and travel, on the way home by tube in order to prolong the pleasure of wearing it – despite incurring some physical discomfort in the process: '*I keep it all on until the bitter end and I sweat to death but I wear it to the bitter end'*.

Men accordingly gained pleasure and pride from their bodies and from aesthetic displays. This was underscored by a celebration of their physical strength in and around the aircraft – their ability to lift heavy objects, to deal with physically challenging passengers and/or to assist in emergency situations were presented as assets that were differentiating factors from female crew. These ascriptions of body autonomy and proficiency are in contrast to some work on women in the same industry (e.g. Tyler and Abbott, 1998; Taylor and Tyler, 2000). Here, the corporate, 'panoptical gaze' is seen as oppressive: more 'reflective of patriarchal norms and instrumentality imposed aesthetic codes, than expressions of self-determined individuality' (Tyler and Abbott, 1998: 437). Male crew, however, appeared to celebrate their bodies as the bearers of an aesthetic ideal as well as a claimed source of strength and security in the day-to-day operations of the cabin.

As Trethewey (1999) argues, by being brought into service bodies must be controlled so that they will 'behave'. In this respect, many crew made reference to the need for endurance as they coped with fatigue from lack of sleep and from irregular, hurried meals – as well as from repressing emotion to present welcoming bodies:

I suppose people could think ... that's not really work ... that must be so easy for you, which isn't true because I'm telling you, you try and do four sector flights, getting up at three in the morning and still smiling when you come off that bloody plane ... so your stomach gets bloated, you feel fat, you feel ugly ... you get fatigued, your skin's awful, you come home all you want to do is have a shower, you stink of plane ...

Within the cabin, the bodily demands and needs of passengers are visible, vocalized and prioritized as a core component of the service process.

In this respect, passengers *are* their bodies, permutations of bodily needs and necessities, while crew must discipline and dispose of their bodies in their service role.

Finally, the presence of male bodies in the 'feminine' space of the cabin altered its meaning so that it became strongly associated with homosexuality. Male bodies, as well as the spaces they occupied, were accordingly 'marked' as different from the heterosexual norm. In this respect, in a 'reversal of gaze' and through 'movements of exhibition' (Irigaray, 1991) as they performed their role, attention was drawn to men's Otherness. Within this 'gay space', men's bodies were objectified and a source of aversion:

> *A group of six girls kept grabbing my arse and one of them was going are you gay because I think you're nice and you're nice looking and I was trying to do the service and they were constantly getting me run around like can I have this now, oh I've changed my mind . . .*

> *When you've got a group of lads on board . . . and basically they look on you as though you're filth because they assume you're gay . . . men look at you in disgust.*

Homophobia was described as endemic among groups of young male passengers as well as in the masculine and heterosexual space of the flight deck. Straight crew often resisted through humour while gay crew, through gestures, speech and body movements, were reported as routinely 'camping it up' in a flamboyant parody of sexual alterity.

The above data and discussion demonstrate, along the lines argued by Witz *et al.* (2003), the embodied nature of service work as well as, from the perspective of Lefebvre (1991), the integrality of bodies with space. Gestures, body movement and expression are implicated in shaping some specifics of a service encounter and these can subtly alter the meanings and emotions of space. As a 'sign-emitting text' (Trethewey, 1999), bodies thus both signify the aesthetics of the organization and are insinuated in the production of meanings attached to space. Visible as Other, men's bodies both mark and are marked by space – essentially corporeal yet practising disembodiment in a disciplinary project of service and care.

Conclusion

This chapter has explored how space and associated temporalities both influence and are influenced by the management of work identities.

More specifically, through the themes of control, resistance and corpo-reality, it has shown how men in a feminized para-professional service role negotiate masculine subjectivities within and through space and how gendered meanings attached to space can impress upon and both challenge and be challenged by the performances and subjectivities of individuals within them.

The performative nature of space is evident firstly in its relational and hierarchical nature (Massey, 2005). In this respect, activities and subjec-tivities of crew, moving rapidly in 'space without place' at 30,000 feet, can be seen to articulate broader power relations below. These relate, for example, to discourses of consumer sovereignty and gender – which are manifest in the practices and power relations of the on-board ser-vice encounter as well in embodied performances and a 'gaze' that is founded on conventional notions of masculinity, femininity and sexual-ity. Equally, we have seen how the 'feminized' space of the cabin, the site for consumption, service and entertainment, is positioned hierarchically (and for male crew often problematically) against the 'masculine' expert and technological space of the flight deck. Spaces are thus separate yet, as Gregson and Rose (2000) point out, also 'threatened, contaminated, stained, enriched' by other spaces.

Performances do not take place in already existing locations – rather space is produced through embodied performances, as both articula-tions and exposures of power (Crouch, 2003; Gregson and Rose, 2000; Massey, 2005). Space can accordingly be seen as a process of doing or becoming (Unwin, 2000) through the citational activities of individu-als within it. A second aspect of performativity therefore concerns the bodily dimensions as well the tensions and instability of space. In this respect, we have seen how a 'masculine' authoritative space created through discourses and activities of safety and security can be easily disrupted and subverted by feminine activities of service and care – creating tensions for men as they manage such contestations of mean-ing. Equally, the presence of male bodies can convert the cabin and aisle as sites of female heterosexuality, encouraged by past and current pro-motional practices suggestive of female service and availability (Tyler and Abbott, 1998; Tyler and Taylor, 1998; Williams, 2003), into a space saturated with and marked by homosexual meanings.

With sometimes painful discursive implications for crew, the aisle is thus precariously suspended between authoritative and deferential space and the cabin as a whole marked by past history and by the body performances of men. Rather than being a 'given passive geometry' (Dodge and Kitchin, 2005), space is 'ontogenetic' in that it is continually brought into existence by the reiterative practices of individuals within them (Lefebvre, 1991; Mackenzie, 2002; Massey, 1994). This recursive view of space implies that it both shapes and is shaped by identity processes – mobilizing and mobilized by social action and, along the lines of Gregson and Rose (2000), shifting with (historically contingent) citational activities and practices it contains.

These citations reinforce dominant discourses and associated subject positions. From Butler, a third aspect of performativity concerns, through the repetition of particular 'codes', its conservative tendencies. Men accordingly move within and draw on space in ways that support dominant conceptions of (deferential) service and, within the feminized space of the cabin, strive in different ways to re-invigorate traditional notions of masculinity. However, while Butler conceptualizes the prospect of deviations as mere 'slippage' or imperfections in performance (Thrift and Dewsbury, 2000), the data presented above may suggest a level of creativity that underpins a more agentic and intentional self.

In this respect, we have highlighted how individuals can draw on, mobilize and transform space through colonization, movement and body displays or by toying with discursive implications of dominant meanings. Male crew thus open up, in a Deleuzian sense, possibilities for creativity and so assist in a rearrangement of self – while a seemingly stable space can be transformed and/or disrupted by the identity performances of conformity, resistance and expertise into arenas of, for example, safety, danger, drama, eroticism or play. Male crew energize space, occasionally diverting it from its purpose to create a theatrical arena for visible (and pleasurable) body displays as well as an active resource in playful inversions of their role. Space is created from which to question and resist power relations embedded in practices and discourses of service and customer care and to undermine as well as reassert dominant understandings of gender. Space thus contains the possibility for the same (Crouch, 2003) as well as for the different, the new and the risky that go beyond slippage, discontinuity or gaps in citation.

Overall, through the themes of control, resistance and corporeality and by combining post-structuralist accounts of gender identity with space, this chapter has drawn attention to the complexity and performativity of space. At the same time, it has shown how the performance of gender is deeply contextual – not in the sense of context as a 'backdrop' to gender expression, but as an active resource in the 'doing' of gender at work.

6
Bodies, Embodiment and Male Nurses

Introduction

This chapter seeks to uncover the significance of bodies within the profession of nursing. Bodies have long been a neglected area of research in organization studies – often invisible despite their centrality in any work context. In this respect, we *are* our bodies and they are therefore deployed to greater and lesser extents in the work we do. It is consequently surprising that the significance of bodies has largely been overlooked – exceptions including those instances where some form of manual labour is required or where bodies are the focus of work. This 'conceptual blindspot' (Grosz, 1994) in mainstream thinking about gender and organization may reflect the Cartesian mind/body dualism in which men and masculinity, through associations with rationality and the higher order of the mind, have been rendered 'bodiless'. Bodies have thus been inferiorized, deviant and visibly tied to the realm of women.

As Connell (2000) points out, bodies matter in that biological difference between men and women play an important part in determining what is seen to be 'masculine' and 'feminine' work. Heavy physical labour, for example, is often deemed more suitable for men and caring roles associated with 'softer' bodies of women. Meanings around masculinity and femininity therefore depend partly on the social definitions of the body. In this respect, as Evans (2004) notes, there has been little work on how men's bodies and dominant social constructions of masculinity shape the experience of men in female-dominated occupations. Here, the masculine body does not comply with associated social expectations. Meanings attached to men's bodies (as rational and disengaged) thus collide with conventional notions of care (emotional, nurturing, supportive) naturalized in the embodied dispositions

93

of women. These aspects of bodies, embodiment and nursing form the basis of this chapter and, after a brief account of the influence of bodies on conceptualizations of gender, are discussed below.

Sex, gender, bodies

Bodies have influenced how we see gender in several ways. At a fundamental level, gender, that is, the socially constructed notion of what it means to be a man or a woman is differentiated from sex as in the biologically based categories of man and woman. This distinction was made in the 1960s by feminists who sought to separate sex as a biological 'given' from gender, seen as a product of social and cultural forces and therefore divorced from biologically determinist meanings. This helped to challenge ideas that hierarchical arrangements based on sex categories were somehow inevitable and 'natural'. The 'natural masculinity thesis' (e.g. Bly, 1990), for example, takes as its foundation the idea that manhood (and hence gender difference) is biologically determined – through genetic programming or hormonal difference. For Bly, men should reconnect with their deep centre or 'essence' in order recapture a masculinity, undermined by what he sees as the feminization of society. From this and related (for example, sociobiological) perspectives, therefore, bodies both explain *and* justify gender difference.

Modernist perspectives such as liberal and radical feminism also promote a sex-linked account of gender – but challenge the justification of hierarchical difference. Both see gender as a stable or solid 'fact' – a role or trait that adheres to the individual and which has some relation to biology. Liberal feminism has a focus on the creation of a level playing field within what are seen as gender-neutral organizations, while radical feminism highlights the problems for women of patriarchal organizational structures. Both perspectives foreground women's biology as an explanatory factor in gender disadvantage. For liberal feminists, women's child-bearing and child-caring role is seen as another variable (such as the necessary level of education and skills) which has the potential to be problematic for organizations as well as for women's career progress – problems that must be 'solved' through equal-opportunity initiatives. Radical feminists such as Ferguson (1984) also focus on biology but adopt a more critical stance. Rather than accepting the implications of women's biology as 'given', they direct attention to patriarchal power and the ways in which men control women's bodies and their sexuality to their own ends – arguing that women need to 'reclaim' control. From these perspectives, bodies partly explain but do not justify gender difference.

As we have seen, post-structuralist accounts see gender as contingent, fluid and fragmentary, rather than as a stable attribute. In this respect, gender is not tied in any determinist sense to biology but needs to be reproduced on an ongoing basis in different interactions and contexts. Rather than seeking to understand the factors that make up gender difference, as in the above modernist accounts, this approach considers how discourse constructs difference and how difference is drawn upon in the performance and display of gender that conform to, or resist, prevailing norms and expectations. For some post-structuralists (e.g. Butler, 1993), these norms and expectations are 'written on' the sexed bodies of men and women. Bodies therefore carry meanings and help authenticate particular performances which then take on the semblance of 'natural' dispositions. In other words, men and women perform or 'do' gender partly through their bodies which becomes sedimented as essentially gendered and universal. Bodies therefore do matter but not in any determinist sense. Instead, the biologically fixed basis and essentialist understandings of the categories of sex are challenged, highlighting the social and cultural meanings attached to sexed bodies as well as their historic location and contingent nature. Bodies matter, not simply because we work with and experience feelings through our bodies, but because bodies carry meanings which have implications for performances of gender. These are discussed below.

Bodies, embodiment and disembodiment

As Morgan *et al.* (2005) point out, bodies can be seen to be pertinent to work in several ways. Firstly, work requires effort which has a bodily dimension. This has most commonly been recognized in the identification of the bodily efforts of manual labour with the male working class. Beyond this, however, bodily effort can be seen in the tiredness we feel, to greater or lesser extents, from the work we do. The demands of emotional labour for example may involve 'burnout' or emotional exhaustion – felt through our bodies.

Secondly, pleasures and pains of work are equally body experiences. This may include feelings of alienation, as predicted by Hochschild's (1983) account of emotional labour, as individuals assume a caring bodily demeanour captured, in the case of cabin crew, in the everlasting smile to more positive feelings of satisfaction and pleasure. As with tiredness from effort, these pleasures and pains are experienced through our bodies – the glow of satisfaction from a job well done to the feelings of frustration (and the headache!) brought on as we deal with difficult situations.

Thirdly, in a Foucauldian sense, we must discipline our bodies to conform to organizational requirements – to produce for example docile bodies, controlled through different organizational techniques. From this perspective, employee bodies have become an important site of control. As Trethewey (1999) argues, by being brought into service bodies must be controlled so that they will 'behave'. This may involve conformity to professional and gendered discourses – of deference, service, care – inscribed on bodies of men and women. Norms of deference or of nurturance are often inscribed on female bodies or on those enacting service and care, influencing the ways individuals walk, sit, interact and occupy space. In the latter respect, as Halford and Leonard (2006a; 2006b) found, 'doing' gender involves bodily performances in and through space: doctors for example demonstrate masculinity and higher status by, among other things, walking freely and with purpose from ward to ward while nurses are often confined, in a display of the 'feminine', to specific locations. Professional norms (of competence, expertise) can also be inscribed on the body through the wearing of uniforms – signifiers also of differences in status as, for example, uniformed bodies are in some contexts positioned against the non-uniformed bodies of more senior personnel.

Finally, all work situations are characterized by different degrees of embodiment and disembodiment. The concept of embodiment captures the meanings attached to bodies referred to above, an awareness of the body that is shaped by wider cultural frameworks and expectations (Morgan *et al.*, 2005). By contrast, disembodiment refers to situations where individuals see themselves and are seen by others as divorced from considerations of the body. In this respect, some work can be seen to be more embodied than others. Manual labour and the care of others, where the source of labour and the chief focus are bodies, can be seen to be explicitly embodied while other work, such as management or administration, may be seen as disembodied in that such work relies on the 'rational mind' with less obvious bodily associations. However, as Hall *et al.* (2007) have recently pointed out, even occupations that require few bodily dimensions demand a body representation that accords with and conveys particular meanings. Estate agency for example is not on the face of it 'bodily' – it does not demand manual labour or body performances of care – but it nevertheless requires a body presentation to clients and customers that conveys particular meanings such as those relating to trust, reliability and business acumen.

Bodies thus carry meanings – meanings which are both gendered and hierarchically arranged. Forms of 'body work' (Wolkowitz, 2003) which involve caring have accordingly been associated with work of women – whose bodies are conceptualized as caring bodies – while work involving the deployment of specific skills or expertise have been associated with men. In a similar vein, women have been seen as more 'embodied' than men, linked to nature and containing bodily associations of fluidity, flux, fecundity and passion (Hassard *et al.*, 2000). Women's bodies have been associated with the private sphere such as the family where 'natural' bodily, emotional and hence lower functions occur. Men by contrast signify the 'organized body' (ibid.) associated with dryness, solidity, containment – a body to be disciplined and controlled. The organization – as rational, ordered, hierarchical – is thus written on the male body. As the 'norm' at work, the disciplined male body is disengaged from its own performance and from reproduction, emotionally under control, symbolically cleaner than women, and the standard against which women, and their bodies are judged problematic. In short, men in general are disembodied in their divorce from bodily considerations – standing for universal personhood as well as for organization and rationality.

However, as Flannigan-Saint-Aubin (1994) points out, male bodies do matter and carry specific meanings that are closely aligned with dominant structuring principles such as patriarchy. In this respect, patriarchal ideology takes the male body as its metaphorical base. Competition and power, as 'watchwords' of patriarchy, are connected to the male body and to individual men's experience of the body. Thus, as Haddon (1988) cited in Flannigan-Saint-Aubin (1994) points out, the phallus-like patriarchy (and one could equally say capitalism) is to be 'potent, penetrating, outward thrusting, initiating, forging ahead into virgin territory, opening the way, swordlike, able to cut through, able to clear or differentiate, goal oriented, to the point, focused, directive, effective, aimed, hitting the mark, string, erect' (Haddon, 1988: 10, cited in Flannigan-Saint-Aubin, 1994: 241). From this perspective, far from being 'disembodied' in that men have tended to reduce women to biology and denied their own corporeality, the male body and the phallus form the metaphorical base of structures of power as well as, from Flannigan-Saint-Aubin, the basis of masculine identity.

Bodies, emotions and emotional labour

These meanings are a far cry from the demands and expectations of embodied performances of care. In fact, despite the recognition of the gendered nature of emotional labour, where service and care carry strong associations with femininity and the female body, the concept of emotional labour has largely overlooked the body. As Warhurst and Nickson (2007) point out, emotional labour 'foregrounds the worker as a mindful feeling self but loses a secure conceptual grip on the worker as an embodied self' (Warhurst and Nickson, 2007: 36). While this has been addressed to some extent by Witz *et al.*'s (2003) work on aesthetic labour as embodied labour, seeking to demonstrate how physical capital in the form of body aesthetics is converted into economic capital by organizations as well as by Warhurst and Nickson (2007) who explored aspects of aesthetic labour in interactive service work, there are a limited number of studies on the embodiment of professional service work where there may be few aesthetic dimensions.

Hochschild's (1983) work on cabin crew and debt collectors went some way to introduce body concerns into work on emotional labour – specifically how the body is deployed in service work or when managing the emotions of others. However, as Witz *et al.* (2003) point out, even in this context, the body is marginal. This may reflect Hochschild's social constructionist approach to the study of emotions, in which issues of the body are subordinated to, for example, labour process concerns as well as the significance afforded to 'deep' over 'surface' acting. Deep acting involves the engagement of the 'inner self' in the expression of feelings, as individuals for example *internalize* the smile. This is seen as largely divorced from the body, at a level of the 'soul', compared with the more corporeal dimension of surface acting, in which the body is used to demonstrate the presentation, the 'putting on' of emotion (for example, a caring expression that lacks the feeling). Thus, as Witz *et al.* point out, 'surface becomes synonymous with the body that is devoid of authenticity, where depth becomes synonymous with the soul as the authentic, feeling core of self' (p. 36). From Wolkowitz (2003) this may serve to reinforce the distinctions drawn between emotional and physical labour in such work and the prioritization of the psychological over bodily effort.

This neglect is surprising given the obvious links between emotions and the body. As Morgan *et al.* (2005) point out, and as we have seen above, we both experience the pleasures and pains of work (and interpret emotions in others) in and through the body. This bodily dimension of work experiences is highlighted in the following story from an Australian nurse in which a patient nearly died through the negligence of two nurses in his ward:

I felt like had actually been hit in the mouth. This is the most awful expe-
rience...I had to face the surgeon....I had to say to these nurses...what
were you thinking?...And I remember going home...I remember thinking
do I want to be here? Do I ever want to go through this again? Um, and I
guess the experience was terrible because I'd been let down by people who
I thought would have known better...and that sort of knocked me around
for quite a bit.

The emotion and turmoil of shock felt by this nurse is partly experienced through the body – described in this instance as a 'hit in the
mouth' and being 'knocked around'. Several nurses recounted how, in
various difficult circumstances, often involving a death, they had been
moved to tears. There is thus an obvious bodily dimension to emotions
experiences at work or elsewhere.

The body is significant in emotional labour and service work in
other ways. Specifically, given that the performance of the worker is
constitutive of the product, bodily characteristics such as gender, age,
personality and other dispositions cannot be separated from that product. As Leidner (1991) has argued, these performances draw on looks,
voices, personalities and emotion as well as physical and intellectual
capabilities. Facial and body displays are crucial to the performance
of emotional labour and to service work generally where embodied
attributes and capacities are often used as a source of competitive
advantage (Warhurst and Nickson, 2007).

From this, there are likely to be strong associations between the body,
emotions and emotional labour. Drawing on interview data from the
male nurses in the study, some of these links are explored below. These
relate to physical effort, discipline and restraint; the intimate care of
bodies; and the marking of men's bodies in the context of nursing care.

Men, bodies and nursing

Bodies are significant to nursing in several ways. Firstly, as Dahle (2005)
notes, much of care work is concrete, bodily and heavy. This bodily
dimension of nursing was recognized early in the profession and contributed to a division of labour, with men assigned to heavy lifting work,
the care of male patients and the mentally ill (often thought to be in
need to physical restraint), that persists today (Evans, 2004). In this
respect in the UK, while 10.9 per cent of nurses are men, in the specialist
area of psychiatry and mental health, with historic links to custodialism and (masculine) associations around the supposed need for physical

strength, this figure rises to 34 per cent (Information Centre for Health and Social Care, 2008).

Research suggests that the co-option of men's bodies in physically demanding nursing work is widespread. Heikes (1991) has referred to a 'he-man' role assigned to male nurses as they are called upon to undertake heavy moving and lifting and Milligan (2001) found male nurses are routinely expected to deal with physically aggressive patients. In the current UK/Australian study, all nurses commented on these expectations. In this respect there was often explicit recognition of the physical advantages of the masculine body and associated meanings of threat and authority. This could, for example, relate simply to differences in voice and tone:

> *As a male because you have a larger tone you can actually lower the tone without raising the volume and actually bring instruction underneath the surrounding sound ... and I think there's also that male like safeness ... like males you know we all have our traditional stories ... there's the hero type side, turning towards men for safety.*

As this nurse suggests, meanings attached to male bodies also come from past history and from narratives of masculinity, which powerfully influence the way men's bodies are perceived. These meanings were often welcomed by men – they were listened to more readily than women and had more authority as a result. Most nurses welcomed a 'protector' role which they presented in a traditional way as masculine chivalry and a concern for the welfare of women. This provided opportunities for men to affirm their masculinity and special contribution to nursing:

> *I may have to look after somebody that's two hundred fifty kilos because you're the only male on and you're working with some sort of wee slips of girls you know? ... I don't mind because I have more ability to do something. It's like anything else; I have physical ability to do something extra so I won't mind to relieve my mates from doing that.*

Men routinely deployed their bodies as 'boundary setters' (Forseth, 2005) in aggressive situations to present an authoritative, reassuring and in some cases intimidating presence. Some nurses described episodes in which, in a masculine display of aggression, they used force to subdue violent patients:

I had him before he got the second hit in, I had him with his arm behind his back facing to the bed and lifted him up, he was about 80 kilos, and on the bed and I said behave, behave. I said I'm bigger than you are and I'm stronger than you are I said security is on its way.

As Monaghan (2002) has argued, when institutionalized and used legitimately in the interests of protection, 'good violence' can be constitutive of masculinity and valour (Monaghan, 2002: 420 cited in Evans, 2004: 19). Not all nurses were so proactive in aggressive displays, acknowledging that meanings attached to the masculine body (for example, of courage, bravery, fearlessness) did not reflect notions of the authentic self:

When you have people who are intoxicated and wanting maybe to throw their weight around, it is helpful to have a male ... if there's a problem with accident and emergency I'm more than happy to go down and just stand there just as a presence ... even though I have to say I'm not actually your aggressive type.

As Evans (2004) points out, this 'enforcer role' is not easily avoided and can, as in the case of the above nurse, who professed to a non-aggressive stance, be inconsistent with personal and professional values. As another nurse commented: *'I'm not an aggressive person naturally, but you've got to act up to the situation ... '*. Thus, irrespective of men's actual body size or personal disposition, men are expected to undertake physically demanding work and to act as disciplinarian in the organization. Evans found that nurses of just average stature were expected to intervene in difficult situations, suggesting that 'variable body capital' in the form of body build and physical characteristics such as strength can become 'the currency of masculinity itself' (Evans, 2004: 18).

From the current study, some men resented these pressures on the grounds that they represented an extra burden and increase in workload as well as a source of anxiety in their routine deployment to 'crisis' situations. Others, as the above quote indicates, self-consciously deployed their bodies, in ways that resonate with Trethewey's (1999) conceptualization of the body as a 'sign-emitting text', to create a particular meaning around an authoritative and regulatory presence.

In some instances, however, these meanings are out of place and men must manage their bodies, for example reducing semblance of body size and volume of voice, in order to present a non-threatening, caring self. Men thus strove to redefine the meanings around the masculine body – speaking in deliberately soft tones to patients or sitting at the end of the bed to reduce the appearance of size. Here men spoke of the need, particularly when dealing with female patients, to create trust – in ways that suggest the necessity to overcome the inherent disadvantages of the male body in the context of some nursing care.

Gender, nursing and the intimate care of bodies

In nursing, bodies can be seen to constitute the social practice of the occupation. As Isaksen (2005) points out, this is a form of work that is both gendered and carries low esteem. Providing intimate hands on care is culturally defined as feminine and generally located within the female domain. Much of the care work that takes place in the private sphere is carried out by women. For example, research cited by Gerstel and Gallagher (2001) suggests that in the family context of sibling contributions to care, the availability of sisters reduces the amount of time men spend with relatives. While brother-only sibling sets draw on the labour of their wives in caring for elderly parents (Matthews and Heidorn, 1998), men with sisters rely on them as primary caregivers (Matthews and Rosner, 1988) (cited in Gerstel and Gallagher, 2001: 200).

The gendered nature of such work may thus have its roots in the assumption that women take responsibility for hands on and intimate care of relatives (children, the elderly) in the home. As Bolton (2005b), citing Lawler (1991), points out, nursing work, women's work and dirty work are inextricably linked through their association with the private realm. The gendered nature of such work is exacerbated by meanings attached to basic body fluids, overloaded with ideas associated with dirt and disgust (Douglas, 1966) and which has low esteem (Dahle, 2005). Medicine is accordingly constructed as an occupation suitable for middle-class men only if interaction with the patient's body is limited and given to (female) nurses. Within the nursing sector itself, there are divisions of status which reflect different relations to the body such as the distinction between basic/general nursing, involving care of the physical and bodily needs of patients and technical nursing, coded more masculine and which carries 'cleaner', that is, more technical tasks and less touching of patients (Wolkowitz, 2002). As Dahle (2005) notes, the tendency for men to move into these more specialist areas represents a 'flight from the body' and a distance from these 'feminine' and more unacceptable aspects of nursing care. This tendency was summarized by one nurse in the present study:

A lot of men in nursing feel that the actual bum wiping is not where they want to be, they want to running the bum wiping nursing.

Care work can thus be seen as dirty work (Isaksen, 2005) so that intimate care is difficult to combine with ideas of masculinity. This 'incompatibility' is highlighted in the following quote, in which a nurse recalled the reaction of his brothers to the news that he was taking up nursing as a profession:

so when I told them I was going to be a nurse they said, you don't need a brain if you want to be a nurse. We can teach black women how to do that work, you know? So that is one kind of stigma I actually experienced because they thought that it was inferior, it was only good enough for black women to do.

Nursing as an embodied practice is thus coded feminine and inferior – as well as 'raced' – and is perceived be of little value and requiring minimum expertise. However, despite common perceptions of such work as 'dirty' and unsuitable for men, male nurses working on the ward – with responsibility for the day-to-day care of patients – often took pride in their ability to carry out such work, celebrating their special skills over the 'squeamishness' of male friends and acquaintances as well as over female colleagues. One nurse commented on his choice of career vis-a-vis those of his male friends:

Some of it's (the work)*upsetting, they couldn't cope with the smells, can't cope with blood, can't cope with opening bodies, with crisis and emergencies and disaster, but particularly just unwell people ... so many males find it quite foreign to take on a role as a nurse.*

Another recalled how, faced with his own child ill with breathing difficulties through a bad cold, he had used a tube and 'sucked out' the mucus from her nose – much to the disgust of his wife. As he commented nonchalantly, '*My wife gagged and went running and I said why not, I figured it would work*'.

Men thus embraced the Other status of such work, creating a distinctive space for the practice of masculinity through meanings associated with endurance and fortitude. These meanings carry heroic qualities and sit in contrast to commonly reported feelings of disgust and fastidiousness. Many men, for example, claimed that female nurses were often reluctant to undertake such 'dirty work' themselves – presenting them as prevaricating to avoid the day-to-day cleaning, showering and bodily care of patients. As Dahle (2005) has argued, it is hard for men to construct a credible masculine identity in nursing work where male surgeons colonize the heroic and often ignore the qualities of bodily-care work of nursing staff. By presenting their abilities in 'masculine' terms and as special qualities, men may thus be helping to create a more satisfying identity.

As discussed earlier, in some contexts men have to manage their masculinity to redefine commonly held assumptions and associated meanings concerning their bodies. In the intimate care of female patients, male nurses must renegotiate meanings which commonly view the masculine body as voyeur, as part of the intrusive 'gaze' which 'invades' the private space of women and against which they require protection. One nurse commented on his midwifery experience:

> *I think the most emotionally charged situation I walked into is a woman who's in pain, who's in labour. I find I'm a man in a woman's world, I've got to establish a rapport, I've got to prove to the woman I'm not going to invade her space or take away her dignity and you've got to build up these things before they actually cost you. And a woman's at a particularly vulnerable spot when she's in labour, she's a woman in a man's world...*

Men often engaged thoughtfully with how, as men, such intimacy should be negotiated and handled and the implications for the women concerned. Self awareness, that is, as masculine subjects, was key to managing these situations. For the following nurse, this involved the need for respect and humility

> *...always have that respect, I suppose that slight humility that you're I suppose...you know, you're a man and you've got to be a little bit, have a little bit of humility and step back sort of allow yourself to um...not cause any aggravation.*

One nurse felt that women suffered these indignities but moved into a space of their own:

> *I mean there's always going to be some things that you have to do, say for example taking vaginal packs out, that sort of thing, that's some of the most intimate things you can be doing to people. Now that has to be done and if you're the nurse on the ward and you happen to be a man who's been allocated to do the patient, then it's something you do, you know. And so*

there's a level of intimacy there, but even in that situation you can still be doing that and the patient can be still ... can be not accepting of your care in some ways and that may sound strange but what I'm trying to get to is that you can do things to people that have to be done, but they may still have a distance, so they'll sort of have ... their own space where they go.

As Twigg (2000) has argued, nakedness in a care situation creates vulnerability which takes a special form because of the asymmetric relations between the carer and the cared for. This vulnerability is likely to be exacerbated for female patients under the nursing care of men. In this respect male nurses engaged thoughtfully with these hierarchical and gendered implications and managed their behaviour (and bodies) accordingly. This is in contrast to how female nurses see men in these and similar roles. Bolton's (2005b) study of female gynaecology nurses, for example, found that women actively pursued the ideology of the 'good woman/the good nurse' in their identification with the vocational and altruistic aspects of nursing. In claiming special expertise in how they cared, they presented male colleagues as dysfunctional in their inability to attend the emotional needs of patients. One ward sister expressed the opinion that men should be 'horse doctors. They would be alright treating animals because they only have to worry about the technical skills involved and not about the patients' emotional well-being' (quote in Bolton, 2005b: 175).

While women in Bolton's study claimed a special status as Other through their uniquely feminine qualities in the 'dirty work' of gynaecology nursing, a similar story could be told for men. Some male nurses may undoubtedly move away from the day-to-day body proximity of general nursing, but others 'do' and 'undo' gender in such work. Men 'do' gender through their cavalier attitude to the 'dirty work' involved, contrasting their ability to deal with such work with the 'squeamishness' of male peers and female colleagues. At the same time, they can be seen to 'undo' gender in their challenge to entrenched attitudes, captured in the ward sister's comments above, that men are unsuited to aspects of intimate care. Instead, men engage self-consciously with gender and work hard to 'manage' their masculinity for the female patients in their care.

The marking of male bodies in nursing care

While men may be valued for their bodies – assigned for example to work that demands physical strength or discipline – they are also 'marked' as different from the female norm. In a context which draws on essential notions of femininity, it is women's bodies that exist as the 'unmarked' case. When men enter these settings their experiences become marked as men's experiences (they are labelled 'male' nurses rather than nurses per se) – their bodies 'matter' in these contexts in several ways.

Firstly, drawing on Connell (2000), men's bodies are out of line with their social definition. As we have seen, nurturance and care are inscribed on the 'softer' bodies of women so there is an incongruity between the meanings attached to male bodies – such as strength, independence and intelligence – and the gendered norms of nursing. These meanings can be captured by the organization and put to instrumental use, as in the co-option of men's bodies for heavy physical work, but can also, as discussed above, cause problems for men and have implications for practices and behaviours at work. Men can thus experience their bodies as 'marked' and as 'matter out of place' (Douglas, 1966) – their body size and other masculine features sitting uncomfortably with the unmarked bodies of women. This is captured in the following quote in which a male health visitor felt the need to manage his body – to be less 'boisterous' to fit with what he perceived as the more restrained dispositions of women:

> ...*I'm tall and big and unshaven and got a big scar on my face...and I think to feel comfortable in a woman's world you have to adapt yourself in many ways...For example, if I was working on a building side I'd be much more boisterous and outspoken, but working as a health visitor with a group of middle aged, middle class women I...didn't feel able really to be myself.*

As Dahle (2005) notes, men can be seen as intruders creating disorder in a system over which women claim jurisdiction. Male nurses are thus often fast-tracked by female nurse managers into more 'body-congruent' specialties and levels of hierarchy and away form the ward (Evans, 2004). From this study, many men felt these pressures. One nurse commented in this respect:

> *There was this constant undercurrent that a. you shouldn't be here, either because you're a bloke or b. because you're too intelligent and you should be a doctor.*

Male bodies are thus 'matter out of place' in the nursing context. A second aspect of body incongruity concerns the association of men's bodies with homosexuality. In this respect, the presence of men in a non-masculine role calls into question and challenges the hetero-sexual norm in the workplace. As Dahle (2005) argues, male nurses are considered deviant through a 'naturalized connection' with homo-sexuality. All nurses in the study acknowledged this association, with sometimes painful implications for identity. As one nurse commented on the 'downside' of his occupational choice:

> *People who said oh, you're a male nurse. The community in generally said oh, a male nurse must be...they considered you gay, they considered you strange; they considered you weird as to why aren't you doing something normal and I just...I had it!*

Heterosexual nurses frequently consigned gay colleagues an Other sta-tus, seen as representatives of their category through the assignment of essentialized characteristics (fun loving, intimate, emotional) not found in the heterosexual male:

> *I've worked in hospitals where you'd be lucky if you were the only non-gay male that was there. And they're phenomenal workers, the tidiest guys I've ever seen and you have the greatest time under the sun. They are phenome-nal workers and the best of friends and they of course do emotionally snap a lot quicker than the general male population. They breakdown in tears, they really fall into the emotional trap, you know, howling with the families and stuff.*

Assumptions of and meanings around homosexuality could have impli-cations for the practice of nursing care. One nurse, treating a 'bushman' who was dying, quickly discovered that physical touching ('pats on the back'; hands on foot') was unwelcome and he subsequently backed off – a situation he put down to discomfort felt being treated by a male nurse.

Men's sexuality and masculinity are thus seen as undesirable, poten-tially dangerous and disruptive in some of the caring work that they are required to do. This brings us to the third way in which men's bodies 'matter' in nursing – namely the sexualization of male nurses' touch (Evans, 2002). This can create discomfort and suspicion on the part of patients, impacting on nurses' own perceptions of their safety while performing intimate caregiving tasks, and leading Evans to refer to male nurses as 'cautious' or vulnerable caregivers. This is contrast to women's touch which is seen as harmless and non-threatening – a natural extension of their caring role. As Evans (1997) points out, the labelling of men as deviant or odd can further explain the choice of gender-congruent specialisms such as mental health, because of its association with physical strength, anaesthetics because of its association with technical prowess and autonomy, and A&E because of their association with technical prowess and cool-headedness. The masculine nature of these areas is further reinforced by their lack of association with feminine nursing traits specifically the need to touch and the delivery of intimate care.

The marking of men's bodies as potentially dangerous, disruptive and problematic can have implications for how intimate care should be managed. One nurse recalled a sense of confusion over the appropriate practice and procedures when he worked in a gynaecology ward:

> *Dealing with or working with females on surgical wards, gynae wards, my managers went through great problems to work out whether I needed a chaperone or not to do a procedure on a female patient. I thought how stupid, I'm a nurse. It doesn't matter whether you're male or female, you've got the skills and the knowledge to do a procedure.*

All male nurses acknowledged these potential problems – often identified as an 'issue' or 'problem' relating to their masculinity – when dealing with women in their care. As the above quote illustrates, confronted with body ascriptions of danger and deviance, men could resist painful implications for subjectivity by drawing on discourses of body integrity, captured in a language of agendered and asexual professional expertise. In this way, meanings attached to the masculine body can be rendered irrelevant through identification with a professional body and the possession of necessary skills and proficiency.

Conclusion

In this chapter we have acknowledged the neglect of the body in much of the work on emotional labour and we have considered the different ways in which bodies may be relevant for the performance of nursing care. While in general terms, men may be considered to be largely 'disembodied' and divorced from considerations of the body, associated with the rational domain of the mind, this association is overturned when men undertake a non-traditional role. As we have seen, while often co-opting men's bodies for instrumental use in the organization, in the context of nursing care men's bodies can be marked as dangerous, disruptive and problematic in ways that resonate with the ways women's bodies have been traditionally viewed.

The chapter has also pointed to ways in which doing gender has a bodily dimension. In other words, we do masculinity and femininity through our bodies, drawing them into displays of appropriate (or inappropriate) gender behaviour. At the same time, bodies are inscribed with meanings, beyond our control, which have implications for how we do gender and for our sense of self. As Butler (2004) has pointed out, we therefore both do and have gender done to us. Bodies are not completely our own in this respect as 'the body has its invariably public dimension; constituted as a social phenomenon in the public sphere, the body is and is not mine' (Butler, 2004: 21). The lived body, that is, the ways in which it is represented and used in specific contexts, is an amalgam of active and passive, of doing and being done to, of signifying and signified which together strongly influence how gender is performed in specific contexts. Male nurses thus draw on traditional body ascriptions to present a particular self, telling stories of prowess and stoicism; they self-consciously co-opt these meanings to produce a desired effect, perhaps in opposition to notions of an authentic self; they manage their bodies to redefine meanings associated with, for example, body size seen as inappropriate for some nursing care; they negotiate the implications of the marking of their bodies in day-to-day practices and present alternative discursive positions. In short, bodies, their meanings and discursive effects as well as their day-to-day 'co-option' form an integral part of doing (and undoing) gender at work.

7
Male Primary School Teachers and the Negotiation of a Professional Identity

Introduction

In this chapter we explore how male primary school teachers negotiate discourses of professionalism and care. This is set in the context of recent changes in the meanings and practices of professionalism which, in teaching as in some other occupations, has led to tensions in terms of the norms and values underpinning day-to-day activities and processes – with implications for identity formation. In this respect the era of marketization and managerialism has meant a change in the structures and practices of professionalism and has signalled a move away from earlier fundamentals of specialist expertise and exclusivity towards a new order that has pervaded both public and private sectors alike. As Dent and Whitehead (2002) point out, the professional that was integral to the 'old' order was seen as someone 'trusted, respected, an individual given class, status, autonomy, social elevation, in return for safeguarding our well-being and applying their professional judgement on the basis of a benign moral or cultural code' (Dent and Whitehead, 2002: 1). As they argue, this autonomous and trusted professional no longer exists, 'swept aside' by the 'relentless, cold, instrumental logic' of the global market (ibid.). Instead, individuals are increasingly subject to external scrutiny and surveillance in the form of 'regimes of accountability', performance indicators and targets. New professional discourses speak of teamworking and of being entrepreneurial, managerial and market-oriented. In that quality and customer/client care have become a driving force in large areas of organizational life, we are all to some extent expected to perform 'professionally'. As Dent and Whitehead argue, and as Grey (1999) has similarly pointed out with regard to managers, we are all professionals now.

While these changes may imply some 'slippage' of identity for those who adhered to and benefited from the old order, such as for those in the 'traditional' professions of medicine, academia, law, it has allowed new opportunities to emerge and with it new identities. In this respect, we can understand 'professional' as a discursive subject position (Dent and Whitehead, 2002) – an ontological location accessed through particular narratives and discourses that legitimize claims to that status in the eyes of self and of others. New discourses of professionalism mean that occupations that might previously have been on the margins of the professional domain, such as primary school teaching and nursing, can now be seen to have a firmer (albeit still insecure) positioning.

Despite some erosion of privilege associated with the broader scope of professional status and the replacement of 'old' professional autonomy with new managerialist regimes of accountability, the call of a professional status can still be strong. Professionalism still retains some association with elitism, status and trust and has an ability, therefore, to bestow social elevation as well to help secure recognition and value for a field of knowledge. As Kerfoot (2002) argues, the notion of professionalism exists as a 'seductive and compelling' discourse, offering the possibility of certainty in terms of identity as well as, more generally, a sense of human 'worthiness' and social standing (Watson, 2002). Lupton (2006) for example, found that desire for social mobility and for a professional status were key factors in men's non-traditional occupational choice. Working class men, disadvantaged by class and who might not have access to higher professional occupations, could enter 'lower level' feminized occupations such as teaching, librarianship or nursing. Certainly, in support of this, in the current UK/Australian study, a desire for a professional status emerged as a strong motivating factor among men, the majority of whom had originated from largely working class backgrounds. More generally, issues of professionalism emerged as a key theme as men made sense of their feelings and experiences of their teaching role and was a significant resource on which to draw as they negotiated some of the conflicts inherent in their work with young children. Before discussing the implications of 'new professionalism' for primary school teaching, some of these challenges and contradictions are considered below.

Challenges and contradictions for men in primary school teaching

Allan (1993) has argued that men in primary education face a double bind. They must enact a masculinity that is 'personally sustainable', and have integrity which is acceptable to those who judge them such as parents, colleagues and managers. At the same time, they must conform to stereotypically feminine qualities in order to establish the sensitive caring relationship necessary for effective teaching at that level. Sargent (2001) also points to the various contradictions men face in attempting to be both 'real teachers' and 'real men'. On this basis, if they perform masculinity, their skills as teachers are questioned; if they perform femininity, their masculinity and their sexuality are called to account.

For Sargent, there are several reasons why men face contradictions and pressures in this context. Firstly, men are under scrutiny for signs of deviant sexual intent. Here men are in danger, as in other 'feminine' occupations, of being labelled gay. In the context of teaching however this is often seen to be synonymous with the potential for child molestation with often painful implications for men navigating the 'fine line' of propriety. Although men want to have the same level of close interaction with the children that female colleagues enjoy, they must also distance themselves in order to avoid the very real dangers of suspicion. As Sargent notes, they then reinforce the very behaviours (for example, of stoic, distant men) which suggest that men are unsuited to primary teaching in the first place. Certainly, a feeling that men were not suited to the demands of teaching small children emerged from many men in the current study. One Australian teacher referred to assumptions that, because he was a man, he would not be able to deal adequately with problems a child might be experiencing:

> *I know that if any of the children have an issue like maybe they're being taunted or something, a parent will immediately assume that I'm not sensitive to the situation...that frustrates me because I'm actually very sensitive and caring....I find I get a lot if OK, you're a man, you're not really in touch, you don't really care, you don't really understand about my daughter's feelings.*

From Sargent's study, there are several possible options open to men that help overcome these contradictions. Men can reject the notion of nurturing as being central to children's learning, preferring instead a focus on less overtly relational areas such as the curriculum. They can defy the rules that dictate that they cannot get close to the children – or they find other compensatory ways of engagement through for example material rewards.

Secondly, men may experience contradictions relating to the expectations that others have of the behaviour and values deemed appropriate for men in these roles. In this respect, as we saw in Chapter 1, there are common assumptions that men will climb the hierarchy to senior management and that they will take on a disciplinary function in their schools. However, as Sargent argues, a lack of interest in being promoted or a resistance to an authority role may be taken as an indication of lack of drive and initiative – and bring them into conflict with managers and female colleagues. While many do pass rapidly into management, some prefer to remain close to professional practice. As we noted in Chapter 1 in terms of career entry dynamics, 'settlers' in particular may reject assumptions of careerism on the part of work colleagues and senior personnel. Men in this category have often come into teaching from other more 'masculine' occupations, rejecting the impersonality of a 'desk job' such as accountancy or administration. They therefore may not always welcome the pressure to ascend the hierarchy into management. From the current study, as one teacher commented in relation to these pressures: '*I just want to be a good class room teacher*'. They may also resent the assumption that they will always take on the most difficult classes or groups. However, as Sargent argues, rejecting these practices brings their masculinity into question – while acceptance further supports and reproduces common assumptions concerning the role of men in primary school teaching.

One common reason for wanting to encourage more men into primary school teaching is that they provide a much needed role model – much needed because of the overwhelming presence of women in schools at primary level and the often absence of fathers in many children's lives. For Sargent, this leads to a third source of contradiction for men. For boys, male teachers are often required to enact a traditional masculinity based on clear boundaries and discipline. This is the masculinity that many parents, with absent or with partners working long hours, wish male teachers to portray. In other words, this is the kind of masculinity that fathers would enact if they were available (disciplinarian, authoritarian, interested in sport, not feminine). However, as one gay teacher in Sargent's study tellingly commented:

You know, it begs the question, like, well, what is their standard? 'Cause it's all, you know, in the eye of the beholder. What is their standard of masculinity? What is masculine for them? If it's the testosterone, beer-drinking, football-playing, bowling-night-on-Wednesday, and poker-night-on-Friday, you know, smoking-the-cigars men, that ain't me, you know (Laughs).

(Sargent, 2001: 122)

This traditional form of masculinity did not therefore always accord with the personal preferences of men. This contradiction could be exacerbated by the type of role model male teachers wish to present to girls. Here, teachers in Sargent's study often explained how they strove to present a more positive image of men in order to counteract perceptions, seen as common in girls' lives, of men as 'abusers' and 'abandoners'. They therefore wanted to present an alternative role model which would give girls a positive experience of men and masculinity. On this basis there were contradictions between what was expected of them in terms of their behaviour towards boys and what they hoped to present to girls. There is consequently, as Sargent argues, 'considerable conflict between modelling stereotypical and counter-stereotypical behaviours especially with girls and boys in the same class room' (Sargent, 2001: 121).

From this we can appreciate some of the complexities and contradictions inherent in the occupational practices of primary school teaching for men. Men in this context are seen as a potential threat to children, leading to cautious behaviour as they negotiate the fine line between relationality and propriety. At the same time, men must manage the contradictions between the cultural image of the mother, dominant in primary school teaching, and expectations that they also perform a form of hegemonic masculinity. Doing gender and 'doing teacher' are therefore fraught with difficulty. If men enact a traditional masculinity, demanded in their role modelling for boys and anticipated by many female colleagues and managers, they reinforce common assumptions concerning the appropriate behaviour of men and reinforce ideas of their often supposed ineptness. If they do teaching in the same way as women (for example, as maternal care), their masculinity and their motivations are called into question. How men negotiate these conflicts and tensions forms the basis for our understanding of the meaning, practices and values of professional identity and the ways in which teachers position them within discourses of care. With this understanding as an end in mind, we now turn to a discussion of the significance of performativity in primary school teaching and of the gendered nature of the so-called 'professionalization project' (Bolton, 2007).

Performativity and primary school teaching

Despite the changes outlined earlier indicating a broader concept of the 'professional', what Lupton has identified as 'lower status' and often female-dominated occupations, are still striving for full professional recognition. The feminized nature of these roles, together with a traditional association with the 'natural' dispositions of women has served to essentialize and hence devalue occupants' skills and knowledge. In this respect, we saw in the last chapter how the entry of men into nursing has been largely welcomed by women on the grounds that their presence would assist in a greater professional recognition for the occupation – and remove it from conceptualizations of devalued bodily care and the role of 'handmaiden' to higher-status and professionally more secure medical men.

As Sargent (2001) notes, the lower the grade level, the more feminine teaching is thought to be. Therefore, while academia has professional status, primary education (age 5–11) has been devalued and associated with the (non-professional) private sphere. Here, teachers spend a long time with their pupils in classrooms that emulate the domestic (Bolton, 2007) and operate in a system that, as Vogt (2002) points out, enforces the maternal subtext and promotes the expression of the 'natural woman'. Primary school teaching has thus had difficulty attracting full professional status and has traditionally been consigned to the (devalued, feminized) 'semi'-professional sphere (Bolton, 2004, 2005a).

As Fournier (1999) argues, professionalism involves a 'performance of legitimacy' in order to establish authenticity. In primary school education, in both Australia and the UK, a managerialist project has been instituted in order to advance the sector's professional status and to improve standards and performance. This has been manifested through a focus on performativity. The concept of performativity in this context has been defined by Whitehead (1998) as

> the emphasis on skills rather than ideas, and the discursive shift from 'human oriented' to where the only question of concern is: 'Is it efficient?' (...)The shift is to a work culture primarily concerned with measurement, performance, targeting and 'objective' assessment and appraisal. All this is embedded within a framework of competition (internal and external) and a funding and financial system which requires government inspired growth together with simultaneous 'efficiency gains'.
>
> (Whitehead, 1998: 207)

In pursuing the goal of performativity and as part of primary schools' 'professionalization project', teacher and school autonomy in the UK has been replaced by the subject-oriented National Curriculum, underpinned by new forms of assessment and inspection. These have been carried out by Office for Standards in Education (Ofsted), established in 1992 as part of a drive to raise standards in education. Similarly, in Australia there has been since the 1990s a shift in policy focus from a concern with inputs to a preoccupation with outputs and standards – exemplified in state-managed curriculum control and accountability and operationalized through a battery of external tests. Within these frameworks, traditional notions of 'care' are often marginalized and redefined. An ethic of care captures the 'relational' aspect of teaching. From Gilligan (1982), this concerns a responsiveness to self and others through attitudes and practices that sustain connection – associated with discourses of nature, altruism and mothering (Vogt, 2002). As Woods and Jeffrey (2002) point out, this humanistic and person-centred concern for social relations has been replaced by a focus on performativity as defined above. This focus has also, they argue, squeezed out a sense of vocationalism, based on an emotional dedication to work. These developments in professionalism and in primary education suggest conflicts between professionalism and care, captured in Sargent's work discussed above. Such conflicts are strongly gendered and have profound gendered implications – explored more fully below.

The professions, primary school teaching and gender

As Davies (1996) has pointed out, the central issue for understanding gender and professionalism turns not so much on the *exclusion* of women, as argued by Witz (1992), but on *how they are included* – in particular on the way their inclusion is 'masked in a discourse of gender that lies at the heart of professional practice itself' (Witz, 1992: 663). In this respect, the concept of professionalism can be seen to have been 'forged in masculine terms' (Bolton, 2007) and to embody a discursive subject that is male (Dent and Whitehead, 2002). This can be seen in both the 'old' and the 'new' orders referred to above.

In terms of the former, cultural connections with masculinity can be seen in the focus on traditional notions of expertise, through for example formalized training and knowledge control, of impartiality through adherence to diagnostic models and a practice of detachment from clients as well as of autonomy whereby professional judgements are made largely divorced from bureaucracy. As Davies (1996) points

out, this 'old' model shares some core assumptions with those of hegemonic masculinity (autonomy, competitiveness, specialist expertise,
independence) and relies largely on the work of women in support and
preparatory functions. Doctors for example can remain detached (bodily, materially, emotionally) from their patients because of the work that
women do as carers in various semi-professional and non-professional
medical domains.

The new order can be seen to be equally masculine. Here, the contemporary focus on accountability, control and performativity, discussed
earlier, has signalled a parallel discourse and practice of managerialism (Dent and Whitehead, 2002). This privileges managers' views over
those of other groups (Watson, 2001) and promotes the application of
management techniques to diverse organizational problems (such as
the drive to improve standards in education) that largely concern a
search for control (Grey, 2002, 2004). As Collinson and Hearn (1994)
point out, the managerial prerogative over key decisions can be seen
as part of a highly masculine discourse based on power and control.
For example, gendered assumptions can be discerned in initiatives such
as performance reviews and performance targets which can be linked
to masculinist concerns with personal power and accountability (e.g.
Hearn, 1994; Kerfoot and Knights, 1993, 1998) as well as having close
associations with the norms of rationality, often predicated on the
exclusion of the feminine (Ross-Smith and Kornberger, 2004).

Contemporary neo-liberal conceptualizations of professionalism, running parallel to managerialism, accordingly carry strong masculine connotations and privilege 'male theories of the polity' (Dillabough, 1999).
As essentially individualistic, competitive and predictable, modern professionalism thus denies qualities culturally assigned to femininity such
as informality, expressiveness and involvement (Bolton, 2007). As we
have seen, in primary education in both Australia and the UK, the State
has embarked on a 'cultural project' with a focus on rationality, objec-
tivity and control – characteristics that share core assumptions with
dominant conceptions of masculinity.

As Bolton (2007) points out, the masculine 'emotion code' of
professionalism emphasizes output, efficiency and performativity, management systems and audit accountability. However, these accepted
masculine codes that make up conceptualizations of the 'competent' and 'professional' teacher contradict the profession's fundamental
reliance on feminine emotionality such as caring, nurturing and process.
The 'masculine project' resolves this paradox by shaping the emotion
work of teaching into a masculine form based on procedural efficiency

and by marginalizing the work supporting children (Bolton, 2007; Vogt, 2002). In the UK, the latter is often delegated to 'non-professionals' in the form of support staff. Thus primary school teaching in this context, as Bolton argues, can be seen to be undergoing both professionalization and de-professionalization as its practices are split between the masculine public (professional) work and the feminine private (non-professional, support) work. There is accordingly, from Vogt (2002), no easy way to bring a concern with caring, evoking connotations of (female) service and vocation, on to the agenda without damaging conventional understandings of competence, (male) professionalism, authority and expertise.

In this respect, notions of the 'competent' or 'rational' teacher support a masculine vision of what it means to be a professional through masculine norms of order and efficiency (Davies, 1996; Dillabough, 1999). Concepts and practices of care and nurturance that have remained central to notions of good teaching, associated with feminine knowledge and attributes, fail therefore to meet the professionalization criteria or match the language and discourse of 'quality' teaching. Instead, as Dillabough (1999) argues, professional identity is increasingly characterized by the teacher's rational capacity to 'behave competently' in the name of student achievement and social/economic change. Teachers can thus be seen as 'reform agents' who subvert their own interests according to objective standards of practice – downgrading the relational nature of teaching and what Gilligan (1982) refers to as an 'ethic of care'.

How do teachers cope with these conflicting pressures? For Sargent, focusing on men, teachers end up doing a 'safe' form of masculinity through compensatory practices (such as the uptake of an 'expert teacher' identity) which often reproduce traditional gender ideologies. From Bolton's (2007) study of men and women, teachers not only draw on symbolic resources of 'woman' but also of masculine rationality and control. Teachers weave their way through demands made on them by the masculine cultural project of professionalism, complying with the need to represent efficiency and performativity and at the same time exhibit a relational bond to the children which the project cannot hope to capture. Similarly, from Vogt (2002), teachers' constructions of professional identities reveal discourses of femininity and masculinity which do not appear to depend on teachers' gender. Vogt found a continuum of 'caring' from ideas of commitment (an inclusive professional identity of caring with links to masculinity) to maternal views of caring (exclusively feminine) the latter often rejected by teachers as undermining their sense of professionalism.

This highlights, from Bolton (2007), that teaching cannot be split into the 'his' and 'hers' of symbolic resources, that is, feminine care and commitment versus masculine control and performance. Instead, activities and practices in the classroom can be seen as a complex human dynamic involving both. However, the recent emphasis on performativity and professionalism suggests that feminine and masculine 'emotion codes' do not carry the same power and influence or attract the same value judgements. In this respect, and not surprisingly, the masculine is prioritized and privileged over the feminine – and the feminine is devalued and marginalized as a result.

How men 'do' professionalism and care

Though individuals perform emotion work and draw on symbolic representations of femininity and masculinity (gendered emotion codes), it is a situated 'doing' accomplished through the lived experiences of women and men within interactional and institutional arenas.

(Bolton, 2007: 21)

As West and Zimmerman (1987) argue, doing gender means engaging in behaviour at risk of gender assessment. In primary school teaching, gender and professional identity clash. As we have seen in other occupational contexts, and as discussed in Sargent's work outlined above, men moving into non-traditional roles must manage the tensions created between gender and role expectations. Men in these contexts can attract disapproval and negative attitudes based on intimations of feminization and homosexuality associated with their gender-atypical occupational choice. As Cammack and Phillips (2002) point out, men who become teachers must struggle with the image of teacher as 'woman'. This may be particularly pertinent in primary schools (DeCorse and Vogtle, 1997), where as we have seen, teaching carries strong maternal associations with the domestic and feminized sphere, undermining its professional status. Perhaps in response, as we found in the case of nursing in the last chapter and despite the preference by some men (particularly settlers) to remain close to professional practice, male teachers may move rapidly up the hierarchy into more gender-congruent managerial and administrative roles. In this respect, in the UK, men comprise 14 per cent of all teachers but hold 41 per cent of headship positions – a figure that rises to 72.2 per cent in the secondary school sector (Department for Children

Schools and Families, 2007). These are matched by similar figure from Australia. Women make up 93.9 per cent of primary school teachers (Australian Bureau of Statistics, 2006) but 60 per cent of headships are occupied by men (DET, 2006).

Professional identities and the secondary school sector

The lack of status associated with primary school teaching emerged from the study as a preoccupation for many teachers. This was frequently set against perceptions of a higher status as well as a more masculine image of the secondary school sector. Here the children are older (11+) and the curriculum is organized around subject specialisms – making claims to the academic and professional domain, in terms of possession of 'fields of knowledge', more secure. From Dent and Whitehead (2002), professional identification is manifest in representation and practice, signifying a particular identity to self and to others. This is illustrated in the following quote, in which an interviewee described his perceptions of a 'typical' primary and secondary school teacher:

> *The image of primary teachers, I think we're seen as lesser teachers than secondary teachers ... don't ask me why I think that but I think that's what we're seen as. If I see primary teacher and secondary teachers, I think of secondary teachers as being men in suits .... in suits and being specialists in certain subjects, whereas primary teachers I see as being jacks of all trades but master of none of them.*

Here, professional identity of secondary teaching is associated with a particular presentation of self (suited, managerial) and the possession and practice of expert knowledge as well with a masculine image. By contrast, the devalued, 'non-serious' and domestic nature of work in primary schools was a common theme:

> *It's because traditionally they* (primary schools) *were seen as the place where you played and you didn't do anything too seriously and you didn't really test anything, so you couldn't really measure anything and society generally thinks little children are a doddle, the littler the child, the easier it is, childcare, baby minding. That's what they think it is and it's that thing of anybody could look after children ... of course when you get to secondary school and you're teaching obviously Science and Maths, capital letter subjects, so that's more specialist. It's subjects rather than looking after children.*

As Dent and Whitehead (2002) point out, for professional status to be legitimized, it must be validated by scientific knowledge – and the professional must succumb to measurement against so-called objective criteria. In reflection of this, the non-rational elements of working with the younger age group embodied in lack of measurement (surprising considering the number of tests in the sector) and play is highlighted. The concept of being a professional, by implication, is associated with being and behaving that privileges specialist and expert knowledge over devalued generalism, affectivity and engagement.

Building and maintaining a professional identity in the sector could thus pose difficulties. Men resisted the semi-professional status which they perceived to be associated with their occupation and its practices in several ways. Some men rejected the instrumentalism which they saw as characteristic of new professionalism and, in their eyes, of secondary education. In the following quote, an interviewee was careful to present himself as highly qualified – the possessor of two degrees – and having an integrity regarding his area of knowledge that was, by implication, lacking in the more mechanistic approach within secondary schools:

> *I didn't want* (to go into secondary education) ... *and the spontaneity, the ability to have a curriculum that was child centred that would enable you to pursue interesting topics. I did a degree in English literature and I got an MA in English literature and I couldn't think of anything worse than being a secondary teacher where you have to shovel Jane Austin down people's throats.*

Recourse to discourses of spontaneity, creativity and child centredness allowed a particular status and interpretation of self that was more sophisticated and in some ways more 'honourable' than the methods, skills and practices perceived to be prevalent in the education of older children.

> *I feel I can be creative here and I suppose my creativity is, I enjoy making learning experiences for the kids and designing worksheets and finding out about work – and the creative aspect I feel I have is fulfilled.*

In a similar vein, primary school work was contrasted with other desk-based occupations:

> *enthusiasm for children would be the most ... I didn't see myself being in a desk job or an office environment. I just thought the politics involved*

with an office environment, I didn't really ... I didn't want to do that. And so ... I wanted to be outside and in a lively profession and because I enjoyed working with children.

A 'lively' profession captures not only the activities around creativity and of working with the 'buzz' of young children but also the emotions of enthusiasm and of a worthwhile, fulfilling deployment of skills. This discursive position was assisted through favourable constructions of difference from other occupational groups – and so the manufacturing of a new 'turn' on the notion of professionalism. Thus, scientific measurement and specialist knowledge, common currency in repertoires of professional practice, were compared unfavourably with newly relevant attributes of creativity, child centredness and meaningful learning engagements – overturning, through their recognition and part deployment, common conceptualizations of primary school teachers as non-serious, non-specialist semi-professionals.

Women as non-professional other

Equally, men positioned themselves against female colleagues. For some men, this allowed the construction of a professional self that was in line with modern managerialist discourses of performativity now dominant in the sector – and distinct from 'non-professional' practices and attitudes of nurturance, triviality and lack of commitment associated with women.

We're (male teachers) *more results oriented and systems oriented and that sort of stuff and it's not that some women aren't either, some women are, but there are a large percentage of women who are there because when they were young they loved kids, and without thinking primary school teaching was the obvious career choice for them ... They don't think much about the art of teaching, the craft of teaching, and how you can teach things better, like you never hear conversations like that at work between women ... they'll be talking about TV shows, or the kids ... whereas we are always talking about, you know, we go whole, part, part, whole, part, part, whole. I mean what do we do, all this sort of curriculum stuff, you know why doesn't this work, why don't we try this ... I guess I can rate more than my female colleagues do, that sort of whole idea that what you are doing needs to be measured and needs to be accountable and needs to be improved ...*

Women's reasons for entering teaching were thus trivialized as 'unthinking' – tied essentially to their embodied dispositions and natural roles as child-bearers. Divorced from nature, and positioned advantageously against women, men's career attitudes could be presented as more 'professional' through the contra-positioning of new management discursive resources (results, curriculum; improvement, experimentation, accountability; commitment) with feminine discourses of trivia and care. In Sargent's (2001) study, men similarly activated discourses of the 'superlative teacher', putting considerable energy into becoming ever more competent. As Kerfoot (2002) argues, 'being a professional' describes the attachment to a way of life that 'privileges instrumentality over other means of human engagement' (Kerfoot, 2002: 85). In the context of teaching, this requires as Bolton (2007) has suggested, a privileging of procedural efficiency over the work supporting children (which, from Sargent, may reflect a desire by men to demonstrate that interactions with children are being properly channelled).

Most men acknowledged that women were better at relational skills and were more sympathetic towards the children – though this was often devalued. One man referred disparagingly to women teachers' *'cosy nursery way of doing things'*. While women were seen to spend time listening to children's problems, they were also portrayed by men as getting 'over involved' in the details of their difficulties. One teacher commented, with some pride, on his contrasting approach to resolving disagreements between children: *'I just tell them go and sort it out and if you can't sort it out by tomorrow then you're in detention'*. Against a preferred masculine identity as no-nonsense disciplinarian, women were aligned with a maternal approach to children in their care. Resonant with Sargent's work, men also tended to present themselves as more academically oriented: *'I do not consider myself a parent or a substitute parent – I am here for their academic progress'*. This approach was seen to be valued by parents who largely welcomed a man as their child's class teacher on the grounds that they were supposedly more able to keep discipline and focus in the classroom.

From my own experience I would have felt that a lot of the parents would expect more, better results and stuff from a male teacher, because they are more disciplined and the children are supposed to have done more work in their class.

By contrast, the demands of discipline were seen to work against the bodily attributes of women – their voices were 'too high', their stature 'too slight' so that they lacked the necessary 'presence' in the classroom.

Professional identity is thus bound up with particular behavioural displays as well as with an attachment to techniques and practices that privilege certain meanings over others (Kerfoot, 2002). In this respect, those who seek to appear as a competent professional will undertake work to control and channel emotion within boundaries deemed appropriate for that status. Men thus practised commitment over women's dilettantism and emotional detachment against women's perceived over-involvement – while elevating work over the private or domestic sphere. Women could thus be seen as a 'repository' for those aspects of primary teaching that detract from its professional status (domesticity, mothering, lack of careerism), enabling the construction of a different (professional) identity for men. In other words, as Kerfoot (2002) points out, the constitution of professional identity must also entail suppression, marginalization and trivialization of undesirable aspects and attributes. Seekers of professionalism must therefore 'work' to express and embody those ideals that support that status while closing off other possibilities of self-expression.

Professionalism and the practice of care

From the above, men created a professional identity that had a close alignment with the managerialist project of performativity, accountability and discipline. In so doing, they positioned female colleagues as Other to their occupationally based sense of self. This is not to say however that men wholeheartedly rejected the 'feminine'. As we have seen, men often draw on discourses of creativity and child centredness, culturally associated with femininity, as they position themselves in relation to the more secure professional status in the secondary sector. Equally, some men took pride in their ability to relate to the children and to 'do' femininity while still maintaining a 'hold' on a masculine identity. They led extra-curriculum activities around sport, acted the disciplinarian and took pride in their more 'formal' approach in the classroom while 'doing' domesticity in classroom activities and in the performance of care. As one man commented in relation to his 'masculine side':

> *My masculine side doesn't lose out at all and the children don't see me in a feminine role because they can see that I do masculine things as well. I also give out the milk and the fruit, so they can see me doing cooking, I cook with them, but they also see me playing outside, I rub their knees when they*

fall over and cut themselves, so I don't think it (masculine side) *misses out at all.*

Other men described skills and attributes required for the job in stereotypically feminine terms, drawing on images of good parenting:

> *You need to be incredibly patient, tolerant, ability to organise and have lots of things on the go all at the same time, be juggling six balls in the air at the same time, be compassionate, there's quite a lot of social work in it. You're sort of a surrogate parent, you probably see the children more than a lot of parents do.*

> *You need to be very patient, extremely patient, you need good communication skills, you need to be able to explain things over and over again in many different ways and forms and you need to be able to relate to children on a level they can understand and at so many different levels because the children are so different and the understanding is very different to each other.*

For some teachers, therefore, practices associated with the 'masculine' project of performativity (planning, preparing, paperwork) were not the 'be all and end all' of teaching and had to be kept in their place. As one teacher commented '*You can do hours and hours of planning but if you can't get down to their level and speak to them on a level they understand then you can plan all you like . . .*

However, associations with femininity in the form of care and intimacy were subject to specific boundaries. As Skelton (1994) and Sargent (2001) have pointed out, the motivation of men teaching young children can be subject to mistrust. Many studies, in support of this, indicate that token men in primary schools experience contradictions around their role: the job requires some forms of caring and physical contact but men's gender role expectations preclude such behaviour and invoke suspicion of paedophilia (Allan, 1993; DeCorse and Vogtle, 1997; Murray, 1996; Sargent, 2001). In Sargent's study, the theme that elicited the most emotional responses from men was that of having to work under a cloud of suspicion, discussed in Chapter 3. Men must therefore 'walk the line of propriety', carefully managing their masculinity and taking precautions to avoid preconceptions and misinterpretations. As Sargent notes, men often kept their distance from children and in so doing helped to reproduce the image that they were not a source of love and nurturing – as well as the idea that men's bodies are a source of danger.

In this respect, in ways that resonate with the experiences of male nurses, men's bodies are 'marked' as potentially paedophilic, their touch carrying meanings associated with sexuality. However, while body proximity is often unavoidable in nursing and forms a major part of its occupational practice, bodily touch in teaching carries more powerful associations with sexual deviance. For a man to sit a child on his lap was particularly problematic. This was put succinctly by one man in Sargent's study: 'That's a big no-no. Women's laps are places of love. Men's are places of danger' (Sargent, 2001: 53). The possibility of arousing suspicion therefore instils considerable fear among male teachers, all of whom, in the context of the present study, raised this as a key issue in their practices of care. As one teacher commented *'there's the fear that as soon as something's said against you, you can lose it all'*.

> *If you've got a child who's really upset and worried and instinct tells you to put your arm around him, but you don't, you get somebody else in there to witness and I think a female teacher, although they have to be very careful, wouldn't have quite that stigma attached to it. It is restricting because you might want to break through to a child and find out what the problem is and just no, you cannot do it any way other than just talking.*

As DeCorse and Vogtle (1997) found, male teachers often discussed the problems associated with physical proximity with children but experienced difficulty expressing their emotions – supporting Tolson's (1977) view that men are often trapped in a public language around, for example, work but have no language for feelings. In support, men's expressions of fear and resentment were often disjointed and incoherent, possibly reflecting a lack of appropriate language and discourse on which to hang their experiences.

Overall, despite a need to distance themselves from the maternal, male teachers practised 'femininity' in their daily activities with the children in their care – and could be critical of the emphasis placed on planning and procedures within the professionalization project. However, in ways that resonate with the 'marking' of male nurses' bodies and the sexualization of male nurses' touch discussed in the last chapter, femininity could be a dangerous discursive domain.

Conclusion

In this chapter we have explored how male primary school teachers manage the contradictions inherent in their role and negotiate between discourses and practices of professionalism and care. The so-called 'professionalization project' (Bolton, 2007) introduced into primary school teaching in both Australia and the UK has helped squeeze out core notions of teaching as nurturance, care, process. This has led commentators (e.g. Bolton, 2007; Vogt, 2002) to suggest conflicts between notions of the competent and professional teacher and the occupation's traditional reliance on emotionality. As both Bolton and Vogt point out, this does not mean however, a simple dichotomy between masculine professionalism/competence and feminine care. As they found, men and women move between these often conflicting discourses and draw on meanings and practices associated with both discursive positions in their day-to-day activities and interactions in the classroom.

This is supported by the results from the present study. Here, male primary school teachers invest – although not always uncritically – in the project of performativity and by and large support the need for accountability, testing and targets. This may well be seen in the context of a desire to 'shore up' a professional identity based on specialist knowledge and academy, otherwise threatened by the occupation's core associations with essentialized femininity. However, at the same time despite some pressures to enact a traditional form of masculinity, they describe an 'ethic of care' (Gilligan, 1982) in their dealings with children. Here they place emphasis on the need for patience, empathy and understanding while practising day-to-day 'femininity' through domesticity (for example, cooking, tidying) as well as physical care.

The notion of care however remains a complex one. In this respect, men seek to distance themselves from pure affectivity, associated with the occupational practices of women, describing a relationality that is based more around the need to provide a supportive and challenging learning environment. This has resonance with Vogt's (2002) continuum of caring and her categorization of 'caring as commitment'. This captures an inclusive concept of the 'good' teacher, aligned with professionalism and focusing on the need to provide a secure environment in order to encourage the best academic performance from pupils. The 'less gendered' caring as commitment, which was found from Vogt's study to have strong purchase in the identities of both men and women, can be contrasted with caring as relatedness, whereby teachers express an interest in the personal situation of each child, caring as in a 'cuddly teacher', involving a high degree of physical contact, and caring as 'mothering' which is highly feminized in its association with motherly love and largely perceived to be incompatible with concepts of professionalism. While men in the study often described practices that conform to Vogt's caring as relatedness, they mainly adhered to the professionally oriented 'commitment' concept of care. They accordingly distanced themselves from the potentially dangerous 'cuddly teacher', given its basis in body proximity, as well as (devalued) maternal notions of care.

The study also points to the dynamic nature of professionalism and of professional identities. As Allan (1993) has argued, male primary school teachers must assert and model 'being a real man' in ways that are personally sustainable and that have integrity – and which are also acceptable to those who evaluate them. Under pressure to conform to stereotypically feminine qualities, in order to establish the sensitive caring relationships necessary to teach children, men must negotiate the meaning of masculinity every day. This may be achieved through personal investment in the masculine 'professionalization' project and support for it practices and principles – together with some distancing from what are perceived to be the feminine aspects of care. The 'work' that men undertake in pursuing this professional ideal points to professionalism as a dynamic concept that has to be constantly affirmed, both to self and to others. Thus, positioned unfavourably in terms of the perceptions of greater claims to professional status by the secondary school sector, male teachers construct a difference based around creativity and child centredness. They therefore overturn the very factors that support that claim (specialist knowledge, formality and academia) to present a different professional 'face' – based on a contrasting and oppositional originality, resourcefulness and (honourable) service to others. Equally, they position women as Other – a repository for those devalued and hence undesirable attributes (lack of commitment, play, the maternal) that interfere with a secure professional status. Professional identities and discourses, in privileging some meanings over others, are thus the sites of struggle and contestation – and are implicated in performances of gender at work.

8
Occupational Image and Social Identity: The Case of Male Librarians

Introduction

In Chapter 1, we identified three groups of men according to the dynamics of their entry into a non-traditional career. These groups were defined as seekers, finders and settlers. In each case, categorization was dependent on the location of the current occupation in men's scale of preferences, whether the occupation comprised a first or subsequent career, the nature of any previous occupation and relative levels of job satisfaction. Thus, seekers and settlers were those who have made an 'active' choice to enter a non-traditional career and where this was their preferred option. Settlers stand out in that they often exhibited a high degree of job satisfaction and moved into their current non-traditional career because of lack of personal fulfilment in earlier more gender-congruent jobs. They then 'settled' in their career, with no plans to leave. Seekers also chose the career but had less commitment in terms of wanting to stay in the occupation. Finders by contrast made a 'passive' choice. Many 'found' the career through a process of compromise in terms of a preferred but inaccessible career option. The career of finders was accordingly 'second best' in the individual's scale of preferences.

From the current study, librarians were in the main in the 'finder' category. They had rarely made an 'active' choice to enter the occupation but had 'found' their way there through the force of different circumstances. In this respect, librarianship was not always high on their scale of preferences. In addition, librarianship has suffered, more than the other occupational groups considered in this book, from a negative image associated with the mundane and with lack of drive and ambition. Against this background, this chapter explores how male librarians, who have often 'fallen into' a non-traditional career, manage their identity. This has been a theme throughout the book. In this respect, we have seen how cabin crew draw on space to resist a subordinated identity, how nurses manage the marking of their bodies as 'matter out of place' in their interactions with patients and how teachers align (feminine) notions of caring with a (masculine) professional identity. As Hickey (2006) points out, there have been few studies that have explored gender identity in the context of librarianship. 'Doing' masculinity in this context may carry particular significance. Librarians stand out not just in terms of the dynamics of their career entry – though this may well be significant in itself – but because of the negative image that attaches to the occupation. These issues are considered in more detail below.

The significance of career entry dynamic

As we saw from Chapter 1, the career entry dynamics of both teachers and nurses exhibit a strong alignment with the characteristics of settlers. They had often experienced a lack of fulfilment in a previous more sex-congruent 'masculine' occupation (the army, accountancy, management) eventually seeking their preferred career, where they 'settled'. Some however were seekers – as were many cabin crew. In this respect, men chose the occupation but did not necessarily have plans to stay. By contrast, librarians were in the main in the 'finder' category (as one librarian commented: *'I've just sort of fallen into it and stayed with it'*). In reflecting on their career choice, many referred to occupations which had been higher on their scale of preferences but which had been inaccessible at the time of the job search and/or career decision. One librarian for example had wanted to go into academia but circumstances had not enabled him to study for the requisite PhD. Another had hoped for a career as a translator, but realized the difficulties of making a good living in that occupation.

Unlike settlers who as we have seen had often moved into the non-traditional occupation from other less preferred jobs, few librarians made this active choice. Similarly, from Carmichael's (1992) study of male librarians, while some had failed at other work before becoming librarians, few had entered as a career change. In this respect, a career change may well signal an active strategy to enter an occupation and so explain its relatively high location on the individual's scale of preferences. Instead, the career decision of male librarians often had an unplanned element or was presented as the result of options closed off:

I was pulling out of teaching and I was unemployed...and it took me a while to find a job. I couldn't get anything else at the time and that was just the first job I was offered...it wasn't like a massive aspiration. I was quite interested in the various aspects of libraries like the books and dealing with the public – but it's almost like what else do you do when you've got an Arts degree?

Many men thought of librarianship as a 'stop-gap' career at the time of entry in the sense that there was an expectation that something different (more exciting, more challenging) would eventually turn up.

I only went into it (librarianship) *because there was nothing else on offer at the time – I never dreamt I would still be here. I assumed that I'd just do it for a couple of years, have the qualification and the experience behind me if you like as an insurance policy...but that I'd be on the look out for something else. But now, it would be difficult to change because I'm not qualified for anything else and I would have to start again.*

All this supports librarians as 'finders' rather than as seekers or settlers. Together with the rather negative image and mundane nature of the job (discussed below), this may have implications for how librarians can rationalize their career choice. In this respect, both teachers and nurses, as settlers and therefore characterized by a tendency to have initiated a career change, have access to a justificatory logic in terms of their non-traditional career choice. Men in these occupations often draw on explanations concerning a desire to extend the affective domain of their lives, largely undeveloped in their previous more masculine sex-typed jobs, to 'make a difference' in the work that they do in terms of helping others, to have the opportunity to travel as well as to gain professional status. Settlers have few if any regrets about their occupational choice – presenting themselves in almost heroic terms as managing to achieve their ambition 'against all the odds' such as disapproval from family and peers and the general upheaval of a career change.

Cabin crew can also activate a justificatory discourse around their chosen career. As we have seen, crew were identified largely as seekers. Many had made an active choice to enter that career but were not planning to 'settle'. While they did not experience the same level of job satisfaction as settlers, they were still able to present their choice in favourable terms. In this respect, they often activated discourses around youth, glamour, fun and adventure – and presented their career as a temporary 'stop-gap' before taking up something more worthwhile and serious.

These logics are largely unavailable to librarians. While providing a service (and for many librarians dealing with the public is the most satisfying aspect of the job), there is difficulty, unlike teachers and nurses, conceptualizing and presenting that service in strongly altruistic or humanistic terms. The mundane nature of the work also contributes to a negative image which is a far cry from representations of adventure and glamour, characteristic of cabin crew. Moreover, having 'fallen into' the occupation, many had progressed up the hierarchically arranged and credentially based graded career structure. They had undertaken further qualifications and training in order to move, for example, from library assistant to the professional status of librarian. Once on this career path, the opportunity costs of a change were simply too great and the ability to transfer skills acquired limited. As one librarian commented rather ruefully: '*I haven't found anything else I've been able to get into*'. Overall, librarians may have a smaller investment in their occupational identity. In addition there are fewer cultural resources on which to draw in managing a sense of self. This is exacerbated by the negative image associated with the job.

The librarian image and masculinity

As Morrisey and Case (1988) argue, men in librarianship are doubly stigmatized. Firstly, they experience the negative stereotypes that attach to women's work in general, such as associations with femininity. In this they encounter similar pressures to men in other non-traditional occupations. In addition, however, they encounter a negative image, discussed below, that attaches to the profession.

What is the nature of this stereotypical image? As Carmichael (1992) has pointed out, librarians are generally seen as powerless, socially inept and unambitious – a stereotype that was recognized by all male librarians interviewed. Moreover, there is a male librarian stereotype which is distinct from the female stereotype. This he describes as effeminate – probably gay – and characterized by lack of social skills, power and ambition. Typical of the descriptions from his sample were 'nerd', 'anal retentive', 'boorish', 'dull' and 'wimp'. From open-ended comments emerged the 'caricature of an unambitious pathetic and sad creature without social graces or skills who hides out in the profession because he cannot succeed in any other work.... dowdy, wearing out-of-date, threadbare or poorly co-ordinated clothes' (Carmichael, 1992: 430).

These associations resonate with meanings given by male librarians in the current study. In this respect, the extent and nature of the negative image may be surprising, given that the sample were all academic librarians, generally seen as a 'cut above' those who work in the non-academic, public library sector. The following quotes capture aspects of this negative image:

Well it's kind of dowdy – not very clued up, obsessed with books. It doesn't come over as very dynamic or interesting.

I did a survey on the street the other day and the lady interviewing me said oh you work in a library do you? I thought only old dears that worked in libraries.

I'm Mr Dusty over there.

My hairdresser was very surprised that I work in a library, he always finds that very unusual that there's someone who works in a library coming into his hairdressing salon which he likes to think is very upmarket and stylish.

A nerdy job.

There's clichés about mundane and everyone's got to be quiet and things like that...you look at the imagery and it tends to be a spinstery type...someone who's fairly matronly and tending to be quite old.

Women in jam-jar glasses, tweed skirt, woolly jumper, mid to late 40s.

A sad boring job...dumb male – a himbo.

As in other non-traditional occupations, the image was overwhelmingly feminine. However, this had less to do with gendered conceptualizations of service and care (as with nursing, teaching and cabin crew) but was associated more with the mundane nature of the work involved. In discussing their day-to-day activities, librarians described the routine nature of such work. This involved cataloguing, issuing books, shelving, binding – as well as answering queries at the front desk. More senior library staff were additionally involved with online cataloguing and cataloguing systems, organizing specialist subject areas and monitoring data quality – such as watching for mistakes made by library assistants. The desk-based and largely clerical nature of such work has, as Henson and Rogers (2001) suggest in the context of clerical employees generally, core associations with femininity – and was presented by some men as a reason for (and so helping to 'naturalize') the predominance of women in the job. This association was based on the mundane nature of tasks involved as well as, at lower levels in the library hierarchy, a lack of control over their execution. While senior librarians may well have more autonomy in this respect, the rule-bound and bureaucratic nature of their work – often seen as carrying limited intrinsic interest – may be seen to 'fit' with emphasized femininity (Connell, 2000) but work against authentic displays of masculinity.

Furthermore, the image as illustrated in the quotes above is aged, with core associations with middle age and its embodiment (old-fashioned dress, glasses). In fact, unlike the other occupational groups (nurses, teachers, cabin crew) age emerged as a defining factor in accounts of men's experiences. This was particularly the case for younger librarian staff who often resisted associations with an older age group (discussed below). In fact, rather than experiencing token status on the basis of gender, as has been the case in other non-traditional contexts, for many men heightened visibility was more associated with age.

The implications of such visibility could be double edged. On the one hand, young men could be given special treatment, similar to the special consideration given to some nurses discussed in Chapter 6. Here men could be treated as a 'favourite son'. As one young man commented: *'I'm called the golden boy – I can do no wrong'*. Even when he over-ordered books and cost the library an unnecessary £600, there was little comment: *'I didn't even get a ticking off for that...I know one person did that a few years ago and he got into quite a lot of trouble for it.*

Another admitted:

> *They* (older female managers) *support me, they listen to me and they're very good. They help you. Margaret's like my mum...it's like having my mum there.*

In a similar vein, Pringle's (1993) study of male secretaries found that younger workers are often incorporated in familial terms as sons – encouraged to perform filial duties in the expectation that they will eventually move on to become autonomous individuals. In support of this, younger librarians often described instances where they were expected to 'listen and learn' from their elders. However, as Carmichael (1992) found, male librarians risk social sanction if they do not aspire to administrative roles both because of the expectations that men are breadwinners and because they are seen to violate the traditionally masculine emphasis on competition. Moreover, from Hickey (2006), displays of autonomy or lack of cooperation in the 'son' role could often lead to charges of male chauvinism and was seen as a threat to the operation of the 'old girls' club'.

In this respect, younger men were often marginalized in the day-to-day informal interactions within the library – left out of conversations and social activities. This is in contrast to the experiences of men in the other occupational groups, discussed in Chapter 3, where men often reported feeling welcomed into the job and where there were few instances of the isolation experienced by similarly placed, that is, token women (e.g. Kanter, 1977). Young male librarians could also be given the physically demanding work (portering, moving heavy trolleys, re-shelving) and the more menial tasks. One young man in his twenties reflected back on his previous experience working in a public library:

> *They* (female librarians) *were all middle aged and I was about eighteen and they just ignored me really and I did the filing and photocopying and stuff and they gave me really useless jobs ... I did it for 6 months and then I moved on. I was really glad to get out of there.*

This supports Hickey's (2006) study of male librarians, in which differences were drawn on the basis of age as well as gender. While gender was viewed as a foundational aspect of difference, age also featured prominently in male librarians' perceptions, suggesting this factor may be significant in how younger non-traditional employees engage with others in their workplaces. In both this (Hickey, 2006) and the current study, older men were not treated in this way.

Finally, the image carried devalued associations with 'bookishness' captured in the label 'nerd'. These connotations also have a gender and age dimension in that they often relate to men (as in the particular case of the label 'nerd') and concern perceptions of an age-inappropriate pursuit of intellectual rather than social or popular activities. The nerd is someone, usually a young man, who might be considered a loner by peers – unpopular and seen as socially and sexually inept, attracting social rejection as a result. The rather asexual image of the librarian may serve to diminish intimations of homosexuality, powerfully indicated in perceptions of other non-traditional occupations. In this respect, unlike in Carmichael's (1992) study where homosexuality was integral to the male librarian image, none of the men interviewed discussed sexuality as of any significance in the popular stereotype. Women were equally asexual and presented as old fashioned and 'spinstery'. While this image may conform to some conceptions of femininity (unadventurous, cautious), there is little purchase here however with dominant conceptions of masculinity, even within 'new man' discourses (Knights, 2001) which place emphasis on aspects of affectivity.

Overall, the image of the librarian is largely a negative one. While some aspects of this image may apply to all librarians, irrespective of gender, from Carmichael (1992), there is a specific image that relates solely and, he argues, more negatively to men. Unlike Carmichael's study, there appears to be little evidence from the current study of associations with homosexuality – the image is largely asexual in character – but results point to core associations between librarianship and femininity. This is based largely on the mundane nature of the work involved – often deemed appropriate for women but not for men. In addition, the image is aged, linked to perceptions of librarians as middle-aged, old-fashioned and conservative.

It is worth noting that from a US-based study of librarians (Morrisey and Case, 1988), the male librarians' perceptions of themselves as an occupational and gendered group was significantly different from their actual image. The perceived image was in fact more negative than the actual – suggesting that male librarians see themselves in a worse light than the general population actually pictures them. This led Morrisey and Case to suggest that male librarians may in fact be fighting an image that does not exist. However, the strength and prevalence of the stereotype suggests that librarianship does have an image problem (Carmichael, 1992; Hickey, 2006) with likely implications for identity and for self-esteem for men in the occupation.

Social identity and librarianship

In terms of identity, as we have seen from Chapter 2 as well as from evidence relating to the experiences of men in the other occupational groups, individuals define themselves in terms of others. In this respect identity can be seen to be relational – dependent on relations with others and with larger collectives. The concept of social identity captures this relational aspect of self and can be defined as the self-concept that emerges through an individual's association or affiliation with a social group (Tajfel and Turner, 1985). From social identity theory, people classify themselves and others according to social categories, enabling the individual to locate him or herself in the social environment. They thus construct a sense of self that is relational and comparative in the sense that these constructions are based on relations to and comparisons with other categories (Ashforth and Mael, 2004). Organizations

and/or occupations, as social categories, can thus provide identity capital, embodying characteristics that then become prototypical for their
members. Given that an individual partly defines him or herself in social
categorical terms, any negative image attached to a group may well
trigger the need for identity repair work on the part of members.

Theories of social identity (e.g. Ashforth and Mael, 2004; Baumeister and Leary, 1995; Breckler and Greenwald, 1986; Tajfel and Turner,
1985) draw a distinction between those aspects of self-concept that
differentiate the self from others and those aspects that reflect assimilation to others and significant groups. This is based on a perceived
distinction between the personal and the social self. Brewer and Gardner (2004) point to a further distinction implicit in these accounts
namely between two levels of social selves – those that derive from
interpersonal relationships and interdependence with specific others
and those that derive from membership in larger, more impersonal
collectives or social categories. They summarize this distinction as
follows:

> Both interpersonal and collective identities are social extensions of
> the self but differ in whether the social connections are personal-
> ized bonds of attachment or impersonal bonds derived from common
> identification with some symbolic group or social category. Prototyp-
> ical interpersonal identities are those derived from intimate dyadic
> relationships such as parent–child, lovers and friendships, but they
> also include identities from membership in small face to face groups
> that are essentially networks of such dyadic relationships. Collec-
> tive social identities on the other hand do not require personal
> relationships among group members.
>
> (Brewer and Gardner, 2004: 67)

As Turner *et al.* (1987), cited in Brewer and Gardner, further explain,
social identity entails a depersonalized sense of self, 'a shift towards the
perception of self as an interchangeable exemplar of some social category and away from the perception of self as a unique person' (Turner
et al., 1987: 50 cited in Brewer and Gardner, 2004: 67). For Brewer and
Gardner, the difference between interpersonal and collective identities
is a matter of the level of inclusiveness. As they point out, some social
identities can be construed as either interpersonal relationships or as
collective identities. Relationships can be experienced as based on specific roles (for example, doctor–patient) or in terms of membership of
a general social category (medical professionals). This resonates with

other work (e.g. Greenwald and Breckler, 1985) which draws distinctions between 'private', 'public' and 'collective' facets of the self. The public self represents those aspects of self-concept that are sensitive to the evaluation of significant others (that is, influenced by and based upon interactions and relationships with those others) and the collective self reflects the internalization of norms and values of important reference groups (that is, those aspects of identity that are influenced by group identification). It is the collective self that corresponds to the concept of social identity as represented in social identity theory.

Social identity thus captures that part of self that emerges through belonging (association, affiliation) to a social group (Tajfel and Turner, 1985) where bonds are impersonally derived from common identification with that social category. When social identities are activated, salient features of members of that group influence (impress upon) self-concept (Brewer, 1991). More specifically, as Brewer and Gardner note, in-group membership plays a role in the formation of self at different levels. Firstly, in-groups provide the 'frame of reference for self-evaluation at the individual level and for the selection of significant others at the interpersonal level' (Brewer and Gardner, 2004: 70). In other words, we compare ourselves to others in that group and transfer trait attributes to ourselves. Secondly, in-groups are compared with relevant out-groups. We accordingly look for traits and characteristics that we share with the group and which make us distinct from other groups. On this basis personal and collective selves can be seen partly interdependent.

As argued above, given that an individual partly defines himself or herself in social categorical terms, any negative image attached to a group may well trigger the need for identity repair work on the part of members. As Elsbach and Kramer (2004) argue, organizational identity threats cause members to deploy tactics to maintain positive perceptions of what the group stands for. In this respect, from Dutton *et al.* (1994), it is important to distinguish between members' perceived social identity (that is, what members themselves believe are the distinctive and enduring aspects of their social category) and their construed external identity (that is, what members think outsiders believe are the distinctive and enduring attributes of their social category). In this respect, as we have seen above from Morrisey and Case (1988), male librarians may well be overly pessimistic in terms of their popular image: the male librarian sees himself in a worse light than the general population actually pictures him.

Male librarians' response to negative stereotyping

How do male librarians respond to these potential threats to identity? The findings from the current study suggest that men distanced themselves from the negative image of the male librarian in several ways. Firstly, as we found in the last chapter with our discussion of primary school teachers and their quest for professional status, men constructed women as Other – a repository for those undesirable elements that help create an insecure identity. In laying claim to professional status, male teachers often consigned to women those meanings (for example, around domesticity, mothering, lack of commitment) that serve to undermine that claim. Similarly, in librarianship, older men in particular presented women as lacking in ambition and suited for the more mundane elements of the job:

> *A lot of women who work in the library … a lot of them don't seem to be particularly seeking out higher positions … they're quite happy with their job, they enjoy their job and that's the main thing.*

> *One thing women are particularly good at is the basic sort of housekeeping … rather much the same way as most women are really good at running a home right down to trivial things like dusting and keeping the shelves clean*

Women as a separate categorical group are thus made to embody those aspects of the more general image (lack of ambition, lack of adventure, pleasure from the mundane) that may be uncomfortable for men. In addition, men often aligned themselves with more gender-congruent aspects of the job such as its technical requirements. This was assisted by library work's recent 're-invention' in terms of a greater involvement in information technology, allowing new titles to emerge. These include, from Piper and Collamer (2001) 'information broker, information specialist, information manager, knowledge manager and cyberarian' (Piper and Collamer, 2001: 407). As Carmichael (1992) found, male librarians often activated these labels as signifiers of prestige and power – even though the work might in fact be the same. Taken together, it could be argued that men create a more positive image for themselves as a group (that is, of male librarians) by activating more gender-congruent and more highly valued traits around technical expertise, whilst differentiating themselves from the category of women. This may reflect and be assisted by different conceptualizations of librarianship. From Morrisey and Case's (1988) study, women were found to look at librarianship from a helping or interpersonal communication perspective while men had an orientation towards processes of dispensing information.

Secondly, librarians selectively highlighted other facets of group membership and hence of self that were in direct contrast to the identity implied by their occupational choice. This often related to an involvement in sport – an antidote to the 'dusty' and physically inept image of the 'nerd'. Many were active in competitive sports (football, rugby, rowing) that demanded investment in time and energy. One young man was keen to present himself as a part-time DJ – and spoke of how his long hair and dress code had at first caused consternation among his older colleagues:

> *I wear big boots sometimes and camouflage trousers and a big woolly top – at first when I got all the earrings they were a bit funny towards me. I mean once I came in and I'd dyed my hair raven black and they talked to me about that . . . a yob that what's they took me for . . .*

This librarian thus resisted the middle-aged image implicated in the popular stereotype – invoking classification schemes (DJ, yob) that are in opposition to the devalued characteristics of the social group. As Elsbach and Kramer (2004) have argued, individuals often highlight the positive dimension of their identities that are unrelated to the source of identity threat as a response to that threat (see also Ashforth and Mael, 2004). In the above case, interestingly, a negative image was invoked (yob) in order to overturn a different form of negativity (dusty librarian). In so doing, from Swann (1987), individuals may conspicuously display self-verifying personal identity cues, such as dress and physical appearance.

Thirdly, men drew on different and higher-status classification systems. They accordingly gave accounts of themselves early on in the interview that positioned them, in terms of social classification, outside the library context. One man explained that he was a writer and that his library work enabled him to continue his writing on a part-time basis. Another was pursuing an acting career while a third was doing a PhD and hoping to enter academia. Several librarians spoke of how they preferred to identify themselves with the university in which the library was located rather than with librarianship *per se*. In response to the following question: 'When you meet people for the first time and they ask about your job, how do you respond?' – the following librarians admitted:

I say I work for (Business School) *and that I help students with their queries and stuff – if I say I look after the business school, that sounds a bit better, with business information, that sounds more impressive.*

I do feel embarrassed when I say I'm a librarian, I have to play on my context and say I work at (University) *and then I gradually have to be more specific.*

This conforms to work on social identity (e.g. Elsbach and Kramer, 2004; Hogg and Abrams, 1988) which suggest, in a similar vein to the above, that when membership of one social category is identity-threatening, an individual can restore a positive sense of self by selectively increasing the salience of other, better-respected groups – in this case the classification category of academia.

Finally, some male librarians located themselves within the occupational group but summoned more flattering but hitherto unrecognized features. Nearly all librarians referred to the more 'technical' aspects of the job, referred to earlier in this chapter – positioning themselves as information and/or knowledge managers, in the forefront of research and social change. One librarian commented in relation to same question above:

You get that feeling when you look into their eyes and you think you don't know anything about the job really. The information economy is going to take off, it's going to be huge in the future so it's really more fool them.

Juxtapositioning the assumed negativity of the librarian image (seen in their eyes) with the reality of the new world of knowledge management, this librarian was able to construct a comfortable space within the devalued classification. In positioning himself as having special, albeit unrecognized, expertise he highlighted the ignorance (more fool them) of his detractors. A similar outcome emerged from Elsbach and Kramer's (2004) study of organizational identity threats. Here individuals often invoked comparisons based on more flattering dimensions and which presented them as having the advantage. In the following quote, a librarian similarly presented the qualities required for the job as highly specific and unrecognized. Only those (notably gendered male) with the necessary technical and academic research expertise, such as those possessed by himself, could truly appreciate the skills required:

Librarianship has a funny image doesn't it? And my post-graduate degree was in information science, so I could say technically I'm an information

scientist... it doesn't come across as dynamic or interesting although it is
when you get into it. But I think men who have done research, that kind of
academic background can really understand what it is about.

Some librarians focused on the service aspect of the job, highlighting
the special expertise required in answering queries:

I developed the ability to deal with customers and find out what they want,
which may not actually be what they're asking for. You need to work out
whether they're actually asking for the right thing, if they go off on the
wrong track they can waste a lot of time.

I like helping students with their inquiries. A lot of students have a fear
of using the library and having done two degrees now, I'm able to get to
grips with their problems quite quickly and show them how to approach
their problems... you need to understand what they are looking for and
how to approach their research needs... you're providing pastoral support
to a certain degree.

Where there is a discrepancy between individual's beliefs about the value
of their social identity categorization and the value attributed by outsiders, strategies may therefore include the highlighting and reification
of features of the job – assigning to the tasks involved a skill and competence that is presented as largely unrecognized or appreciated only by
other professionals. Overall, this suggests a proficiency in managing and
manipulating the boundaries between social categorizations in order to
create a comfortable sense of self. As Elsbach and Kramer (2004) note in
this respect:

The portrait of the individual that emerges is that of a cognitively flexible, adaptive and opportunistic social perceiver, one who
responds to identity threatening events by highlighting *personal*
membership in select social categories to make salient his or her positive identity attributes, favourable status among peers and favourable
similarity or uniqueness relative to others.

(Elsbach and Kramer, 2004: 475)

In this way, librarians exhibit a form and level of 'hybridity' in their
social categorizations as they engage in an ongoing 'dialogue' with
different groups and as they attempt to slip out from the negativity associated with their occupational category. The concept of hybridity – the
formation of heterogeneous identities that might not be seen to always

go together (Albert and Whetten, 2004) – captures the networks of identities available to an individual, the coalitions that are activated as well as personal strategies of resistance. It highlights how individuals construct their identities beyond dichotomous stereotypes (male/female; masculine/feminine; young/old; black/white) and how they seek to evade being 'pinned down' by them. Thus men locate themselves within the general category of librarian but draw on perceptions and understandings of other better-respected groups (for example, academic researchers) for validation; they hold up the negative perceptions of an imaginary group, to ridicule and diminish their foundations ('more fool them'); drawing on discourses of technical expertise and commitment, they situate themselves within the more specific male librarian category to differentiate themselves from women; they activate other social identities (musician, DJ, sportsman, PhD student) to neutralize the identity-threatening implications of their occupational category; they align themselves with the category and signifier of their employing (university) organization. Librarians can thus be seen to move between different social categorizations and to form 'strategic alliances' with as well as 'strategic distancing' from other groups.

Conclusion

We started this chapter by identifying male librarians as 'finders'. Unlike nurses and teachers, who had often entered the profession as a second and highly preferred career, and unlike cabin crew, who had often made an active choice to enjoy life and 'take to the skies', male librarians often 'found' the career through a process of compromise. For many, it was 'second best' in that there is a preferred (but hitherto inaccessible) option. For some, the decision to remain within the hierarchical structure of the profession, in the absence of a more challenging alternative, was tinged with disappointment and regret.

This more precarious positioning is likely to have implications for how male librarians manage their identity within a non-traditional occupational context. Male librarians neither experience nor can they easily draw on vocationalism as a discursive resource, as is the case with many nurses and teachers – and their work is far from glamorous or adventurous, a justificatory logic employed by cabin crew. Moreover, they encounter a negative image which, on the face of it, affords few opportunities to create a counter ideology and facilitate an alternative presentation of self. This has led Morrisey and Case (1988) to argue that male librarians are 'doubly stigmatized' – encountering damaging associations with femininity and an image (unambitious, unadventurous, socially inept) that hinders constructions of masculinity.

This image as we have seen is both gendered and aged. In fact, unlike the other non-traditional occupations considered, age combines with gender to define the experiences, through heightened visibility, of many young men. In this respect, while work on men in other non-traditional contexts has indicated beneficial outcomes from men's 'token' status (e.g. Heikes, 1991; Simpson, 2005), these benefits do not appear to extend to young male librarians. Such work has often been set against the detrimental implications of token status for women – in the form of marginalization, exclusion and enforced conformity to belittling and confining 'role traps' (Kanter, 1977). Men in female-dominated occupations have been found, as discussed in Chapter 3, to benefit from their difference from women through assumptions of careerism and enhanced leadership skills. Results from this study of librarians suggest that the nature and extent of these benefits may, however, be overstated in this particular setting. While often 'cared for' by older women, young men can also encounter marginalization and exclusion. Pressed into 'son' roles, with associated expectations of respectful deference, young men can experience negative sanctions, similar to those experienced by women in Kanter's (1977) study, if they fail to conform.

As Ghidina (1992) has argued, occupational role is usually afforded greater importance in defining social status than other categorizations. This reflects the varying levels of status and prestige given to different occupations and the centrality of the occupational role for self-definition as well as definition by others. The implications of low-status work for identity can therefore be profound and is likely to trigger the need for identity repair work to secure a sense of self. The negative image attached to librarianship poses such problems for men. As we have seen, the nature of this image as well as the materiality (and often mundane nature) of the work that librarians undertake afford few cultural resources on which to draw secure alternative meanings.

However, to be 'livable' (Butler, 2004), librarianship must allow men the opportunity for some renegotiation of identity and a way of managing or redefining the negative image. To make sense of these processes we have drawn on the concept of social identity – which highlights the relational (and comparative) dimension of identity in terms of individuals' location within and sense of belonging to different groups. Drawing on this notion, we have seen how men construct women as Other, a repository for those undesirable traits and values embedded in the negative image; how at a personal level, they selectively highlight those facets of self (and hence other belongings) that are oppositional to the image implied by the job; how they increase the salience of other better-respected groups in narratives of self; and how they create a more comfortable space within the devalued group by summoning and drawing on more flattering and hitherto largely unrecognized attributers and features. Through these different strategies, male librarians manage 'identity dissonance' (Ashforth and Mael, 2004) caused by disparity between perceptions of occupational identity and the identity seemingly attributed by outsiders. They thus restore and affirm a positive perception of self and enable a more favourable presentation to others. By drawing and redrawing boundaries between the different dimensions of social identity, and by selectively highlighting (and concealing) other personal and social categorizations, they both manage their identity and disrupt the negative stereotype. Thus, rather than thinking of the different dimensions of self as ordered, integrated and ultimately holistic, this suggests that they are instead separate, fragmented and often in conflict with each other – a hybrid identity in which the constituent parts do not always fit easily with each other. Individuals accordingly 'call up' oppositional categories, create contrasting dimensions as well as activating parallel discourses in their identity work.

9
Reflexivity and Constructions of Difference in the Context of Nursing Care

Introduction

This chapter explores processes of reflexivity as men and women consider gendered attitudes and practices. In the context of nursing, it investigates how men see women and how women see men in their work roles. In line with the key themes that have been explored in the occupations that have made up this book, it considers the skills and aptitudes that each is seen to bring to the job, how men and women view the other's performance as care-givers and the experiences and challenges of working with and/or managing the other group. Men in 'female'-oriented caring roles, such as nursing, challenge traditional notions of gender, which, as some authors suggest (Adkins, 2003; Bourdieu, 1990; McNay, 2000), can provide a fertile ground for critical reflexivity as both men and women attempt to align 'new' practices with existing power relations. To be reflexive about gender is to 'have a particular awareness that stems from cogitating, studying or thinking carefully' (Martin, 2006: 260). Reflexivity in this context is taken to mean the critical awareness that arises from a self-conscious relation with the Other (McNay, 2000). From Ricoeur (1991), this involves a self-conscious shaping of identity that is achieved as individuals make sense of divergent, emergent and ever-changing roles, experiences and practices.

Reflexivity, transformation and gender

Theories of reflexivity have made links between changes in late capitalism and the potential for identity transformation (Beck *et al.*, 1994; Giddens, 1992). The loosening of broader social structures in

determining individual experience and absence of social solidarity associated with late modernity, linked to the decline in the relevance of
'grand narratives' in making sense of social and power relations, have
from this perspective led to a greater freedom for individual expres-
sivity and self-determination. Individuals are thus increasingly 'freed'
from structures (Lash, 1993) to fashion themselves, through deployment
of 'practices of the self' and self-conscious self-stylization (Foucault,
1985) or reflexive self-management (Giddens, 1992). Taken with a
de-traditionalization associated with the feminization of labour markets and the move of women from the private to public spheres – as
well as the supposed uptake of 'feminine' ways of working – individuals
are encouraged to critically reflect on their social conditions. From this
perspective, there is a potential for a breakdown of or challenge to gender relations. In the context of the present study, this could include
the implications arising from the move of men into 'feminine' occupations and the ways in which women are required to accommodate them.
Reflexivity is accordingly a self-conscious shaping of identity (Adkins,
2003) and identity a 'reflexive enterprise' (Giddens, 1991) which, given
these conditions, is likely to involve a heightened critical awareness
vis-a-vis gender.

Thus as Beck *et al.* (1994) argue, 'reflexive modernity' (that is, the
increased capacities for reflexivity associated with the decline in the
significance of social structures) is a likely trigger for change as agents
reflect on the social conditions they face. From Giddens (1992),
increased reflexivity undermines traditional rules, norms and expectations and so has transformative potential as individuals, in an emancipatory process, refashion identities. With respect to gender, this can
lead to a deconstruction of dominant norms and expectations, so
challenging conventional notions of masculinity and femininity. From
this perspective, there is thus a direct link between reflexivity and
transformation.

Embedded in these accounts is the idea that reflexivity emerges from
dissonance. From McNay (2000), drawing on Bourdieu, dissonance
occurs through a mismatch between existing power relations on the
one hand and current attitudes and practices on the other. In Bourdieusian terms, reflexivity is constituted where there is lack of fit between
habitus and field. Habitus refers to how individuals develop attitudes
and dispositions and how they engage in practice and with others. The
habitus is accordingly a set of personal and durable characteristics –
our sense of self that shapes attitudes and behaviours and which has
been acquired and learnt from the field. The latter comprises the sets

of institutions, rules and conventions that produce and authorize certain activities (Virkki, 2008). The habitus is thus the site of individual internalizations of the 'rules of the game' in a specific field and through which social reproduction takes place. These fields are overlapping – with their own logic and limits on practice. While not locked together, habitus and field are by and large compatible. The field sets limits to practice – though at the same time the actions of agents shape the habitus of the field and hence the field itself (Adkins, 2003).

What concerns us here is the potential for a lack of fit between habitus and field. This possibility has been presented as arising from the entry of women into the public domain – signalling the transposition of the female habitus into public socioeconomic fields (our interest of course is the reverse – namely the introduction of male habitus into what might be seen as 'feminine' fields). As McNay argues, this may lead to a 'distantiation' or part removal of the individual from constitutive structures as in the above example leading perhaps to a questioning of patriarchy on the part of women moving into previously all-male occupations and organizational settings. Complexity and difference associated with dissonance may therefore lead to greater awareness and critical reflection on norms and expectations that have not previously been the subject of scrutiny as individuals negotiate in daily-practices conflictual roles.

This moves reflexivity away from an orientation, promoted by the reflexive modernization thesis characteristic of Giddens, which conceives of reflexivity as a cognitive, individually based capacity and of subjects as existing outside of social worlds but able to cognitively and objectively reflect on that world (Adkins, 2003; Lash, 1993). Instead, reflexivity is intrinsically linked to the everyday, embedded in situation (Adkins, 2003) and with a collective dimension (Lash, 1993) as individuals make sense of and share meanings and practices that ultimately shape perceptions and action. This more situated and collective account conceives of reflexivity as a conscious, situated reflection on categories of habit and on shared meanings. In terms of gender, this allows for some transformation as the 'undoing' of the synchronicity of habitus and field leads to possibilities for critical reflection on 'the (previously unconscious and unthought) norms, rules and habits governing gender' (Adkins, 2003: 27).

In this respect, as both McNay (2000) and Adkins (2003) argue, theories of reflexive transformation may overestimate the extent of reflexivity and its transformative powers. From McNay, the emphasis on conscious self-monitoring and creativity overlooks the more enduring reactive aspects of identity and overestimates the significance and extent of 'expressive possibilities' available to men and women. In this respect, while gender identity is not 'an essential horizon', there are many pre-reflexive aspects of masculine and feminine behaviour which question the processes of identity transformation highlighted in some theories of reflexivity. Martin (2006) for example has pointed to the many 'unreflexive' practices of gender in work contexts and the sometimes harmful implications for men and women. She refers here to how men 'act like men' in ways that reinforce and mobilize stereotypes – practising masculinity to bring favour from other men but with little or no regard for the sometimes damaging effect on women. This is supported by Whitehead (2004) who argues that men are largely unable to see the gendered nature of the worlds in which they live. While feminism has given women both language and political verification enabling reflexivity required for 'epistemological and ontological transformation', men's reflexivity is 'blocked' within a dominant discourse. In fact, 'new manhood' is less about changing masculinities and more about men's strategic responses to perceived loss of gendered power.

There are therefore embodied and embedded aspects of identity that are less amenable to reflexive transformation or re-interpretation – and which may be enacted at a pre-reflexive level. As McNay points out, despite women's entry into the labour market and into areas of work previously occupied by men, indicative that some conventional arrangements of gender have been dismantled, other aspects have become entrenched. Women for example still take on the burden of emotional responsibilities in both public and private spheres, expected to deny self and be available for the support and care of others despite possible inclinations to the contrary.

Furthermore, if reflexivity is seen as emerging from the distantiation provoked by conflict and tension, for example between habitus and field, and as these tensions are unlikely to be uniform in intensity and type across different fields, then reflexivity will not be evenly generated. Thus, even as some aspects of gender identity are de-stabilized, suggestive of a loosening of dominant conceptions of masculinity and femininity, others become entrenched. Reflexivity is therefore not a generalized or universal capacity but arises unevenly from individual's embeddedness in different power relations so there will be an irregular or uneven de-traditionalization of gender.

Adkins (2003) further critiques the link between reflexivity and transformation. In this respect, reflexivity is not so much associated with the freedom to question and critically deconstruct rules and norms that

govern gender, but may be better conceptualized as a 'habit' of gender in late modernity. Rather than de-stabilizing, reflexivity can be seen
to be tied to arrangements of gender that are becoming increasingly
demanded and integral to corporate success. This can be seen in the
ways in which workers reflexively use gender in their work contexts.
Adkins refers here to McDowell's (1997) study of financial service workers in the City of London who use gender in different ways in encounters
with clients (for example, choosing an 'executive bimbo look' or that
of 'smart professional'). In support of this view, reflexivity is increasingly demanded in training and management (e.g. Chia, 1996; Grey,
2002) as successful management is seen as integral to self-awareness
and an ability to think critically and reflect on the behaviour and attitudes of themselves and those around them. Reflexivity can therefore
be linked to (gendered) positions of privilege and exclusion and to a
reworking of gender that may not involve a transformation. Reflexivity may routinely enter into everyday life as a matter of course – with
limited transformative powers.

Reflexivity, identity and the other

Reflexivity has been defined here as the self-conscious shaping of
identity and a critical awareness that arises from a self-conscious relation with the Other. Reflexivity has thus been associated with post-
structuralist thinking on identity on the grounds that, released from
structures, identities become a project of the self – discursively produced in the day-to-day actions, interactions and communications. As
we have seen in previous chapters, gendered identity is accordingly fluid
and uncertain and filled with tensions and contradictions as individuals in a reflexive manner mobilize, negotiate and renegotiate gender in
day-to-day activities.

   As McNay (2000) argues, this may overlook the more enduring, reactive aspects of identity and a level of coherence to self may be submerged
by the post-structuralist emphasis on the fragmented, contradictory and
dispersed nature of subjectivity. She argues for a temporalized understanding of self that has unity but which also is dynamic through
time – as individuals make sense of experiences, organizing them along
a temporal dimension and gathering events together to present a meaningful structure. Drawing on Ricoeur (1991) she argues this can be done
through narrative as individuals impute meaning and coherence to the
flux of events in a way that gives shape to identity and which can never
achieve closure because of the emergence of new possibilities.

Narrative therefore shares with post-structuralism the constructed nature of identity but incorporates a greater level of coherence and, because of the constraints imposed by narration (for example, to maintain a comfortable or authentic sense of self), a smaller degree of transformative powers. Furthermore, while acknowledging the relational nature of identity, McNay argues that post-structuralist accounts are based on an exclusionary dynamic vis-a-vis the Other whereby identity is asserted through the rejection of difference that is unsettling to the sense of self. Men therefore align themselves with a desirable One whilst differentiating themselves in relation to a devalued and feminine Other (Ainsworth and Hardy, 2004). However, as McNay argues, there are a range of possibilities available when men and women are faced with complexity and alterity that may go beyond exclusion, denial or resistance and which may embrace acceptance and reciprocity – issues we considered in Chapter 2. While identity presupposes some exclusion, this does not mean that exclusion becomes the essence of subjectivity. On this basis, there can be other less defensive ways of relating to the Other which may be based on creativity and which could result in new forms of interaction. From this perspective, reflexivity is the potential to relate to the Other in an open manner – a capacity to tolerate alterity and to be able to resolve apparent contradictions in a meaningful way. As McNay argues, individuals 'map' the different strands of their lives – the 'ebb and flow' of experiences and the multiplicity of time forms – into a form of coherence whilst at the same time managing complexity, plurality and instability. Outcomes are sometimes emancipatory and sometimes not, so that any change in gender relations is often uneven and not necessarily synchronous.

This has resonance with this study of men, situated in non-traditional work contexts. The movement of men into occupations traditionally held as 'feminine' may be seen as part of a 'de-traditionalization' of gender and trigger reflexivity as men and women make sense of and share meanings relating to the day-to-day situated activities and practices. From the above, the experience of dissonance may lead to awareness of and critical reflection on norms, attitudes and behaviours that have previously passed unnoticed. In this respect, male and female nurses were asked to reflect on the significance of gender in their working lives in terms of perceptions of difference in skills brought to the job and in terms of nursing care, as well as more generally to explore the challenges faced working with or managing the 'other' group.

Women discussing men

Highlighting the relational nature of identity, both men and women drew on sameness and difference in the stories they recounted of each other. Women in particular drew on universal notions of professionalism to establish sameness:

> *No I think their values all pretty much the same – you know we have our public duty principles and we make it very clear that these are what the expectation is – I think our integrity and honesty and selflessness is universal.*

Women also drew on discourses of professionalism to highlight difference. Male presence was welcomed as it was seen to assist in the trend towards a greater level of professionalism within nursing – though it was generally recognized that men gravitated towards management, research and education and away from traditional nursing care. In this respect, however, rather than problematizing this careerism as being at women's expense, female nurses presented men as deserving, justifying their career advantage. In so doing, they positioned themselves, rather unsympathetically, as lacking, deficient and dysfunctional. Rather than being the focus of critique, faster progress was justified by calling up gender differences in career focus and by appealing to breadwinner discourses:

> *Men can often end up being the primary breadwinner – if only for a time – I don't necessarily begrudge them it.*

> *Men have a clearer focus as to what they want than women necessarily have ... and they probably do get there quicker but I don't think they necessarily deserve to be criticized for it. I think more females need to look around at themselves and criticize themselves more. I think sometimes they are to blame for it.*

Several women were critical of men's reluctance to take on the 'drudgery', body proximity and traditional 'caring' of general nursing. Men were seen to avoid the 'hard slog' of this 'mind-numbing' role (*it's quite a rare bird a male nurse as far as caring capabilities'*). Instead, women saw them as more suited to the technology around diagnostics and to prefer the medical model of nursing care as well as the excitement of accident and emergency.

However, men were valued for their special contribution and for the cultural resources they were seen to bring to the profession which helped to overcome associations with a 'subservient role'. Male presence was also seen to bring a balance to what was perceived as a dysfunctional all-female group:

I think some of the things men bring is a strength of men in terms of their position in society that women do not necessarily exercise.

They probably bring a good balance ... a strength to the profession when it is more evenly balanced

you get less bitching and back biting with men around.

Women were also critical of their own perceived inability to make decisions. Here, women's emotions and a tendency to get side-tracked by the insignificant were seen to get in the way of effective decision-making and were contrasted with a greater sense of focus on the part of men.

They (men) *have a different frame of reference and focus as to what's important and what's not and some of that is that women do get lost in the insignificance sometimes.*

Women can't see the wood for the trees sometimes – it can be quite crippling for getting things done ... they can never make up their minds, very indecisive. Men cut to the chase more quickly.

Men's presence – an embodiment of authority – led to feelings of security and certainty in sometimes stressful situations:

That authoritative person, the maleness makes – trying to deal with all the complexity, I think there is a comfort in having someone who just cuts through ... I don't think there's any doubt that one of the things that create most anxiety in health settings is uncertainty – about what it is that can be achieved with patients ... if things don't go well or aren't done properly, so that kind of uncertainty and desire for predictability and it's people who can just walk into a situation and by their own behavior, by appearing clear about what needs to be done, even in the face of all that uncertainty. I do think that some of that's a gender kind of thing and I think that male nurses probably bring that in.

In much of their reflections on gender issues, women thus activated traditional notions of masculinity and femininity. These reflections are likely to have been facilitated by a dissonance arising from the presence of men in a traditionally feminine role that called into question conventional notions of masculinity and femininity. Such reflexivity, however, rather than leading to a challenge to existing gender power relations, served to further support them. While women were critical of men's tendency to move into technology and away from day-to-day bodily care, they accepted and justified, by calling on traditional breadwinner discourses, perceptions of faster career progress. At the same time, they drew on 'masculine' professionalism and rationality as well as on the benefits, through 'balance', that men were seen to bring to 'dysfunctional' all-female groups. In some of these constructions, women blamed and devalued themselves. Men accordingly were afforded a privilege (as One) and women concomitantly devalued (as Other) in gender constructions that women justified through recourse to gender-typical explanations.

Men discussing women

While women, in reflecting on their relationship and attitudes towards men in their occupational context, were largely supportive of dominant gender norms, men engaged with gender at different reflexive levels. At one extreme, unlike women who all engaged thoughtfully (though not necessarily critically) with issues of gender, a few men drew unquestioningly on entrenched repertoires and were unreflexive in their accounts of working with women. Here, women were aligned unproblematically with domestic or trivial roles (one man referred disparagingly to women doing 'fluffy stuff like tidying up the blanket' and to their 'twittering' in a corner) while others dismissed the significance of gender as 'not a problem', claiming in an unquestioning manner gender (and their masculinity) to be a non-issue in the work context.

Men in addition drew on difference to both support *and* subvert traditional gender norms. In terms of the former, men supported gender norms as they considered gender difference and reflected on the implications for their own sense of self and experience. In so doing, they drew tentative conclusions (couched in qualifying terms such as 'probably' or 'I think') that were based on traditional notions:

> *I think so . . . they* (men)*do things differently. Yes I think they probably just cut to the chase and get on with it . . .*

I'd say...that female nurses are more emotional – more emotionally tied to their patients

...just thinking about it now, I guess I feel I'm just a bit more detached, without affecting the way I do the job, just keeping myself at a bit more of a distance.

In a similar vein to women's accounts discussed above, some men therefore engaged thoughtfully with difference but in a 'non-radical' manner. Women were variously portrayed as better able to express and deal with emotions but less able to make quick decisions while men were seen as more detached and able to bend the rules – adding value through humour and a more relaxed attitude to group dynamics.

A few men engaged with difference at a deeper level – challenging traditional gender norms, recognizing gendered hierarchies and engaging with a 'feminine' self. As we saw from Chapter 6, some men for example acknowledged the meanings attached to masculinity and monitored their behaviour accordingly, arguing for a need for humility and sensitivity towards, particularly female, patients in their care.

Several men commented critically on the dismissive treatment of female nurses by male doctors and on the subservience of women. In the following quote, a nurse recognizes the cultural privileges of masculinity in the work context:

Males will get listened to in conversations more readily than I think the females...I see it time and time again and it's just a cultural thing. You know the males seem to be able to dominate conversations and get their own way. The other side of that of course is that females are almost conditioned to accept that.

These advantages were often tied to what were perceived as differences in body dispositions and ascriptions. The male body could mobilize meanings that were seen to support an authoritative presence – a lower voice could be associated with safety, for example, and aligned with the traditional protective role of men. As we saw in Chapter 2, men could deploy in a reflexive manner their masculinity, self-consciously manipulating meanings associated with masculine body dimensions, to present an authoritative, reassuring and in some cases intimidating presence, even though, as in the quote below, this was seen as performance that was often reluctant and did not reflect notions of the authentic self:

> *I find working in A&E that because you're a man you've got to deal with the aggro...I'm not an aggressive person naturally but you've got to act up to the situation, act assertively, act aggressively so that they don't think you're a pussy. And you've got to do it, go in there, you can't sort of sit down and procrastinate you've got to do it there and then you know. As soon as you walk into a situation, assess it, deal with it.*

RS: Is that quite hard to do?

> *I find that it's proving hard to do because we're a man in a woman's world. It's like they're saying, I call upon you to diffuse the situation in A&E because you're a man.*

Other men however (on the grounds of equality of treatment) actively resisted traditional gender norms, refusing for example to lift heavy patients or take on disciplinary or security roles.

Reflexivity could thus be based on a recognition of the implications of gendered hierarchies, but in a way that was supportive of traditional gender norms (for example, of the authoritative male, vulnerable female). At the same time, men reflected on conventional notions of masculinity and considered how this impacted on their ability to undertake more 'feminine' roles. Many referred to their feeling of inadequacy and lack of expertise in dealing with highly emotionally charged situations, linking this with a masculine preference for detachment and control, and acknowledged female nurses' capabilities in this respect. Others claimed little difficulty in what was seen as their 'feminine' side – resisting conventional notions of masculinity. Many gave illustrations of their proficiency in 'caring' and feminine roles. As one man commented:

> *the actual essence of nursing is to nourish, to nurture, and I think that's instinctively a female thing to be able to give that intense, because it's not just to care, it's to care intensely and I think that's essentially a feminine thing, so I think I think as a nurse, but thinking as a nurse is thinking as a woman.*

Overall, men could thus exhibit unreflexive approaches to gender or could engage reflexively at different levels. In so doing men could support or subvert dominant values – in critical recognition of gender hierarchies, drawing self-consciously on masculinity to present a particular(for example, authoritative self) or by engaging in a self-conscious manner with 'feminized' and 'non-masculine' behaviours.

Conclusion

This chapter set out to explore the nature and extent of reflexivity as men and women engage with each other in the context of nursing care. The analysis presented above throws light on various issues relating to gender and reflexivity.

Firstly, while post-structuralist accounts of identity have pointed to the transformative nature of reflexivity (e.g. Beck *et al.*, 1994; Giddens, 1991; Lash, 1993), associated partly with the decline in structures as identity-determining principles (and so the ability to self-consciously shape one's identity) and partly with the supposed de-traditionalization of gender norms, this research questions along the lines of McNay (2000) the nature and extent of these transformative powers. Both men and women engage reflexively with gender and for many, the outcome is supportive rather than subversive of traditional gender norms. For some men, self-conscious adoption of traditional masculinity is used in an instrumental way to pursue organization goals – resonant with McDowell's (1997) study of city workers referred to above and lending possible weight to Adkins (2003) argument that reflexivity can be seen as a 'habit' of gender. At the same time, from McNay (2000), gender is viewed by some men in particular at a pre-reflexive level, pointing to the entrenched nature of gendered hierarchies.

Secondly, results point to some gender difference in the nature and level of reflexivity undertaken. In this respect, unlike Whitehead's (2004) conclusions concerning the lack of gender reflexivity among men, male nurses engaged with gender issues perhaps in a more var-ied and a deeper level. While women were critically aware of difference (for example, men's reluctance to undertake traditional 'caring' roles; the tendency for men to be fast-tracked in their career), male advan-tage was justified through recourse to traditional gendered discourses around male breadwinner roles or the professionalism that the presence of men was seen to bring. In positioning men as the One – deserving, privileged, valued – women saw themselves mirrored as Other, that is, as abject, devalued and the subject of critique. Unlike this group of women, men by contrast could be unreflexive, assuming a male privilege or dis-missing the salience of gender in their work roles while others could be differentially reflexive with varied implications vis-a-vis the support given to or the subversion of traditional gendered norms.

This is not to say that men have greater powers of reflexivity than women (or vice versa). Rather, as McNay (2000) has argued, de-traditionalization of gender is likely to depend on levels of dissonance and distantiation experienced. In Bourdieusian terms, dissonance will emanate from a mismatch between habitus (that is, sets of dispositions and orientations that define behaviour and subjectivity) and field (that is, the social space with its specific rules, in which individuals act and react). While for women, the entry of men into nursing may throw into question some assumptions concerning gender-appropriate behaviour and trigger possible processes of questioning and resolution, there will be less of a dissonance between (gendered) habitus and field than for men.

Here, dissonance is likely to arise as 'masculine' perceptions and values collide with a 'feminine' context or field provoking higher levels of distantiation from constitutive organizational and occupational structures. While men in Whitehead's study of further education managers may not have the opportunity to 'stand outside' of dominant discourse to reflect on its meanings and implications, given the often-cited alignment of management and dominant conceptions of masculinity, men in feminine contexts may have access to alternative discourses from which to challenge the hegemonic 'malestream'. Moreover, as discussed earlier, men's entry into a non-traditional career may not always be an easy one, eliciting possible disapproval from family and peers. Men are therefore likely to have thought carefully about their career choice and to have already undertaken some 'reflectivity'. Their entry and pre-entry may thus encourage a heightened critical awareness and reflection on the social conditions faced, as evidenced in some of the responses outlined above from men. Here the relationship with the Other has emerged as possibly more complex and complicated, as discussed in Chapter 2, than a simple rejection or dismissal as in some post-structuralist accounts. Moreover if, as McNay points out, experiences of dissonance are likely to be uneven through occupancy of different fields, then while some aspects of gender relations may be questioned, others as we have seen above may become further entrenched. When men enter non-traditional occupations, reflexivity is differentially triggered and challenge to gender norms is patchy and incomplete.

10
Conclusion

This book has focused on the experiences of men in four gender-atypical occupations involving levels of service and care, namely cabin crew, nursing, primary school teaching and librarianship. It has explored career issues and career dynamics, the implications of men's 'token' status for experiences in the organization, perceptions of gender differences in occupational practices around emotional labour, and how men manage potential mismatch between gender and occupational identity. On this basis, the book has done two things. Firstly, it has highlighted some key issues pertaining to men's experiences in gender atypical roles, furthering our understanding of their relevance in accounts of gender. These issues, forming the basis of the first part of the book, concern identity, visibility and emotions. Secondly, it has explored the significance of occupational context and, by adopting a different lens in each case, has given some fresh insight into meanings and practices at the intersection between subject positions and occupationally based discourses of work. Through these general and occupationally specific themes, the book has thrown light on how men 'do gender' and 'do difference' in organizations.

Identity, visibility and emotions

The themes of identity, visibility and emotions help bind the diverse accounts of men together as well as providing a frame through which men's experiences can be better read. Separately, the themes help dismantle and uncover some of the complexities inherent in men's contradictory subject positions. Together they allow a deeper understanding of the challenges men face. These challenges include the identity implications of visibility, the emotions that accompany contradictions in their

159

roles and in performances of service and care, and the ways in which men manage identity by moving within and between different discursive locations.

Chapters 2, 3 and 4 have considered the significance of each theme for understanding men's experiences in their gender-atypical roles. In terms of identity, Chapter 2 drew on the One and the Other to explore how men manage tensions between gender and occupational identity and the ontological insecurities that are inherent in performing a nontraditional role – themes that were also apparent in later chapters. In this respect, men's location as One, a status associated with masculinity, can be fragmented and uncertain – and threatened by proximity and associations with the Other. Equally, the Other can be colonized and partly brought into the One as men reframe emotionality and care in masculine terms. Alterity can be a challenging, painful and sometimes pleasurable experience for men – it can impress subordinated identities or support rewarding and less conventional selves. Overall, location in the One is never complete and can be a source of ontological insecurity while alterity is multidimensional and fragmented – evading capture from defining categories, and fluid in the boundaries that are often drawn between the two.

In terms of visibility, we have seen from Chapter 3 how men's token status can have implications for men in work contexts that are dominated numerically by women. Heightened visibility can be a source of pleasure and of pain. Men can benefit through, for example, assumptions of careerism and of special expertise and by being exposed, as a result, to developmental opportunities – often enjoying the attention that visibility brings. On the other hand, men become visible as gendered subjects in their non-traditional role, their bodies marked as deviant and out of place and their behaviour subjected to a normalizing and controlling gaze. As we have seen, these undesirable consequences of visibility may encourage men to seek some of the cultural and material privileges of the invisibility within the norm.

From Chapter 4, issues around emotions and emotional labour emerged as central to understanding men's experiences and behaviours in these contexts, not least because such work draws on skills and aptitudes that relate to service and care. Here, we have seen how the mobilization of feminine emotions can be a source of power and status for men. By appropriating emotions and bringing them into the masculine domain, associated skills and aptitudes can be divorced from essentialized and devalued notions of femininity. Equally, men can position themselves favourably against traditional notions of masculinity in their avowed capacity for nurturance and care. This supports the notion of a deferential and gendered division of emotional labour which may have positive identity implications for men.

These themes have been considered in their respective chapters as almost separate phenomena that are implicated in how men undertake gender-incongruent work and how they experience their non-traditional work context. However, the themes of identity, visibility and emotions are not separate categorizations but are interdependent and interweave in complex ways. First and foremost, identity is a theme that runs throughout the book and is central to our understanding of men's experiences as well as their values, attitudes and practices. From Morgan (1992) the work context is a central arena for the manufacture of masculine identity and in non-traditional occupations, this core aspect of identity is under threat. Implications for identity are consequently profound as men manage the contradictions inherent in the performances of gender and of their occupational role.

In this respect, both visibility and emotions are implicated in how men manage identity. For example, visibility can confer a special status on embodied performances of emotional labour, with positive identity effects, but at the same time the marking of men's bodies can have painful implications for men's sense of self. As we have seen, these encounters with alterity can encourage men to seek the privileges of invisibility – and the marginal and uncertain nature of men's relationship with the dominant centre can trigger negative emotions (anger, resentment, envy) towards higher-status men. In this way, identity can be seen to be expressed through emotions – not just these negative emotions but also for example through pleasure and pride – and to be involved in the work of constructing and negotiating identity.

At the same time, visible as gendered subjects, in a context where masculinity is 'on the line', men experience the visibility of their bodies and of their masculinity in some of the work they do – attracting pressures to co-opt their masculinity in traditional ways and activating the demand for emotions pertaining to security, discipline and authority. Equally, men may work to manage their masculinity (voice, demeanour) and their embodied performances to comply with more appropriate and non-assertive notions of care. Heightened visibility may also offer the opportunity to 'reveal' some aspects of emotional labour, concealed within essentialized notions of femininity when performed by women. Visible status can then be seen to give the opportunity to reframe discourses of care into oppositional attributes and practices that have special value and significance when undertaken by men and to help sustain a more sophisticated identity that avoids discourses of servitude and subordination otherwise implied by the job.

The occupational contexts

To different degrees, identity, visibility and emotions are also themes that run through accounts of occupational context that comprise Part II of the book – highlighting similarities and differences in experiences. Chapter 5 thus explored how, through the themes of control, resistance and corporeality, male crew negotiate subjectivities within and through space and how gendered meanings attached to space can impress upon and both challenge and be challenged by the performances and subjectivities of individuals within them. Highlighting the instabilities of space, the chapter explored the ways in which meanings are drawn upon to manage an identity and how those meanings also impress on the subjectivities of male crew. In this respect, a 'masculine' authoritative space created through discourses and activities of safety and security can be easily disrupted and subverted by feminine activities of deferential service and emotional labour, and create often emotionally charged tensions for men as they manage such contestations of meaning. Equally, men must manage their identity in a space that is saturated with and marked by homosexual meanings and manage the implications of a gaze that is founded on conventional notions of masculinity, femininity and sexuality. Visibility and emotions are accordingly implicated in the ways in which space both shapes and is shaped by identity processes.

In Chapter 6, we saw how in the context of male nurses, gender identity has a bodily dimension and that bodies carry meanings that can conform to or disrupt its social practice. Both signifying and signified, active and passive, bodies have implications for doing gender identity and 'having gender done' in specific work contexts. Male nurses draw on and resist traditional body ascriptions to present a particular self (the paternal protector, the independent non-conformist, the disciplinarian), sometimes co-opting dominant meanings for instrumental ends, sometimes managing their bodies in a self-conscious manner in their interactions with patients. Men draw on and are defined by their bodies, visible in the incongruity between masculine bodily ascriptions and the practices of nursing care. Embodied, visible, emotional – men manage the meanings their bodies convey. At the same time, from Chapter 9 while female nurses are largely accepting of the gender order, male nurses were shown to exhibit different levels of reflexivity and variously accept and/or challenge traditional gender norms.

Chapter 7 explored how male primary school teachers negotiate between discourses and practices of professionalism and care and how men draw on, resist and move between these often conflicting discursive positions. Men partly invest in the project of performativity to support a professional identity but at the same time describe an ethic of care – based not on pure affectivity, culturally coded feminine and with dangerous associations with body proximity, but on a more gender-neutral and professionally oriented commitment to a challenging learning environment. The chapter highlighted the dynamic nature of professional identities, the visibility and marking of masculinity in men's interactions with young children as well as the need for identity work to pursue the professional ideal.

The last occupation, librarianship, was the focus of Chapter 8. Through the concept of social identity, the chapter considered the implications of visibility based on gender and age and how men move between social categorizations to manage the challenges to identity implied by the negative image of the job. With few cultural resources available to help to secure alternative meanings, men selectively highlight those facets of self and belongings that are oppositional to that image and increase the salience of other better-respected groups in narratives of self. This helps to create a form of hybridity based on a fragmented notion of identity that is disintegrated rather than integrated and where the constituent parts do not always fit easily with each other. Gender, age and visibility interact in the context of the meanings attached to the job to create a need for considerable identity (and emotion) work to manage the discursive effects of these negative associations.

From these brief accounts we can see the centrality of identity in understanding and interpreting men's experiences in their non-traditional work contexts as well as the significance of emotions and implications of (in)visibility. We can also see commonalities in terms of some of the processes and practices involved. In this respect, making sense of men's experience, through the difference lenses presented, has highlighted the dynamic, fluid and contradictory nature of underlying processes. Spaces can be seen as dynamic and unstable, full of contradictory meanings that have implications for crew as they (often creatively) manage their identity; in different ways, men negotiate the contradictions within embodied practices of nursing, both drawing on and defying dominant meanings; male teachers activate, resist and move between the conflicting discursive positions of professionalism and care; by differentially aligning with and separating from social groups, librarians create a fragmented, hybrid identity based on varieties of belonging. This brings to light movements, transitions, temporary positionings and the blurring of boundaries as well as creativity, complexity and contradiction. Men in these contexts cannot draw on existing organizationally situated masculine discourses to support a gendered subjectivity and must instead activate and negotiate new meanings – managing tensions and contradictions 'from scratch'. The exact nature of these negotiations is, however, context and organizationally specific, dependent partly on the nature of the expectations that impinge on how men 'do' service and care and partly on the cultural resources available to men to negotiate and fashion new, different discursive positions.

In Chapter 1, it was recognized that an understanding of the experiences of men in non-traditional occupations is vital if sex-stereotypic work–career boundaries are to be challenged and breached. This was set in the context of the persistence of gender-based occupational segregation and the ongoing strength of stereotypes as to what comprises men's and women's work. From Chapter 9, a supposed de-traditionalization of gender norms associated in particular with the movement of women into the labour market and into areas that were previously colonized by men, can be seen to create the conditions, through reflexivity, for identity transformation, that is, the ability for men and women to self-consciously shape their identity. In the context of the present study, it could be supposed that the movement of men into gender-atypical occupations would create a similar potential.

The contradictions that men face in their non-traditional role together with the absence of mainstream masculine discourse may well signal a re-fashioning of identities in the creative ways suggested above. From Chapter 9, however, what emerges is a patchy and uneven transformation. Men (and some women) appear adept at reflecting on gender issues, but the results in terms of attitudes and practice occasionally support and occasionally subvert traditional gender norms.

Doing and undoing gender

The above discussion suggests an orientation to gender that can uncover complexities and contradiction in subjective experiences. On this basis, the book has been informed by post-structuralist accounts. These have complexity, ambiguity and fluidity as central themes, drawing on the concept of discourse to understand gender relations and the ways in which individuals negotiate and manage gendered identities. This also allows a focus on multiple masculinities and how they co-exist in institutionally specific relations of hierarchy and exclusion; on the active construction of masculinities and the dynamics of difference; on the gender work involved – the internal complexities and contradictions – in practices and interactions; and on how men's bodies are implicated in gender constructions and masculine expressions. Far from a static category – a stable attribute that 'attaches' to the individual – masculinity and gender generally are therefore active and activated in specific interactional performances.

On this basis, the theoretical orientation of the book has been identified as one of a situated 'doing' of gender. As we saw in Chapter 1, drawing on symbolic interactionism and on social constructionism, West and Zimmerman's (1987) original conceptualization conceived of gender as an accomplishment, actively produced through interaction and so moved away from perceptions of gender as a stable attribute of the individual. This accomplishment is achieved in local situations according to normative conceptions of gender which serve to naturalize its appearance. Thus, norms of appropriate gender behaviour may be seen to vary in different occupational contexts: cabin crew, for example, can draw on (sexed, gendered) meanings attached to air travel which allow a more flamboyant display of alterity which would be out of place in a hospital or school. Nurses and cabin crew can be expected to deploy masculine body characteristics to subdue disruptive patients or passengers, while body attributes may be less relevant in gender assessment of male librarians. It is through these and other norms that individuals are held 'accountable' to their performances.

Accountability captures the regulatory force of normative conceptions of what it means to be a woman or a man. In this respect, behaviour is assessed by others according to norms of acceptability within the institutional or organizational arena in which the 'doing' of gender takes place. In this study, we have seen that this can have discursive implications as men experience ontological insecurity through the effects of the disapproving 'gaze' of other men (friends, acquaintances, family members) signalling a problematic deviance from the (heterosexual) masculine norm. Accountability can also have material consequences for the occupational practices as men for example are pressed into gender-congruent activities such as portering, heavy lifting or discipline and with possible sanctions imposed if men are judged as failing to meet expectations in these respects.

More recently, these and other authors (e.g. Fenstermaker and West, 2002) have moved from an orientation of doing gender to one of doing difference. This has allowed a more dynamic conceptualization of difference, as created and re-created in situated interaction – with the potential to move away from gender as the sole orientation in managing our sense of self. In this respect, doing difference allows for a greater alignment with post-structuralist thinking on gender as a multiplicity of difference and of identity as produced through interaction and discourse – as well as for the potential for gender to intersect with other defining aspects of subjectivity and experience such as race, class and sexuality. Difference is thus multiplicitous – both contestable and unstable – drawn upon as part of (gender) identity work.

This has resonance with Butler's theory of gender performativity, a concept drawn on in Chapter 5 to explore how male crew manage identity in and through space. For Butler, gender is performative in that it is produced through language or discourse in a way that reproduces, via the repetition of norms and normative practices, what gender is supposed to be. The power of discourse thus lies in its ability to 'enact what it names' – to both constitute and produce gender through regulatory practices, similar to West and Zimmerman's accountability but which are, from Butler's perspective, framed within a compulsory heterosexuality.

While Butler's early work (1990) suggests that the reiteration and repetition of norms might offer some possibility for agency, resistance and change, it is her later work that explicitly addresses gender 'undoing' (Butler, 2004). Here, in the contexts of homosexuality, incest and transsexuality, she highlights the ambiguous, incomplete and fluid nature of gender identity as well as the potential for its transgression. In a similar vein, arguing for a need to include 'undoing' in performances of gender, Deutsch (2007) suggests the concept of gender 'doing' leaves little room for dismantling gender difference or diminishing gender inequity and oppression. For Deutsch 'doing' can theoretically capture both conformity and resistance to gendered norms, a stance supported by Moloney and Fenstermaker (2002), but the focus on accountability as a regulatory (and institutionally based) mechanism in the sense of being 'at risk' of gender assessment, tilts the balance towards conformity. On this basis, it is 'easy to see why men and women would comply and difficult to explain why they would resist' (Deutsch, 2007: 109).

The single conceptualization of 'doing' may not therefore adequately capture the dismantling of and resistance to difference. In support, Deutsch points to empirical applications of the 'doing' framework to studies of men and women in unconventional occupational contexts. Many of these studies draw conclusions in terms of the preservation, rather than disruption, of the gender order – suggesting the need for a different conceptualization to help uncover and render visible potential for challenge and erasure as well as the re-creation of difference.

'Undoing' goes some way to address the weakness outlined above – and recent interest in the potential and possibilities of the concept is evidenced in a special issue of *Gender Work and Organization* devoted to this topic (see Pullen and Knights, 2007). Undoing captures the social interactions, and associated discourses can reduce or challenge difference (Deutsch, 2007). Undoing therefore alerts us to the ways in which difference is drawn upon, activated and denied to dismantle or disrupt traditional notions of gender. In the context of the present study, the analysis of the experiences of men in gender-atypical occupations allows a dramatization of difference which may be rendered more visible than in other more conventional contexts. At the same time, it helps us move away from an interpretation of men's experiences which places emphasis on separation and distance from the feminine as well as, in a similar vein to Deutsch's critique above, away from an orientation in which masculinity is reaffirmed rather than disrupted and challenged.

Doing and undoing in difference in non-traditional work contexts

This is not to deny that separation, distance and reaffirmation occur. As we have found, male crew claim special expertise in managing unruly passengers and in maintaining safety on the plane as differentiating factors that separate them from female co-workers; male primary school teachers draw on discourses of masculine professionalism which is presented as different from the more maternally based approach of women; male nurses gravitate towards gender-congruent specialisms such as mental health and A&E, and differentiate from women by presenting their capacity to 'care' within a masculinist logic of rationality and detachment.

However, to interpret men's accounts of themselves solely in terms of separation and distance is to miss the complex ways in which doing and undoing difference unfolds. Men draw on difference to reconstruct a masculinity threatened and rendered insecure through associations with femininity. For example, an occupationally based masculinity can be reinvigorated around technical competence and professionalism, or the demand for security and discipline – thereby partly reproducing and naturalizing the gendered organization of work. Men colonize the feminine, rendering relational skills visible and of value by calling up discourses of rationality and detachment and bringing them into the masculine domain. At the same time, men comfortably engage with behaviour and practices culturally coded feminine: teachers engage patiently with the young children in their classroom; librarians stamp books and catalogue returns; cabin crew gossip with colleagues and serve tea and coffee; nurses change dressings and attach babies to the breast. In other words, while some aspects of occupational identity may be resisted and challenged, others will be simultaneously embraced. Some elements in gender relations may be questioned, others may become further entrenched and still others quietly transformed in day-to-day activities of service and care. By entering a non-traditional occupation, men therefore simultaneously 'do' and 'undo' gender in different ways and with different levels of contestation and challenge. As in Hall *et al.*'s (2007) study of men in hairdressing, estate agency and fire-fighting, through various embodied practices, men conform to, draw on and resist gendered stereotypes associated with their occupation. Men therefore act to reinforce as well as to destabilize gender in its stereotypical forms.

As intimated earlier, the extension of doing gender into doing difference has allowed a more complicated enquiry into the relational nature of identity construction and its reliance on dynamics of difference. Some of these dynamics have been revealed in this study of men. In this respect, men have been found to *flatten* difference, drawing for example on common, supposedly gender-irrelevant notions of occupational integrity and practice. They *activate* difference in their experiences of alterity: homosexual (and some 'straight') cabin crew 'camp it up' in their relations with pilots and as they confront a highly masculinized heterosexuality; librarians *invoke difference* by calling up other more flattering categorizations that remove them from associations with the mundane. Male cabin crew have been shown to *make creative use* of difference, as they draw in an ironic fashion on alterity, in order to resist a subordinated identity. Male nurses work to *deny* difference as they seek alignment to higher-status men – while at the same time they *resist and struggle against* the differences that are subsequently displayed. Men *embrace* difference, inviting it in as they claim a special status within the feminine domain, describing their immersion in practices associated with feminine notions of care. Nurses and cabin crew *play with* difference in informal work spaces as they gain pleasure from and claim a comfort with the feminine. Through levels of reflexivity, men self-consciously *acknowledge* difference, working to diminish the impact of potentially intimidating representations of masculinity (as in voice tone, body size) in the practices of care. They *make strategic use* of difference – as nurses for example deploy masculinity in potentially threatening situations to signal authority and control, even though this is presented as contrary to personal dispositions by some men. Men therefore 'do' a traditional masculinity while also, through reflexive recognition of its deployment, contribute to its undoing.

These dynamics of difference alert us to the complicated ways in which men do gender and do difference, as well as to their undoing, in organizations. Lines of inclusion and exclusion, rendered more visible through the experiences of men in non-traditional work contexts, are not fixed or totally definitive, but are from Fournier (2002) 'contingent, temporal and liable to shift' and are drawn in complicated ways to define a sense of self.

Researching men

In Chapter 1, the modest claim of the book was made namely to further our understanding of men's subjective experiences in the specificities of their gender-atypical work contexts and of how they themselves make sense of those experiences as they manage a sense of self. In so doing, the book has added to existing work on men and masculinity – developed originally to redress their absence in mainstream academic research.

As Mac an Ghaill (1994) has argued, this absence has reflected the universal nature of men's 'first-class' status. Men have been seen as the normative standard case – their dominance and universality precluding the need for further analysis. Their subjectivity and experiences have been construed as constituting objective knowledge, while women's activities have been 'privatized and written out of history'. The universalization of men's experiences has allowed a neglect of gender and has obscured gender power relations as well as the male advantage. Therefore, as Collinson and Hearn (1994) have argued, literature on organizations has traditionally failed to problematize gender, men or masculinity. From their perspective, by placing men and masculinity at the centre of the analysis, we can try to overcome past tendencies to view men as generically human. By particularizing men's knowledge claims, pretensions to universality can be challenged. Moreover, the study of men and masculinity can serve to 'take the focus off women' as the (one and only) problem to be explained – and help to diversify and differentiate men's experiences beyond a single focus on patriarchy, the conceptual entity that had under some previous feminist research, incorporated the totality of gender relations.

This book therefore goes some way to redress the above imbalance and to explore men's experiences as gendered subjects, that is, not as the universal standard case but as men. It is by making men and masculinity explicit, as Collinson and Hearn (1994) have argued, that we can simultaneously and paradoxically assist in the de-centring of men and masculinity in discourse. This involves making problematic the ways in which men and masculinity may be conventionally seen to be at the centre of discourse and more generally as the dominants' foundation.

This raises the question of how we can research men when they have been the centre of knowledge and of power. How then do we study men, focusing on the lived experiences of their lives, without reproducing another patriarchally based 'vision' and a consciousness that re-excludes women and femininities? From Brod and Kaufman (1994), some of these problems can be overcome if men and masculinities are consistently located within relations of power – positioned with women as well as with other men. As Messner (1992) suggests, this may involve a 'tricky balancing act' of integrating personal experiences of, for example, lack of power with the 'promise' and the reality of masculine privilege. It is through the concrete examination of men's lives that the social mechanisms of male power over women and over other men are revealed. For Connell (1987) these political tensions can be understood if a feminist approach is adopted that focuses on process and struggle around hegemonic and subordinated masculinities. This may for example involve an exploration of how men create difference and exclude women – or how they create rituals, reaffirm symbolic differences, establish internal hierarchies and exclude, dominate, stigmatize women and non-conforming men.

Through the research sites presented some of these processes and struggles have been revealed. As such, the book has explored the complexities inherent within gender relations and the micro-practices of power – as men have activated difference, drawn on sameness and colonized (revalued) characteristics of marginalized groups. These research sites have presented fertile ground for highlighting some of these complicated gender practices which might otherwise be hidden from view. In this respect, as Sargent (2001) points out, it is through the study of men in non-traditional roles that we can uncover men's unique experiences of gender and, by inquiring into their subjective experiences of the gender order, reveal how men feel as men. 'Non-hegemonic' men may be at 'ground zero' of a potential chain reaction of change – and the consequence of their presence may 'produce artefacts that we can read and thus gain insights into gender that were previously hidden.' (Sargent, 2001: 11). As Morgan (1992) has argued, the biographies of such men can reveal challenges to the gender order through their simultaneous experiences of marginalization and privilege. By uncovering men's unique experiences of gender in these contexts, we can further our understanding of the sex/gender system as a whole. This encourages an analysis of the relationships between hegemonic and subordinated masculinities and how this can lead to the subordination of both men and women. These understandings may become more possible in contexts where contradictions within and challenges to the gender order are afforded greater visibility – such as where masculinity is under strain in non-traditional roles.

Final comments

This book has explored various aspects of men's non-traditional occupational experience in four 'feminine' occupations from career entry dynamics to how men see women and women see men in these roles. Through the themes of identity, visibility and emotions, as well as through their intersection, it has provided a lens for uncovering some of the difficulties and challenges encountered as men manage identities in gender-atypical contexts. By exploring issues pertaining to each occupation (space, bodies, professionalism, social identity), it has highlighted the occupationally specific nature of some of these experiences and of the ways in which men draw on, activate and negotiate difference. In this respect, as discussed in Chapter 1, it is not argued here that these are the only lenses through which to understand how men manage gender in these contexts. Post-structuralist-influenced research is based on the principle of the possibility of a plurality of views and multiple meanings. This book presents one of many possible interpretations and understandings, but I hope it will go some way to uncover the complexities involved in 'doing' gender in organizations and, more specifically, how men negotiate between masculinity and femininity and manage difference in work involving service and care.

References

Acker, J. (1990) 'Hierarchies, Jobs, Bodies: A Theory of Gendered Organization', *Gender & Society*, 4: 139–158.

Adib, A. and Guerrier, Y. (2003) 'The Interlocking of Gender with Nationality, Race, Ethnicity and Class: The Narratives of Women in Hotel Work', *Gender Work and Organization*, 10 (4): 413–432.

Adkins, L. (1995) *Gendered Work*. Buckingham: Open University Press.

Adkins, L. (2001) 'Cultural Feminisation: Money, Sex and Power for Women', *Signs*, 26 (3): 669–695.

Adkins, L. (2003) 'Reflexivity: Freedom or Habit of Gender', *Theory, Culture and Society*, 20 (6): 21–42.

Ainsworth, S. and Hardy, C. (2004) 'Critical Discourse Analysis and Identity: Why Bother?' *Critical Discourser Studies*, 1 (2): 225–259.

Albert, S. and Whetten, D. (2004) 'Organizational Identity', in M.J. Hatch and M. Schultz (Eds) *Organizational Identity* (pp. 89–118). Oxford: Oxford University Press.

Albrow, M. (1992) 'Sine Ira et Studio or Do Organizations have Feelings', *Organization Studies*, 13 (3): 313–329.

Allan, J. (1993) 'Male Elementary Teachers, Experiences and Perspectives', in C. Williams (Ed) *Doing Women's Work: Men in Non-Traditional Occupations* (pp. 10–28). London: Sage.

Alvesson, M. (1998) 'Gender Relations and Identity at Work: A Case Study of Masculinities and Femininities in an Advertising Agency', *Human Relations*, 51 (8): 969–1005.

Alvesson, M. and Deetz, S. (2000) *Doing Critical Management Research*. London: Sage.

Amble, N. and Gjerberg, E. (2003) 'Emotional Labour and Mastering Practice', *Sosiologisk tidsskrift*, 11 (3): 248–272.

Ashcraft, K. (2006) 'Back to Work: Sights/Sites of Difference in Gender and Organizational Communication Studies', in Bonnie J. Dow and Julia T. Wood (Eds) *The Sage Handbook of Gender and Communication* (pp. 97–122). Thousand Oaks, CA: Sage.

Ashforth, B. and Mael, F. (2004) 'Social Identity Theory and the Organization', in M.J. Hatch and M. Schultz (Eds) *Organizational Identity: A Reader* (pp. 134–160). Oxford: Oxford University Press.

Australia Bureau of Statistics. (2006) *Schools*. Canberra.

Australian Institute of Health and Welfare. (2007) *Nursing and Midwifery Labour Force*, Labour Force Series No 39. Canberra: AIHW.

Baldry, C. (1999) 'Space – The Final Frontier', *Sociology*, 33 (3): 535–553.

Barrett, F. (1996) 'The Organizational Construction of Hegemonic Masculinity: The Case of the US Navy', *Gender Work and Organization*, 3 (3): 129–141.

Barrett, F. (2001) 'Hegemonic Masculinity: The US Navy', in S. Whitehead and F. Barrett (Eds) *The Masculinities Reader* (pp. 77–99). Cambridge: Polity Press.

172

Baumeister, R. and Leary, M. (1995) 'The Need to Belong: Desire for Interpersonal Attachments as a Fundamental Human Motivation', *Psychological Bulletin*, 117: 479–529.

Beck, U., Giddens, A. and Lash, S. (1994) *Reflexive Modernisation: Politics, Tradition and Aesthetics in the Modern Social Order*. Cambridge: Polity Press.

Beech, N. and McInnes, P. (2005) 'Now where was I? Questioning Assumptions of Consistent Identity', in A. Pullen and S. Linstead (Eds) *Organization and Identity* (pp. 23–42). London: Routledge.

Benwell, B. and Stokoe, E. (2006) *Discourse and Identity*. Edinburgh: Edinburgh University Press.

Biskup, P. (August 1994) 'Gender and Status in Australian Librarianship: Some Issues', *Australian Library Journal*, 165–179.

Bly, R. (1990) *Iron John*. New York: Addison-Wesley.

Bologh, R. (1990) *Love or Greatness: Max Weber and Masculine Thinking – A Feminist Enquiry*. London: Unwin Hyman.

Bolton, S. (2004) 'Conceptual Confusions: Emotion Work as Skilled Work', in C. Warhurst, E. Keep and I. Grugulis (Eds) *The Skills That Matter* (pp. 19–37). London: Palgrave.

Bolton, S. (2005a) *Emotion Management in the Workplace*. London: Palgrave.

Bolton, S. (2005b) 'Women's Work, Dirty Work: The Gynaecology Nurse as Other', *Gender Work and Organization*, 12 (2): 169–186.

Bolton, S. (2007) 'Emotion Work as Human Connection: Gendered Emotion Codes in Teaching Primary Children with Emotional and Behavioural Difficulties', in P. Lewis and R. Simpson (Eds) *Gendering Emotions in Organizations* (pp. 17–34). Basingstoke, Hampshire: Palgrave Macmillan.

Bolton, S. and Boyd, C. (2003) 'Trolley Dolly or Skilled Emotion Manager? Moving on from Hochschild's Managed Heart', *Work Employment and Society*, 17 (2): 289–308.

Bourdieu, P. (1990) *In Other Words: Towards a Reflexive Sociology*. Cambridge: Polity Press.

Bradley, H. (1993) 'Across the Great Divide', in C. Williams (Ed) *Doing Women's Work: Men in Non-Traditional Occupations* (pp. 10–28). London: Sage.

Brannen, M. (2005) 'Once More with Feeling: Ethnographic Reflections on the Mediation of Tensions in a Small Team of Call Centre Workers', *Gender Work and Organization*, 2 (5): 420–439.

Breckler, S. and Greenwald, A. (1986) 'Motivational Facets of the Self', in E. Higgins and R. Sorrentino (Eds) *Handbook of Motivation and Cognition* (Vol. 1, pp. 62–80). New York: Guilford Press.

Brewer, M. (1991) 'The Social Self: On Being the Same and Different at the Same Time', *Personality and Social Psychology Bulletin*, 17: 475–482.

Brewer, M. and Gardner, W. (2004) 'Who is This "We"? Levels of Collective Identity and Self Representations', in M.J. Hatch and M. Schultz (Eds) *Organizational Identity* (pp. 66–88). Oxford: Oxford University Press.

Brod, H. and Kaufman, M. (Eds) (1994) *Theorizing Masculinity*. London: Sage.

Bruni, A. and Gherardi, S. (2002) 'Omega's Story: The Heterogeneous Engineering of a Gendered Professional Self', in M. Dent and S. Whitehead (Eds) *Managing Professional Identities: Knowledge Performativity and the New Professional* (pp. 174–200). London: Routledge.

Butler, J. (1990) *Gender Trouble: Feminism and the Subversion of Identity*. London: Routledge.

Butler, J. (1993) *Bodies that Matter: On the Discursive Limits of Sex*. London: Routledge.

Butler, J. (1994) 'Gender as Performance: An Interview with Judith Butler', *Radical Philosophy*, 67: 32–39.

Butler, J. (1999) *Gender Trouble: Feminism and the Subversion of Identity*. London: Routledge.

Butler, J. (2004) *Undoing Gender*. New York and London: Routledge.

Cameron, C. (2001) 'Promise or Problem? A Review of the Literature of Men Working in Early Childhood Services', *Gender Work and Organization*, 8 (4): 430–453.

Cammack, J. and Phillips, D. (2002) 'Discourses and Subjectivities of the Gendered Teacher', *Gender and Education*, 14 (2): 123–133.

Carmichael, J. (October–December 1992) 'The Male Librarian and the Feminine Image: A Survey of Stereotype, Status and Gender Perceptions', *Library and Information Science Research*, 14: 411–446.

Chia, R. (1996) 'Teaching Paradigm Shifting in Management Education: University Business Schools and the Entrepreneurial Imagination', *Journal of Management Studies*, 33 (4): 409–428.

Chung, Y. and Harman, L. (1994) 'Career Interests and Aspirations of Gay Men', *Journal of Vocational Behaviour*, 45: 223–239.

Chusmir, L. (1990) 'Men who Make Non-traditional Career Choices', *Journal of Counselling and Development*, 69: 11–15.

Cockburn, C. (1983) *Brothers: Male Dominance and Technological Change*. London: Pluto Press.

Cockburn, C. (1985) *Machinery of Dominance*. London: Pluto Press.

Cockburn, C. (1991) *In the Way of Women*. London: MacMillan.

Collinson, D. (1994) 'Strategies of Resistance: Power, Knowledge and Subjectivity in the Workplace', in J. Jermier, D. Knights and W. Nord (Eds) *Resistance and Power in Organizations* (pp. 26–38). London: Routledge.

Collinson, D. (2003) 'Identities and Insecurities: Selves at Work', *Organization*, 10 (3): 527–548.

Collinson, D. and Hearn, J. (1994) 'Naming Men as Men: Implications for Work, Organization and Management', *Gender Work and Organization*, 1 (1): 2–22.

Connell, R. (1987) *Gender and Power*. Cambridge: Polity Press.

Connell, R. (1995) *Masculinities*. California: University of California Press.

Connell, R. (2000) *The Men and the Boys*. Cambridge: Polity Press.

Creswell, J. (2007) *Qualitative Inquiry and Research Design, Choosing among Five Approaches*. London: Sage.

Cross, S. and Bagilhole, B. (2002) 'Girl's Jobs for the Boys? Men, Masculinity and Non-traditional Occupations', *Gender Work and Organization*, 9 (2): 204–226.

Crouch, D. (2003) 'Spacing, Performing and Becoming: Tangles in the Mundane', *Environment and Planning*, 35: 1945–1960.

Czarniawska, B. and Hopfl, H. (2002) 'Casting the Other: Introduction', in B. Czarniawska and H. Hopfl (Eds) *Casting the Other: The Production and Maintenance of Inequalities in Work Organizations* (pp. 1–6). London and New York: Routledge.

Dahle, R. (2005) 'Men Bodies and Nursing', in D. Morgan, B. Brandth and E. Kvande (Eds) *Gender Bodies and Work* (pp. 127–138). Hampshire: Ashgate.

Davies, C. (1996) 'The Sociology of the Professions and the Professions of Gender', *Sociology*, 30 (4): 661–678.

Davies, A. and Thomas, R. (2004) 'Gendering Resistance in the Public Services', in R. Thomas, A. Mills and J. Helms Mills (Eds) *Identity Politics at Work: Resisting Gender, Gendering Resistance* (pp. 105–122). London: Routledge.

De Beauvoir, S. (1949) *The Second Sex*. Jonathen Cape: London.

DeCorse, C. and Vogtle, S. (1997) 'In a Complex Voice: The Contradictions of Male Elementary Teachers' Career Choice and Professional Identity', *Journal of Teacher Education*, 48: 37–46.

Dellinger, K. (Winter 2002) 'Wearing Gender and Sexuality "On Your Sleeve": Dress Norms and the Importance of Occupational and Organizational Culture at Work', *Gender Issues*, 3–25.

Dent, M. and Whitehead, S. (2002) 'Configuring the New Professional', in M. Dent and S. Whitehead (Eds) *Managing Professional Identities: Knowledge, Performativity and the 'New' Professional* (pp. 1–16). London: Routledge.

Department for Children, Schools and Families. (DCSF) (January 2007) *School Workforce in England*. London.

Deutsch, F. (2007) 'Undoing Gender', *Gender & Society*, 21 (1): 106–127.

Dillabough, J. (1999) 'Gender Politics and Conceptions of the Modern Teacher: Women, Identity and Professionalism', *British Journal of the Sociology of Education*, 20 (3): 373–394.

Dodge, M. and Kitchin, R. (2005) 'Code and the Transduction of Space', *Annals of the Association of American Geographers*, 95 (1): 162–178.

Douglas, M. (1966) *Purity and Danger: An Analysis of Concepts of Pollution and Taboos*. London: Routledge and Kegan Paul.

Dutton, J., Dukerich, J. and Harquail, C. (1994) 'Organizational Images and Member Identification', *Administrative Science Quarterly*, 39: 239–263.

Eagly, A. (1987) *Sex Differences in Social Behaviour: A Social Role Interpretation*. Hillsdale, NJ: Erlbaum.

Eagly, A., Wood, W. and Diekman, A. (2000) 'Social Role Theory of Sex Differences and Similarities: A Current Appraisal', in Eckes, T. and Trautner, H. (Eds) *The Developmental Social Psychology of Gender* (pp. 363–390). Mahwah, NJ: Erlbaum.

Elsbach, K. and Kramer, R. (2004) 'Organizational Identity Threats', in M.J. Hatch and M. Schultz (Eds) *Organizational Identity: A Reader* (pp. 469–509). Oxford: Oxford University Press.

Ely, R. and Padavic, I. (2007) 'A Feminist Analysis of Organizational Research in Sex Differences', *Academy of Management Review*, 32 (4): 1121–1143.

Eriksson, P. and Kovalainen, A. (2008) *Qualitative Methods in Business Research*. London: Sage.

Essers, E. and Benschop, Y. (2007) 'Enterprising Identities: Female Entrepreneurs of Moroccan or Turkish Origin', *Organization Studies*, 28 (1):49–69.

Evans, J. (1992) 'A Historical Study of Men in Nursing', *Journal of Advanced Nursing*, 26: 232–236.

Evans, J. (1997) 'Men in Nursing: Exploring the Male Nurse Experience', *Nursing Enquiry*, 4: 142–145.

Evans, J. (1997) 'Men in Nursing: Issues of Gender Segregation and Hidden Advantage', *Journal of Advanced Nursing*, 26: 226–231.

Equal Opportunities Commission EOC. (2006) *Facts about Men and Women in Great Britain*. UK: Manchester.

Evans, J. (2002) 'Cautious Caregivers: Gender Stereotypes and the Sexualisation of Men Nurses' Touch', *Journal of Advanced Nursing*, 40 (4): 441–448.

Evans, J. (2004) 'Bodies Matter: Men Masculinity and the Gendered Division of Labour in Nursing', *Journal of Occupational Science*, 11 (1): 14–22.

Faludi, S. (1992) *Backlash: The Undeclared War against Women*. London: Chatto and Windus.

Farmer, H. and Chung, Y. (1995) 'Variables Related to Career Commitment, Mastery, Motivation and Level of Career Aspiration among College Students', *Journal of Career Development*, 21 (4): 265–278.

Fassinger, R. (1991) 'The Hidden Minority: Issues and Challenges of Working with Lesbian Women and Gay Men', *The Counseling Psychologist*, 19: 157–176.

Fenstermaker, S. and West, C. (Eds) (2002) *Doing Gender, Doing Difference*. London: Routledge.

Ferguson, K. (1984) *The Feminist Case Against Bureaucracy*. Philadelphia: Temple University Press.

Fineman, S. (2000) *Emotions in Organizations*. London: Sage.

Flannigan-Saint-Aubin, A. (1994) 'The Male Body and Literary Metaphors for Masculinity', in H. Brod and M. Kaufman (Eds) *Theorizing Masculinity* (pp. 239–258). London: Sage.

Fletcher, J. (1999) *Disappearing Acts: Gender Power and Relational Practices at Work*. Cambridge, MA: MIT Press.

Fletcher, J. (2003) 'The Greatly Exaggerated Demise of Heroic Leadership: Gender Power and the Myth of the Female Advantage', in R.J. Ely, E. Foldy and M.A. Scully (Eds) *Reader in Gender Work and Organization* (pp. 204–210). Victoria Australia: Blackwell.

Floge, L. and Merrill, D. (1986) 'Tokenism Reconsidered: Male Nurses and Female Physicians in a Hospital Setting', *Social Forces*, 64 (4): 925–947.

Fondas, N. (1997) 'Feminization Unveiled: Management Qualities in Contemporary Writings', *Academy of Management Review*, 22 (1): 257–282.

Forseth, U. (2005) 'Gender Matters? Exploring How Gender is Negotiated in Service Encounters', *Gender Work and Organization*, 12 (5): 440–459.

Foucault, M. (1977) *Discipline and Punish: The Birth of the Prison*. Harmondsworth: Penguin.

Foucault, M. (1985) *The Use of Pleasure*. Harmondsworth: Penguin.

Fournier, V. (1999) 'The Appeal to "Professionalism" as a Disciplinary Mechanism', *The Sociological Review*, 47 (2): 280–307.

Fournier, V. (2002) 'Keeping the Veil of Otherness: Practising Disconnection', in B. Czarniawska and H. Hopfl (Eds) *Casting the Other: The Production and Maintenance of Inequalities in Work Organizations* (pp. 68–88). London: Routledge.

Frank, B. (1993) 'The "New Men's Studies" and Feminism: Promise or Danger?' in T. Haddad (Ed) *Men and Masculinities: A Critical Anthology* (pp. 333–343). Toronto: Canadian Scholars press.

Galbraith, M. (1992) 'Understanding the Career Choices of Men in Elementary Education', *Journal of Educational Research*, 85 (4): 246–253.

Gatens, M. (1991) *Feminism and Philosophy: Perspectives on Difference and Equality*. Cambridge: Polity Press.

Geertz, C. (1973) *The Interpretation of Cultures*. New York: Basic Books.

Gerstel, N. and Gallagher, S. (2001) 'Men's Care-Giving: Gender and the Contingent Nature of Care', *Gender and Society*, 15 (2): 197–217.

Gherardi, S. (1995) *Gender, Symbolism and Organizational Culture*. London: Sage.

Gherardi, S. and Poggio, B. (2001) 'Creating and Recreating Gender in Organizations', *Journal of World Business*, 36 (3): 245–259.

Ghidina, M. (1992) 'Social Relations and the Definition of Work: Identity Management in a Low Status Occupation', *Qualitative Sociology*, 15 (1): 73–85.

Giddens, A. (1991) *Modernity and Self Identity: Self and Society in the Late Modern Age*. Cambridge: Polity Press.

Giddens, A. (1992) *The Transformation of Intimacy: Sexuality, Love and Eroticism in Modern Societies*. Cambridge: Polity Press.

Gilligan, C. (1982) *In a Different Voice: Psychological Theory and Women's Development*, Cambridge, MA: Harvard University Press.

Goffman, I. (1959) *The Presentation of Self in Everyday Life*. Harmondsworth: Penguin Books.

Goffman, E. (1980) *The Presentation of Self in Everyday Life*, 8th Edition. London: Penguin.

Goleman, D. (2004) 'What Makes a Leader?' *Harvard Business Review*, 82 (1): 82–91.

Gottfredson, L. (1981) 'Circumscription and Compromise: A Developmental Theory of Occupational Aspirations', *Journal of Counselling Psychology*, 28: 545–579.

Gottfredson, L. and Lapan, R. (1997) 'Assessing Gender Based Circumscription of Occupational Aspirations', *Journal of Career Assessment*, 5 (4): 419–441.

Greenwald, A. and Breckler, S. (1985) 'To Whom the Self Presented?' in B. Schlenker (Ed) *The Self and Social Life* (pp. 39–52). New York: McGraws Hill.

Gregson, N. and Rose, G. (2000) 'Taking Butler Elsewhere: Performativities, Spatialities and Subjectivities', *Environment and Planning D: Society and Space*, 18: 433–452.

Grey, C. (1999) ' "We are all Managers Now"; "We Always Were": On the Development and Demise of Management', *Journal of Management Studies*, 36 (5): 561–585.

Grey, C. (2002) 'What are Business Schools for?' *Journal of Management Education*, 26 (5): 496–511.

Grey, C. (2004) 'Reinventing Business Schools: The Contribution of Critical Management Education', *Academy of Management Learning and Development*, 3 (2):178–187.

Grosz, E. (1994) *Volatile Bodies: Towards a Corporeal Feminism*. London: Allen and Unwin.

Guerrier, Y. and Adib, A. (2004) 'Gendered Identities in the Work of Overseas Tour Reps', *Gender Work and Organization*, 13 (3): 334–350.

Gutek, B., Cherry, B., Bhappu, A., Scheneider, S. and Woolf, L. (2000) 'Features of Service Relationships and Encounters', *Work and Occupations*, 27 (3): 319–352.

Haddon, G. (1988) *Body Metaphors: Releasing God-Feminine in All of Us*. New York: Crossroads.

Hakim, C. (2000) *Work–Lifestyle Choices in the 21st Century*. Oxford: Oxford University Press.

Halford, S. and Leonard, P. (2006a) 'Place, Space and Time: The Fragmentation of Workplace Subjectivities. *Organizational Studies*. 27 (5): 657–676.

Halford, S. and Leonard, P. (2006b) *Negotiating Gendered Identities at Work: Place, Space and Time*. Basingstoke, Hampshire: Palgrave MacMillan.

Hall, E. (1993) 'Smiling, Deferring and Flirting: Doing Gender by Giving Good Service', *Work and Occupations*, 20 (4): 452–471.

Hall, A., Hockey, J. and Robinson, V. (2007) 'Occupational Cultures and the Embodiment of Masculinity: Hairdressing, Estate Agency and Firefighting', *Gender Work and Organization*, 14 (6): 535–551.

Haraway, D. *Simians, Cyborgs and Women: The Reinvention of Nature*. New York and London: Routledge.

Harding, S. (Ed) (1987) *Feminism and Methodology*. Bloomington, IN: University Press.

Hassard, J., Holliday, R. and Willmott, H. (2000) *Body and Organization*. London: Sage.

Hearn, J. (1993) 'Emotive Subjects: Organizational Men, Organizational Masculinities and the (De)construction of Emotions', in S. Fineman (Ed) *Emotion in Organization* (pp. 142–166). London: Sage.

Hearn, J. (1994) 'Changing Men and Changing Management: Social Change, Social Research and Social Action', in M. Davidson and R. Burke (Eds) *Women in Management: Current Research Issues* (pp. 192–212). London: Paul Chapman.

Hearn, J. (1996) 'Deconstructing the Dominant: Making the One(s) the Other(s)', *Organization*, 3 (4): 611–626.

Heikes, E. (1991) 'When Men are in the Minority: The Case of Men in Nursing', *The Sociological Quarterly*, 32 (3): 389–401.

Heilman, M. (1997) 'Sex Discrimination and the Affirmative Action Remedy: The Role of Sex Stereotypes', *Journal of Business Ethics*, 16 (9): 877–899.

Henson, K. and Rogers, J.K. (2001) ' "Why Marcia You've Changed!" Male Temporary Clerical Workers Doing Masculinity in a Feminized Occupation', *Gender and Society*, 15 (2): 218–238.

Hickey, A. (May 2006) 'Cataloguing Men: Charting the Male Librarian's Experience Through the Perceptions and Positions of Men in Libraries', *The Journal of Academic Librarianship*, 32 (3): 286–295.

Hochschild, A. (1983) *The Managed Heart: Commercialisation of Feeling*. Berkeley: University of California Press.

Hogg, M. and Abrams, D. (1988) *Social Identifications: A Social Psychology of Intergroup Relations and Group Processes*. London: Routledge.

Holland, J. (1959) 'A Theory of Vocational Choice', *Journal of Counselling Psychology*, 6: 35–45.

Holland, J. (1962) 'Some Explorations of a Theory of Vocational Choice', *Psychologial Monographs*, 76 (26): 1–545.

Holland, J. (1966) *The Psychology of Vocational Choice*, Waltham, MA: Blaisdell.

Holland, J. (1982) 'The SDS Helps Both Females and Males: A Comment', *Vocational Guidance Quarterly*, 30 (3): 195–197.

Information Centre for Health and Social Care. (March 2008) *NHS Staff 1997–2007*.

Irigaray, L. (1985) *The Sex Which is Not One*. Ithaca: Cornell University Press.

Irigaray, L. (1991) *Philosophy of the Feminine*. London: Routledge.
Isaksen, L. (2005) 'Gender and Care: The Role of Cultural Ideas of Dirt and Disgust', in D. Morgan, B. Brandth and E. Kvande (Eds) *Gender Bodies and Work* (pp. 115–126). Hampshire: Ashgate.
Jacobs, J. (1989) *Revolving Doors: Sex Segregation and Women's Careers*. Stanford, CA: Stanford University Press.
James, N. (1993) 'Divisions of Emotional Labour: Disclosure and Cancer', in S. Fineman (Ed) *Emotion in Organization* (pp. 94–117). London: Sage.
Jardine, A. (1985) *Gynesis: Configurations of Woman and Modernity*. Ithaca: Cornell University press.
Johnson, P., Buehring, A., Cassell, C. and Symon, G. (2006) 'Evaluating Qualitative Research: Towards a Contingent Criteriology', *International Journal of Management Reviews*, 8 (3): 131–156.
Kanter, R. (1977) *Men and Women of the Corporation*. New York: Basic Books.
Kaufman, M. (1994) 'Men, Feminism and Men's Contradictory Experiences of Power', in H. Brod and M. Kaufman (Eds) *Theorizing Masculinities* (pp. 142–164). London: Sage.
Keenoy, T. and Oswick, C. (2003) 'Organizing Textscapes', *Organization Studies*, 25 (1): 135–142.
Kelan, E. (2008) 'Emotions in a Rational Profession: The Gendering of Skills in ICT Work', *Gender Work and Organization*, 15 (1): 49–71.
Kerfoot, D. (2002) 'Managing the "Professional" Man', in M. Dent and S. Whitehead (Ed) *Managing Professional Identities: Knowledge, Performativity and the "New" Professional* (pp. 81–95). London: Routledge.
Kerfoot, D. and Knights, D. (1993) 'Management Masculinity and Manipulation: From Paternalism to Corporate Strategy in Financial Services in Britain', *Journal of Management Studies*, 30 (4): 659–677.
Kerfoot, D. and Knights, D. (1998) 'Managing Masculinity in Contemporary Organizational Life: A Man(agerial) Project, *Organization*, 5 (1): 7–26.
Kimmel, M. (1994) 'Masculinity as Homophobia: Fear Shame and Silence in the Construction of Gender Identity', in H. Brod and M. Kaufman (Eds) *Theorising Masculinities* (pp. 119–141), London: Sage.
Knights, D. (December 2001) 'The "New Economy" and the "New Man": Virtual Transitions or Transitional Virtualities', *Keynote Address to Asia-Pacific Researchers in Organization Studies Conference*. Hong Kong: Baptist University.
Knights, D. and McCabe, D. (2001) 'A Different World: Shifting Masculinities in the Transition to Call Centres', *Organization*, 8 (4): 619–645.
Knights, D. and Surman, E. (2008) 'Editorial: Addressing the Gender Gap in Studies of Emotion', *Gender, Work and Organization*, 15 (1): 1–8.
Kondo, D. (1990) *Crafting Selves: Power, Gender and Discourses of Identity in a Japanese Workplace*. Chicago: University of Chicago Press.
Korczynski, M. (2001) 'The Contradictions of Service Work: The Call Centre as Customer Oriented Bureaucracy', in A. Sturdy and I. Grugulis and H. Willmott (Eds) *Customer Service: Empowerment or Entrapment* (pp. 79–101). Basingstoke: Palgrave MacMillan.
Korczynski, M. (2003) 'Communities of Coping: Collective Emotional Labour in Service Work', *Organization*, 10 (1): 55–79.
Kornberger, M. and Clegg, S. (2004) 'Bringing Space Back in: Organizing the Generative Building', *Organization Studies*, 25 (7): 1095–1114.

Lash, S. (1993) 'Reflexive Modernization: The Aesthetic Dimension', *Theory Culture and Society*, 10 (1): 1–23.

Lefebvre, H. (1991) *The Production of Space*. Trans. D. Nicholson-Smith. Oxford, UK: Blackwell.

Legge, K. (1987) 'Women in Personnel Management', in A. Spence and D. Podmore (Eds) *In a Man's World* (pp. 33–60). London: Tavistock.

Leidner, R. (1991) 'Serving Hamburgers and Selling Insurance: Gender Work and Identity in Interactive Service Jobs', *Gender and Society*, 5 (2): 154–177.

Leonard, P. (2002) 'Organizing Gender? Looking at Metaphors as Frames of Meaning in Gender/Organization Texts', *Gender Work and Organization*, 9 (1): 60–80.

Lewis, P. (2005) 'Suppression or Expression: An Exploration of Emotion Management in a Special Care Baby Unit', *Work Employment and Society*, 19 (3): 565–581.

Lewis, P. (2007) 'Emotion Work and Emotion Space in a Special Care Baby Unit', in P. Lewis and R. Simpson (Eds) *Gendering Emotions in Organizations* (pp. 75–88). Basingstoke, Hampshire: Palgrave.

Lewis, P. and Simpson, R. (2007) (Eds) *Gendering Emotion in Organizations*. London: Palgrave.

Lupton, B. (2000) 'Maintaining Masculinity: Men Who do Women's Work', *British Journal of Management*, 11, S33–S48.

Lupton, B. (2006) 'Explaining Men's Entry into Female Concentrated Occupations: Issues of Masculinity and Class', *Gender Work and Organization*, 13 (2): 103.

Mac an Ghaill, M. (1994) *The Making of Men*. Philadelphia: Open University Press.

Macdonald, C. and Sirianni, C. (1996) *Working in the Service Society*. Philadelphia: Temple University Press.

Mackenzie, A. (2002) *Transductions: Bodies and Machines at Speed*. London: Continuum Press.

Maddock, S. (1999) *Challenging Women: Gender Culture and Organization*. London: Sage.

Moloney, M. and Fenstermaker, S. (2002) 'Performance and Accomplishment: Reconciling Feminist Conceptions of Gender', in S. Fenstermaker and C. West (Eds) *Doing Gender, Doing Difference* (pp. 189–204). London: Routledge.

Mangan, P. (1994) 'Private Lives', *Nursing Times*, 90 (14): 60.

Marsh, K. and Musson, G. (2008) 'Men at Work and Home: Managing Emotion in Telework', *Gender Work and Organization*, 15 (1): 31–48.

Martin, P.Y. (2003) ' "Said and Done" versus "Saying and Doing": Gendering Practices, Practicing Gender at Work', *Gender and Society*, 17 (3): 342–366.

Martin, P.Y. (2006) 'Practising Gender at Work: Further Thoughts on Reflexivity', *Gender Work and Organization*, 13 (3): 254–276.

Massey, D. (1994) *Space, Place and Gender*. London: Methuan.

Massey, D. (2005) *For Space*. London: Sage.

Matthews, S. and Heidorn, J. (1998) 'Meeting Filial Responsibilities in Brother Only Sibling Groups', *Journal of Gerontology: Social Science*, 53B: S278–S286.

Matthews, S. and Rosner, T. (1988) 'Shared Filial Responsibility: The Family as Primary Caregiver', *Journal of Marriage and the Family*, 50: 185–195.

McDowell, L. (1997) *Capital Culture: Gender at Work in the City*. Oxford: Blackwell.

McDowell, L. and Pringle, R. (1992) *Defining Women*. Buckingham: The Open University Polity Press.

McNay, L. (2000) *Gender and Agency: Reconfiguring the Subject in Feminist and Social Theory*. Cambridge: Polity Press.

Messner, M. (1992) *Power at Play: Sports and the Problem of Masculinity*. Boston, MA: Beacon Press.

Metcalfe, B. and Linstead, A. (2003) 'Gendering Teamwork: Re-Writing the Feminine', *Gender Work and Organization*, 10 (1): 94–119.

Milligan, F. (2001) 'The Concept of Care in Male Nurse Work: An Ontological Hermeneutic Study in Acute Hospitals', *Journal of Advanced Nursing*, 35 (1): 7–16.

Mills, A. (1995) 'Cockpits, Hangars, Boys and Galleys: Corporate Masculinities and the Development of British Airways', *Gender Work and Organization*, 5 (3): 172–188.

Monaghan, L. (2002) 'Regulating "Unruly" Bodies: Work Tasks, Conflict and Violence in Britain's Night-Time Economy', *British Journal of Sociology*, 53 (3): 403–429.

Morgan, D. (1992) *Discovering Men*. London: Routledge.

Morgan, D., Brandth, B. and Kvande, E. (2005) 'Thinking About Gender, Bodies and Work', in D. Morgan, B. Brandth and E. Kvande (Eds) *Gender Bodies and Work* (pp. 1–18). Hampshire: Ashgate.

Morgan, G. and Knights, D. (1991) 'Gendering Jobs: Corporate Strategy, Managerial Control and the Dynamics of Job Segregation', *Work Employment and Society*, 5 (2): 181–200.

Morris, A. and Feldman, D. (1996) 'The Dimensions, Antecedents and Consequences of Emotional Labour', *Academy of Management Review*, 21 (4): 996–1010.

Morrisey, L. and Case, D. (September1988) 'There Goes My Image: Perceptions of Male Librarians by Students, Colleagues and Self', *College and Research Libraries*, 453–464.

Mulholland, K. (2002) 'Gender Emotional Labour and teamworking in a call centre', *Personnel Review*, 31 (3): 283–303.

Mumby, D. and Putnam, L. (1992) 'A Feminist Reading of Bounded Rationality', *Academy of Management Review*, 17 (3): 465–496.

Murray, S. (1996) '"We all love Charles": Men in Childcare and the Social Construction of Gender', *Gender and Society*, 10 (4): 368–385.

NSW Department of Education and Training. (2006) Annual Report 2006 DET Sydney. 84–85.

Parkin, W. (1993) 'The Public and the Private: Gender Sexuality and Emotion', in S. Fineman (Ed) *Emotion in Organizations* (pp. 167–189). London: Sage.

Perriton, L. (1999) 'The Provocative and Evocative Gaze upon Women in Management Development', *Gender and Education*, 11 (3): 295–307.

Pierce, J.L. (1995) *Gender Trials. Emotional Lives in Contemporary Law Firms*. Berkeley, CA: University of Californai Press.

Pierce, J. (2003) 'Racing for Innocence: Whiteness, Corporate Culture and the Backlash Against Affirmative Action', *Qualitative Sociology*, 26 (1): 53–70.

Piper, P. and Collamer, B. (September 2001) 'Male Librarians: Men in a Feminized Profession', *Journal of Academic Librarianship*, 27 (5): 406–411.

Powell, G. and Butterfield, D. (2003) 'Gender, Gender Identity and Aspirations', *Women in Management Review*, 18 (1, 2): 88–96.

Prasad, A. and Prasad, P. (2000) 'Everyday Struggles at the Workplace: The Nature and Implications of Routine Resistance in Contemporary Organizations', *Research in the Sociology of Organizations*, 15: 225–257.

Pringle, R. (1993) 'Male Secretaries', in C. Williams (Ed) *Doing Women's Work: Men in Non-traditional Occupations* (pp. 128–151). London: Sage.

Pullen, A. (2006) *Managing Identity*. London: Palgrave.

Pullen, A. and Knights, D. (2007) 'Undoing Gender in Organizations', *Gender, Work and Organization*, 14 (6): 505–511.

Pullen, A. and Linstead, S. (2005) *Organization and Identity*. London: Routledge.

Pullen, A. and Simpson, R. (November 2007) 'When the One becomes the Other: Men and Difference in Non-Traditional Occupations', *ASCOS Conference*. Auckland.

Rajchman, J. (1991) *Truth and Eros: Foucault, Lacan, and the Question of Ethics.* London: Taylor and Francis.

Ricoeur, P. (1991) 'Life: A Story in Search of a Narrator', in M. Valdes (Ed) *A Ricoeur Reader: Reflection and Imagination* (pp. 67–84). Hemel Hempstead: Harvester Wheatsheaf.

Robinson, S. (2000) *Marked Men: White Masculinity in Crisis*. New York: Columbia University Press.

Rose, G. (1999) 'Performing Space', in D. Massey, J. Allen and P. Sarre (Eds) *Human Geography Today* (pp. 65–72). Cambridge: Polity Press.

Ross-Smith, A. and Kornberger, M. (2004) 'Gendered Rationality: A Genealogical Exploration of the Philosophical and Sociological Conceptions of Rationality, Masculinity and Organization', *Gender Work and Organization*, 11 (3): 280–305.

Ross-Smith, A., Kornberger, M., Anandakumar, A. and Chesterman, C. (2007) 'Women Executives: Managing Emotions at the Top', in P. Lewis and R.Simpson (Eds) *Gendering Emotion in Organizations* (pp. 35–56). London: Palgrave.

Sargent, P. (2001) *Real Men or Real Teachers: Contradictions in the Lives of Men Elementary School Teachers*. Harriman, TN: Men's Studies Press.

Sass, J. (2000) 'Emotional Labour as Cultural Performance: The Communication of Care Giving in a Nonprofit Nursing Home', *Western Journal of Communications*, 64 (3): 330–358.

Schann, M. (1983) 'Career Plans of Men and Women in Gender Dominant Professions', *Journal of Vocational Behaviour*, 22: 343–356.

Schwandt (1994) 'Three Epistemological Stances for Qualitative Inquiry: Interpretivism, Hermeneutics and Social Constructionism', in N. Denzin and Y. Lincoln (Eds) *The Handbook of Qualitative Research* (pp 189–214). Thousand Oaks, CA: Sage.

Shu, X. and Marini, M. (1998) 'Gender-Related Change in Occupational Aspirations',*Sociology of Education*, 71 (1): 43–67.

Simpson, R. (1997) 'Have Times Changed? Career Barriers and the Token Woman Manager', *British Journal of Management*, 8: 121–129.

Simpson, R. (2000) 'Gender Mix and Organizational Fit: How Gender Imbalance at Different Levels of the Organization Impacts on Women Managers', *Women In Management Review*, 15 (1): 5–20.

Simpson, R. (2004) 'Masculinity at Work: The Experiences of Men in Female Dominated Occupations', *Work, Employment and Society*, 18 (2): 349–368.

Simpson, R. (2005) 'Men in Non-traditional Occupations: Career Entry, Career Orientation and Experience of Role Strain', *Gender Work and Organization*, 12 (4): 363–380.

Simpson, R. (2007) 'Emotional Labour and Identity Work of Men in Caring Roles', in P. Lewis and R.Simpson (Eds) *Gendering Emotion in Organizations* (pp. 57–74). London: Palgrave.

Simpson, R. and Lewis, P. (2005) 'An Investigation of Silence and a Scrutiny of Transparency: Re-Examining Gender and Organization Literature Through the Concepts of Voice and Visibility',*Human Relations*, 58 (10): 1253–1275.

Skelton, C. (1994) 'Sex, Male Teachers and Young Children', *Gender and Education*, 6: 87–93.

Snow, E. (Winter 1989) 'Theorizing the Male Gaze: Some Problems', *Representations*, 25: 30–41.

Squires, T. (1995) *Men in Nursing*, RN 58 (7): 26–28.

Sturdy, A. (1998) 'Customer Care in a Consumer Society: Smiling and Sometimes Meaning It?', *Organization*, 5 (1): 2–53.

Sturdy, A. (2002) 'Knowing the Unknowable: A discussion of Methodological and Theoretical Issues in Emotion Research in Organization Studies', *Organization*, 10 (1): 81–105.

Sturdy, A. and Fineman, S. (2001) 'Struggles for the Control of Affect', in A. Sturdy, I. Grugulis and H. Willmott (Eds) *Customer Service* (pp. 135–156). Basingstoke: Macmillan.

Sveningsson, S. and Alvesson, M. (2003) 'Managing Managerial Identities: Organizational Fragmentation, Discourse and Identity Struggle', *Human Relations*, 56: 1163–1193.

Swan, E. (2008) 'You Make me Feel Like a Woman: Therapeutic Cultures and the Contagion of Femininity', *Gender Work and Organization*, 15 (1): 88–107.

Swann, W. (1987) 'Identity Negotiations: Where two Roads Meet', *Journal of Personality and Social Psychology*, 53: 1038–1051.

Tajfel, H. and Turner, J. (1985) 'The Social Identity Theory of Intergroup Behaviour', in S. Worchel and W. Austin (Eds) *Psychology of Intergroup Relations*, 2nd Edition (pp. 7–24). Chicago: Nelson Hall.

Taylor, S. and Tyler, M. (2000) 'Emotional Labour and Sexual Difference in the Airline industry', *Work Employment and Society*, 14 (1): 77–95.

Thomas, R. and Linstead, A. (2002) 'Losing the Plot? Middle Managers and Identity', *Organization*, 9 (1): 71–93.

Thomas, R., Mills, A. and Mills, J. (2004) 'Introduction: Resisting Gender, Gendering Resistance', in R. Thomas, A. Mills and J. Mills (Eds) *Identity Politics at Work: Resisting Gender, Gendering Resistance* (pp. 1–19). London: Routledge.

Thrift, N. and Dewsbury, J. (2000) 'Dead Geographies—and How to Make Them Live', *Environment and Planning D: Society and Space*, 18 (4): 411–432.

Tolson, S.A. (1977) *The Limits of Masculinity*. London: Tavistock.

Townley, B. (1992) 'In the Eye of the Gaze: The Constitutive Role of Performance Appraisal', in B. Townley, P. Barrar and C. Cooper (Eds) *Managing Organizations* (pp. 185–202). London: Routledge.

Trethewey, A. (1999) 'Disciplined Bodies: Women's Embodied Identities at Work', *Organization Studies*, 20 (3): 423–450.

Turner, J., Hogg, M., Oakes, P., Reicher, S. and Wetherell, M. (1987) *Rediscovering the Social Group: A Self Categorization Theory*. Oxford: Blackwell.

Twigg, J. (2000) *Bathing, the Body and Community Care*. London: Routledge.

Tyler, M. (2005) 'Women in Change Management: Simone De Beauvoir and the Co-optation of Women's Otherness', *Journal of Organizational Change Management*, 18 (6): 561–577.

Tyler, M. and Abbott, P. (1998) 'Chocs Away: Weight Watching in the Contemporary Airline Industry', *Sociology*, 32 (3): 433–450.

Tyler, M. and Taylor, S. (1998) 'The Exchange of Aesthetics: Women's Work and "The Gift"', *Gender Work and Organization*, 5 (3): 165–171.

Unwin, T. (2000) 'A Waste of Space? Towards a Critical Understanding of the Social Production of Space...', *The Institute of British Geographers*, 25 (11): 11–29.

Virkki, T. (2008) 'The Art of Pacifying an Aggressive Client: "Feminine" Skills and Preventing Violence in Caring Work', *Gender Work and Organization*, 15 (1): 72–87.

Vogt, F. (2002) 'A Caring Teacher: Explorations into Primary School Teachers' Professional Identity and Ethic of Care', *Gender and Education*, 14 (3): 251–264.

Walby, S. (1986) *Patriarchy at Work*. Cambridge: Polity Press.

Ward, J. (2008) 'Sexualities', in *Work and Organizations: Stories by Gay Men and Women in the Workplace at the Beginning of the Twenty-first Century*. London: Routledge.

Warhurst, C. and Nickson, D. (2007) 'Employee Experience of Aesthetic Labour in Retail and Hospitality', *Work Employment and Society*, 21 (1): 103–120.

Watson, T. (2001) 'Beyond Managism: Negotiated Narratives and Critical Management Education in Practice', *British Journal of Management*, 12: 385–396.

Watson, T. (2002) 'Speaking Professionally: Occupational Anxiety and Discursive Ingenuity among Human Resource Specialists', in M. Dent and S. Whitehead (Eds) *Managing Professional Identities: Knowledge, Performativity and the 'New' Professional* (pp. 99–115). London: Routledge.

Weedon, C. (1993) *Feminist Practice and Poststructuralist Theory* 2nd Edition. Oxford: Blackwell.

West, C. and Fenstermaker, S. (1995) 'Doing Difference', *Gender and Society*, 9 (1): 8–37.

West, C. and Zimmerman, D. (1987) 'Doing Gender', *Gender and Society*, 1: 121–151.

West, C. and Zimmerman, D. (2002) 'Doing Gender', in S. Fenstermaker and C. West (Eds) *Doing Gender, Doing Difference* (pp. 3–24). London: Routledge.

Whitehead, S. (1998) 'Disrupted Selves: Resistance and Identity Work in the Managerial Arena', *Gender and Education*, 10 (2): 199–215.

Whitehead, S. (2002) *Men and Masculinities*. Cambridge: Polity.

Whitehead, S. (2004) 'Man: The Invisible Gendered Subject', in S. Whitehead and F. Barrett (Eds) *The Masculinities Reader* (pp. 351–368). Cambridge: Polity Press.

Wigfield, A., Battle, A., Keller, L. and Eccles, J. (2002) 'Sex Differences in Motivation, Self Concept, Career Aspiration and Career Choice: Implications for Cognitive Development', in A. McGillicuddy-De Lisi and R. De-Lisi (Eds) *Biology, Society and Behaviour: The Development of Sex Differences in Cognition* (pp. 93–124). Westport, CT: Ablex.

Williams, C. (1993) (Ed) *Doing Women's Work: Men in Non-Traditional Occupations.* London: Sage.

Williams, C. (1995) *Still in a Man's World: Men Who Do Women's Work.* London: University of California Press.

Williams, C. (2003) 'Sky Service: The Demands of Emotional Labour in the Airline Industry', *Gender Work and Organization*, 10 (5): 513–550.

Williams, L. and Villemez, W. (1993) 'Seeker and Finders: Male Entry and Exit in Female Dominated Jobs', in C. Williams (Ed) *Doing Women's Work: Men in Non-Traditional Occupations* (pp. 64–90). London: Sage.

Witz, A. (1992) *Professions and Patriarchy.* London: Routledge.

Witz, A., Warhurst, C. and Nickson, D. (2003) 'The Labour of Aesthetics and the Aesthetics of Organization', *Organization*, 10 (1): 33–54.

Wolf, N. (1990) *The Beauty Myth.* London: Vintage.

Wolkowitz, C. (2002) 'The Social Relations of Body Work', *Work Employment and Society*, 16 (3): 497–510.

Wolkowitz, C. (2003) 'The Social Relations of Body Work', *Work Employment and Society*, 16 (3): 497–510.

Woods, P. and Jeffrey, B. (2002) 'The Reconstruction of Primary Teachers' Identities', *British Journal of Sociology of Education*, 23 (1): 89–106.

Wouters, C. (1989) 'The Sociology of Emotion and Flight Attendants: Hochschild's Managed Heart', *Culture and Society*, 6: 95–123.

Zimmer, L. (1988) 'Tokenism and Women in the Workplace: The Limits of Gender Neutral Theory', *Social Problems*, 35: 64–77.

Index

CPSIA information can be obtained at www.ICGtesting.com
Printed in the USA
LVOW112123130212

268559LV00004B/21/P